D1598450

"WE MUST BE FEARLESS"

"We Must Be Fearless"

The Woman Suffrage Movement in Indiana

Anita Morgan

Indiana Historical Society Press | Indianapolis 2020

Printed in the United States of America

This book is a publication of the
Indiana Historical Society Press
Eugene and Marilyn Glick Indiana History Center
450 West Ohio Street
Indianapolis, Indiana 46202-3269 USA
www.indianahistory.org
Telephone orders 1-800-447-1830
Fax orders 1-317-234-0562
Online orders @ http://shop.indianahistory.org

The paper in this publication meets the minimum requirements of American National Standard for Information Sciences—Permanence of Paper for Printed Library Materials, ANSI Z39. 48–1984 ♾

Library of Congress Cataloging-in-Publication Data

Names: Morgan, Anita J., author.
Title: "We must be fearless" : the woman suffrage movement in Indiana / Anita Morgan.
Description: Indianapolis, Indiana : Indiana Historical Society Press, [2020] | Includes bibliographical references and index.
Identifiers: LCCN 2019038061 (print) | LCCN 2019038062 (ebook) | ISBN 9780871954381 (hardback) | ISBN 9780871954398 (epub)
Subjects: LCSH: Women—Suffrage—Indiana—History. | Suffragists—Indiana.
Classification: LCC JK1911.I5 M67 2020 (print) | LCC JK1911.I5 (ebook) | DDC 324.6/209772—dc23
LC record available at https://lccn.loc.gov/2019038061
LC ebook record available at https://lccn.loc.gov/2019038062

To the people who encourage me to study the past
and keep me grounded in the present:
Jeremy, Christy, and Teddy

"We Must Be Fearless": The Woman Suffrage Movement in Indiana
was made possible by contributions from the following individuals:

Nancy Fyffe
Marie E. Kingdon
Mary Jane Meeker-Stogsdill
Katherine Tyler Scott
Susan Smithburn

Also supported by the Carter Family Quasi Fund, a fund of
Central Indiana Community Foundation; The Braly Family Foundation;
the Indiana Women's Suffrage Centennial Commission;
and the Indianapolis Woman's Club.

Contents

Acknowledgments		ix
Introduction		1
Chapter 1	"The Power to Protect Herself"	15
Chapter 2	War Work	35
Chapter 3	Victory and Defeat	55
Chapter 4	"So Slight an Organization"	79
Chapter 5	"Women to the Left of Them, Women to the Right of Them"	101
Chapter 6	"We Must Be Fearless"	137
Chapter 7	"Working together . . . there is nothing we cannot accomplish"	167
Notes		207
Index		231

Acknowledgments

There are several organizations to thank for their help with this work. A sabbatical leave from the School of Liberal Arts at Indiana University–Purdue University Indianapolis gave me the time to finish the project. Volunteers at the Herbert Hoover Presidential Library searched the James. P. Goodrich Papers for suffrage correspondence. Keenan Salla at the Indiana State Archives quickly responded to requests and explained the organization of some of its World War I collections and governors' papers. The Indiana State Archives is an essential resource for anyone doing research in Indiana history. Both the collections and the staff deserve to be housed in a better building. Numerous thoughtful, helpful people with the Rare Books and Manuscript division at the Indiana State Library, the Indiana Historical Society William H. Smith Memorial Library, and the Lilly Library at Indiana University provided skillful assistance, advice, and patience during my research visits. Thank you also to *USA Today* for allowing the use of images from the *Indianapolis Star* and the *Indianapolis News*. Sue King, archivist at the Morrisson-Reeves Library in Richmond, Indiana, provided the photograph of the young Doctor Mary Thomas, which she received from Elaine Gepford and the Mincer family descendants. Susan Ross, the granddaughter of Carrie Barnes Ross, provided the photograph of her grandmother and also verified some family history. Many thanks to Ross for its use and thanks to A'Lelia Bundles for making the electronic introduction to Ross.

Many individuals need to be thanked including some of the outstanding students found at IUPUI. The School of Liberal Arts awarded undergraduate student Cassandra Anderson a Crisler Scholarship so that she could translate the Indianapolis German-language newspaper, the *Indiana Tribüne*, for me. She and Doctor Thorsten Carstensen of IUPUI did important work in an underutilized source. Former IUPUI graduate student Jennifer Kalvaitis's thesis work on the 1917 suffrage bills was extremely important to my research and I greatly appreciate her taking the time from her busy schedule working with History Day in Wisconsin to read my analysis of the 1917 Indiana legislative session. Another IUPUI graduate student, Eric Hamilton, studied Amanda Way and Doctor Mary Thomas for his thesis and that work proved to be invaluable for studying the origins of the suffrage movement in Indiana. As an IUPUI undergraduate, Nathan Gallagher researched the Indiana Woman's Suffrage Association and his findings, for which he received the IUPUI History

Department's Thelander Award, also helped with framing some of this book. Finally, Cara Crane, another former IUPUI student and now a historian, read the antebellum chapters and offered encouragement and humor at a crucial time in the completion of this work.

Women's historians are a supportive community. Indiana Historical Bureau historians Jill Weiss Simins and Nicole Poletika passed along research, encouraging conversation, general support, and friendship. Marcia Caudell, reference and government services supervisor with the Indiana State Library, believed in this project and offered encouragement whenever we talked. Two other women's historians and friends offered support near the end of this project. My colleague at IUPUI, Nancy Robertson, read two troublesome chapters and offered advice, editing, words of wisdom, and encouragement. Nancy Gabin of Purdue University did not read the manuscript, although she offered to do so, but her knowledge of Indiana women's history and a lively conversation about a few key suffragists lifted my spirits and made the final weeks much easier.

Ray E. Boomhower at the Indiana Historical Society Press never gave up on this project even when the chapters were somewhat delayed by my heavy teaching schedule. He and fellow IHS Press editor Kathy Breen straightened out my sometimes twisted prose, worked with me on photographs, and likely completed many other behind-the- scenes activities that I know nothing about but which made this book possible. Thank you to them for everything they did. Any errors, of course, remain my own.

Last, but never least, my family helped me more than they know. Jerry Morgan did not read any of this manuscript nor did he complain about the time I spent on it. His quiet, calm presence and his continuation of life as usual made the work go easier. My son, Jeremy Hackerd, has always encouraged me in my work even though having a historian for a parent can be difficult since on some days the past simply takes you out of the present. He is also a historian and discussing history with him is a highlight of any day. My daughter-in-law, Christy, does not realize how important she was to the decision to finally write a book that had percolated in my mind for several years. She attended a women's march in Indianapolis a few years ago and on that day, I happened to be with my son, and my grandson, Teddy. When she telephoned to check in with us, Teddy asked if she was marching. She said yes and, as only a three-year-old can do, Teddy proceeded to march around the room and yelled, "I'm marching with you, Mommy!" That day has stuck with me. Women in Indiana have acted politically since at least 1851, so the march in

Indianapolis was nothing new. I knew, however, that few women, or men, had read about the long history of women's persistent activism in the state or prior rallies and marches for women held with or without their families' support. That was a story that needed to be told. I hope I have given the bold, Hoosier women of the past the recognition they so richly deserve.

Introduction

"THE GREAT WOMAN'S MOVEMENT"

An Indiana suffragist could be almost anyone. She was a sister, daughter, mother, mother-in-law, and a wife. She was a doctor, a minister, a lawyer, a teacher, a factory worker, a newspaper columnist or editor, a typesetter, an African American entrepreneur, a social worker, the First Lady of Indiana, a farmer, a volunteer, and a woman who worked at home. She was the daughter and granddaughter of immigrants, usually German. She was a prohibitionist, an advocate for world peace, a housing reformer, a literary club member, an advocate of municipal playgrounds, and a supporter of health care for African Americans. She had attended Northwestern Christian University (Butler University), Vassar, Central College of Physicians and Surgeons (Indianapolis), Indianapolis Law School, Berea College, University of Chicago, Columbia University, Harvard, or had no formal education. She lived in a city, town, village, or on a farm. She was a Quaker, a Methodist, a Unitarian, a Jew, a Catholic, a member of the African Methodist Episcopal Church, or a member of any number of other religious groups. She was a Republican, a Democrat, a Woman's Party member, or a Socialist. She was a lobbyist and a politician even though she could not vote. The men in her life probably supported woman's suffrage, too.

Many people know the familiar names—Doctor Mary Thomas, Amanda Way, May Wright Sewall, Grace Julian Clarke, Helen Gougar, Zerelda Wallace, and Doctor Amelia Keller. They probably do not know about Martha McKay, Sara Messing Stern, Doctor Hannah Graham, Laura Donnan, Carrie Barnes, Luella McWhirter, Marie Edwards, Charity Dye, Harriet Noble, Sara and Eldena Lauter, Emma Swank, and Frances Berry Coston. Many different organizations worked for women to gain the vote—the Indiana Woman's Rights Association, Indiana Woman's Suffrage Association, Equal Suffrage Association, Branch Number 7, First Colored Woman's Suffrage Club, Woman's Franchise League, Woman's Legislative Council, and the National Council of Jewish Women. Sometimes suffrage groups cooperated and sometimes they did not. Personalities, priorities, techniques, and goals sometimes led to discord and anger. Still, it took every organization and every woman to win the vote.

Antisuffrage agitators said women should not vote because they would neglect their children, cause tension in their homes, and add an unnecessary burden to women's lives. Others feared that women would lose their moral influence on society if they engaged in the rough-and-tumble world of politics—how could a woman retain high moral standards if she went to the polls on election day and participated in the chaos and corruption that apparently lurked there? Some men and women feared that once women could vote, they might want to run for office. Brewers feared that woman suffrage would bring about strict laws on the production and consumption of alcohol or lead to outright prohibition. Industrialists feared that women voters might help enact tough labor regulations, especially for women and children. And, some feared that woman suffrage meant more African Americans would have the vote.

This book is a popular history of the woman suffrage movement in Indiana and the women who often had in common only one thing—a belief that Hoosier women should vote. This is not the book to read if you are looking for academic arguments or a who's who of historians who have studied woman suffrage, although it will hopefully inspire historians to conduct more research on women in Indiana. Academic arguments figure into the analysis of the story this book tells, but it is not the major point of the book. Instead, this book is a narrative history of the sixty-nine years of the woman's rights movement in Indiana. The people who acted, what they did, and the results of their efforts are the focus. Through this story, it also places the state's women more firmly into the history of Indiana, the Midwest, and the nation.

It begins with a twenty-three-year-old Winchester resident, Amanda Way, who called for the first woman's rights meeting in Indiana in 1851 and ends with the ratification of the Nineteenth Amendment by the Indiana state legislature on January 16, 1920, under the oversight of Winchester native son, Governor James P. Goodrich. The womans suffrage movement in Indiana changed a great deal across the sixty-nine years of its existence. Annual meetings and internal debates over resolutions about what could be done to improve women's lives led to the presentation of petitions to the state legislature and attempts to vote without a woman suffrage law on the books. There were usually two woman suffrage groups in the state at any one time and their accomplishments waxed and waned due to conflicts between state suffrage leaders, an absence of leaders in some parts of the state, Hoosier suffragists' activity in national women's organizations that took them out of the state for extended periods of time, and political tricks by antisuffrage legislators. Once technology improved, suffragists adopted automobile tours to take their message throughout Indiana's many small towns. They held street meetings complete with Votes for Women banners and yellow (the color of the

Indiana suffrage movement) streamers. At one point, suffrage groups joined each other in a march to the Indiana Statehouse, where they pinned yellow Votes for Women sashes on legislators. One of the most powerful women's political groups in the state, the Woman's Franchise League, established its headquarters in the Odd Fellows Building in downtown Indianapolis. From its twelfth-floor office, the group mounted an effective, statewide suffrage campaign. To supplement the high-profile office space, suffragists prodded the state government to also give them an office at the statehouse, which made for even more effective lobbying. Suffragists spoke to and corresponded with the leaders of Indiana's political parties and with governors. They became a force to be reckoned with and they knew it. Their stellar organizational skills let them reach out to women and men across the state and their powerful voices twice pushed suffrage bills through the Indiana General Assembly, only to lose both to arcane rules and a state constitution that defied common sense. Even when they lost lawsuits against suffrage bills in court, suffragists were assured by judges that they personally agreed with women voting, but that the law defined how their rulings would go.[1]

Hoosier suffragists were part of the "great woman's movement," as prominent suffragist and skillful politician Clarke put it. This movement consisted of an array of organizations that sometimes overlapped in their goals and membership in what historians refer to as the women's club movement. Club members pursued temperance, housing reform, child labor laws, labor laws for women, access to healthy foods, municipal suffrage, better pay for women teachers, the creation of state parks, and several other changes to state laws through those groups. Some members also supported suffrage, and some did not. This book, however, focuses squarely on winning the vote and will mention other women's organizations and their important reform measures only when necessary to explain the connections between suffragists and other issues that either impeded or enhanced the chance to win the vote. It is somewhat constrained by the available sources. Other than Clarke and McWhirter, Hoosier suffragists left behind only minimal personal documentation. Meeting minutes and newspaper reports fill in some of the gaps, but more information would have made for richer personal stories. As you meet the suffragists, you will notice that some women are recognized by their first names and some by their husband's names. To bring suffragists out of the shadows, if a woman's first name could be found, she will be referred to by that name. "Mrs. Ovid Butler Jameson" becomes "Mary Tarkington (Mrs. Ovid Butler) Jameson" when you first meet her, and after that, Mary Tarkington Jameson is used. If you never see a woman's first name, but she is instead always referred to by her husband's name, that is because her own name has been lost to history or it is not clear who she was. Through this method of naming women, I hope many important Hoosier women will be restored to their rightful place in the state's story.[2]

A look at attempts by Hoosier women to secure the vote adds much more information to the small amount of data that is generally known about Indiana women's history. Despite steady progress since 2000, historians are woefully behind in delivering what they know about Indiana women to the public. Numerous articles, dissertations, and master's theses document Hoosier women's lives, but most of those works remain buried in academic journals that few people read. Consequently, although we know a great deal about Hoosier women, little of that information has reached beyond the academy. That absence needs to be corrected in part because most people do not know about the important roles Indiana women played in the national suffrage movement. Hoosier women did not just sit back and watch change happen—they were an integral part of that change.

Suffragists across the nation had Indiana ties. For example, Lizzie Bunnell Read got her start in suffrage work in Indiana when she published a woman's rights newspaper, *The Mayflower*, in Peru, before she married and moved to Iowa, where she published a wide-ranging newspaper and presided over the state suffrage organization. Her importance to Iowa suffrage history is seen by her appearance as the only woman whose likeness is found in an 1875 *Atlas of Iowa*. Her work grew in importance elsewhere, but she started in the Hoosier State. Elizabeth Boyton Harbert had been active in Indiana suffrage work before she left her native Crawfordsville after her marriage. She moved to Iowa where, like Read, she at one time presided over the state suffrage organization and argued for woman suffrage before the Iowa legislature. After her family moved to Illinois, she led its state suffrage organization for several years. She also wrote a women's column for the *Chicago Inter-Ocean*. This widely circulated newspaper took her column to women across the Midwest, including to a young Carrie Chapman Catt, who much later in life guided the federal woman suffrage amendment to victory. Years later, Catt let Harbert know how important those columns had been to her development as a suffragist.

When the two national suffrage organizations, the National Woman Suffrage Association and the American Woman Suffrage Association merged in 1890 to form the National American Woman Suffrage Association, two Hoosiers on the board of the NWSA (Sewall and Gougar) and two Hoosiers on the board of the AWSA (William Dudley Foulke and Thomas) helped to negotiate the terms of the reorganization. Terre Haute's Ida Husted Harper became good friends with national suffrage leaders Susan B. Anthony and Elizabeth Cady Stanton and coauthored a volume of the *History of Woman Suffrage* and wrote Anthony's biography. Harper later authored, on her own, the last two volumes of the *History of Woman Suffrage*. She wrote suffrage-oriented newspaper articles that were distributed throughout the country and led NAWSA's press bureau. At the same time Harper oversaw publicity for NAWSA, Mary Garret Hay, a close friend of Catt, worked as a member of the NAWSA board and as the chair of the national Republican Party's Women's National Executive Committee. Sewall led an international women's organization and served on NAWSA's governing board. Clarke served as a bridge between the suffrage movement and the national board of the General Federation of Women's Clubs and strategized with national suffrage leaders such as Anthony and Harper. Indiana women could be found everywhere from almost the very beginning of the early woman's rights associations.[3]

Another reason to look at Indiana women as they worked for the vote is that the state has a long legacy of suffrage work. The *History of Woman Suffrage*, the "official" history of the suffrage movement, claims that Indiana has one of the oldest state suffrage associations in the United States. The Indiana Woman's Rights Association met for the first time in 1851, just three years after the famed Seneca Falls, New York, woman's rights meeting that proclaimed, "all men *and women* are created equal." Consequently, sixty-nine years of suffrage work makes Indiana an excellent place to view the continuity of suffrage arguments and techniques across time, to look for significant changes in either, and to see how national politics affected state and local suffragists.[4]

In general, we see Hoosier suffragists carrying on their work with a political shrewdness that historians have hidden behind the idea of women's reform work. While men who try to change social, economic, and political environments are called politicians, women are called reformers in part because they could not vote. However, women participated in the political realm by petitioning state legislatures, attending legislative sessions, and personally lobbying lawmakers. Indiana suffragists even addressed the general assembly several times. Eventually Indiana's governors agreed to allocate office space for suffragists in the statehouse. Suffragists, in other words, acted politically and developed a political culture that embraced women from across the state and from all walks of life. Any divisions between Hoosier suffragists do not appear to be based on race or class or even political party leanings, but rather based on political techniques and approaches to secure the vote. Keller, McWhirter, and Clarke were deeply involved in politics, regularly interacted with politicians, and proved to be three of the most consequential political women in Indiana.

Another reason to examine suffrage in Indiana is to demonstrate that no one road led to suffrage in what today is called the Midwest. Recent work on woman suffrage has looked at Iowa, Wisconsin, and a few places on the Great Plains and some of that work emphasizes the influence of settlers from the mid-Atlantic and New England states, sometimes referred to as Yankees, on those states' suffrage organizations. Indiana, the oldest of the midwestern states outside of Ohio, had a unique settlement pattern that makes its suffrage story different from states farther to its west. Indiana's first settlers traveled from the upland South and included North Carolina Quakers who moved to Indiana, in part, because they did not like slavery. Sometimes they traveled to Indiana with former slaves, who then settled with the Quakers or at nearby rural settlements. A preponderance of Quakers participated in the first decades of Indiana suffrage work and coalesced their efforts on four important reforms: improved women's property laws, temperance, abolition, and, beginning in 1851, the vote. Early woman's rights advocates usually supported all four of these issues and extended their efforts to include an expansion of women's options for employment and for higher education. By the time other midwestern states created their suffrage associations, Indiana advocates had long worked with national suffrage leaders and developed pockets of intensive suffrage activism in the state.[5]

In addition to the longevity of the movement, part of the difference between Indiana and some other midwestern states is the continuous presence of African American women at suffrage meetings and the formation of African American woman suffrage organizations in at least three cities—Indianapolis, Marion, and Muncie. The first mention of African American women's involvement in suffrage in Indiana is found at the 1869 Indiana Woman's Rights Association meeting, the first meeting convened after the Civil War. According to one Indianapolis newspaper, "A note from a colored woman was here handed to Mrs. [Mary] Livermore [the evening's speaker] asking if she would be included in the proposed enfranchisement. Mrs. L. responded emphatically, 'Of course you will be included. Certainly, madam. We are all on the same footing.'" It is quite possible African American women attended suffrage meetings before 1869, since Thomas, the primary mover and shaker of the suffrage movement in Indiana for the first thirty years, came from a staunchly abolitionist family and like her fellow Quaker suffrage supporters also participated in it. Further, the people of Richmond, Indiana, knew Thomas for her medical work among the African American community. (When she died, two of the six women pallbearers at her funeral were African American women from the community.) African American women were again present at the Indiana Woman's Suffrage Association meeting in 1882. Wallace made sure the convention knew they could take an active role in the meeting's deliberations.[6]

African Americans in Indiana had always been found in towns and cities in addition to the rural settlements near Quaker strongholds. Towns along the Ohio River and Indianapolis developed substantial African American populations over the decades. When you look at the capital city, Chaney Lively was, depending on the story, the first or second African American to live there when she arrived as Alexander Ralston's housekeeper in 1820. (Ralston designed the distinctive central Circle with radiating diagonal streets that still define the city.) Lively worked for Ralston, took in washing, and possibly took in boarders. By the 1830s she was a married property owner and one of the few women in the city who paid taxes. Indianapolis's African American population steadily grew after 1820 and reached around 22,000 people by 1910 or 9.3 percent of the city's total population, "the highest percentage of any city north of the Ohio River." One historian has stated that "African Americans were as much natives of the city as any other inhabitant of a nineteenth century town . . . because of their early presence they possessed a historical memory of the city's promise and direction." Unlike other northern cities, whose African American populations grew because of migration during World War I, "Indianapolis already contained a sizable African American population as the city itself developed." In Indiana's public-school system, African American students attended school with white students if a separate school for them was not available. In Indianapolis, that meant that elementary schools were segregated, but high schools were not. African American and white students attended Indianapolis High School, later renamed Shortridge High School, and two additional high schools together. This was crucial for the growth of the suffrage movement as black and white teachers worked with black and white suffrage leaders and with their former African American pupils in the city. Butler University, for part of this era, was located just outside the Indianapolis city limits in Irvington. Butler admitted African American students and suffragist Clarke attended Butler around the same time (mid-1880s) as the earliest of these students and was herself the daughter and granddaughter of abolitionists. The interaction between white and African American women suffragists is most easily seen after 1910 and sets Hoosiers apart from most other states in the Midwest.[7]

Finally, a look at Indiana's suffrage movement lets us look at the question of immigration and the right to vote. Compared to states surrounding it, Indiana had a smaller immigrant population for the years from 1851 to 1920. The largest foreign-born population, Germans, were found in cities along the Ohio River, especially Evansville, and in Dubois County, Fort Wayne, and Indianapolis. Like African Americans, Germans came to Indiana early in statehood. A particularly strong presence in Indianapolis led to a variety of institutions and successful businesses led by Germans. Indianapolis's second language was German and was heard on the streets of the city and seen in German-language newspapers. Throughout the state, but especially in Indianapolis, some suffragists were the daughters of German parents. For example, Doctor Amelia Keller and Sara and Eldena Lauter's parents were all German born. Unlike other states farther to the west, Indiana's suffragists were not all "Yankees" who hailed from the mid-Atlantic and New England states. Many were born in the state to either parents born in Indiana or to foreign-born parents. This did not mean, however, that Hoosier suffragists were not upset with men of foreign birth who could vote when they, who were already citizens, could not. Indiana, like some other states, let men of foreign birth vote after they had been in the state for only six months and declared their intention to become naturalized citizens, but were not yet citizens. Voting on "first papers," as this was referred to, irritated suffragists. Because the naturalization process was regulated locally, sometimes men voted for years on first papers, sometimes without becoming citizens within the allotted amount of time to do so.

To further add to the frustrations of what was called "alien suffrage," American-born women who married foreign-born men lost their citizenship until their husbands became citizens because citizenship followed the man and not the woman. An American-born man who married a foreign-born woman granted her citizenship upon their marriage, but not the reverse. This truly vexed suffragists and sometimes they let their tempers flare into nativist rhetoric. This nativist talk by suffragists was not as severe in Indiana as it appears to have been in other states. That does not mean it did not happen, especially when local issues drove the conversation, but the words were not as vitriolic as found elsewhere.[8]

The first chapter of this book introduces the Indiana Woman's Rights Association, which met for the first time at Dublin, Indiana, in 1851. Way and Thomas led the group through its first decade of existence. Most of the early members were Quakers, which meant they believed in equality of the sexes. They were also abolitionists and temperance reformers and hoped that women's votes would help bring about the end of slavery and the creation of stricter drinking laws (or outright prohibition). They also emphasized that women needed access to expanded education and employment opportunities. The IWRA boldly presented the state legislature with a suffrage petition in 1859 when the House of Representatives hosted speeches by Thomas and others. Some critics referred to early suffrage advocates as "strong-minded," which at the time was meant as an insult. "Strong-minded" women dared to speak at large public gatherings, where they argued for women to have access to all areas of life and to vote. This earliest group of advocates also had to deal with critics who claimed their voices were either too soft or too shrill or too nervous sounding and their dress too "mannish."[9]

Chapter 2 looks at the ways that women devoted themselves to "war work" during the Civil War—sending medical supplies, clothing, and food to soldiers, working at the state arsenal, nursing wounded soldiers at home and in the field, maintaining a farm or business in the absence of a husband or father. Suffragists eagerly assumed the burden of war work and hoped that devotion to the Union cause would lead men to recognize their value as citizens, and consequently, that they should be able to vote. They so convinced themselves that this tactic would work that after the 1859 IWRA convention, Indiana suffragists failed to call another meeting until 1869. By then, it was clear that the federal government was not going to reward their war work with suffrage. The 1869 IWRA meeting differed from prewar meetings. Many Republican politicians, former Union officers, and a wide variety of Protestant ministers attended, presumably to show their support for woman suffrage although most of them remained silent throughout the meeting's sessions. Another first for this convention was a statement by a local newspaper that mentioned that African American women attended the conference. While the convention gave its approval to the introduction of a Sixteenth Amendment to the U.S. Constitution that would give women the vote, nothing came of the proposed amendment at the federal level.

Chapter 3 introduces the problems that Indiana suffrage supporters faced with attempts to amend the state constitution to include suffrage for women. The Indiana General Assembly met only every other year. To amend the constitution, an amendment had to pass two separate legislative sessions, which meant that it took two years to make any changes. This long delay, combined with rules that seemed designed to provide legislators with built-in dodges and political tricks to avoid enacting any proposed amendment, meant that the state's governing document proved impossible to amend. The legislative sessions of 1881 and 1883 serve as examples of this political chicanery. Other ruses included a false charge of infidelity against Lafayette suffragist Gougar. While campaigning in 1882 for a Lafayette Republican, who also happened to be a friend of both Gougar and her husband, the local police chief accused Gougar and the candidate of having an affair and threw the town and the state into turmoil. Gougar sued the man for slander and the resulting trial played out as the 1883 legislature fumbled with the 1881 suffrage law. It is probably no coincidence that just as the political tides seemed to be turning for Hoosier women, a false scandal reminded everyone that women who engaged in politics could have their personal lives ruined. The chapter ends with the death of a woman no one could fault, Thomas, who had almost single handedly kept the Indiana suffrage movement on solid footing. Her death left suffragists without a clear leader in the last turbulent decades of the nineteenth century.

Chapter 4 emphasizes the difficulties Hoosier women faced from antisuffrage forces who did not believe that women should vote and who feared that suffrage would bring about the prohibition of alcohol. The issue at heart was the mixing of suffrage and prohibition as the state Woman's Christian Temperance Union gathered strength in numbers during those years. It did not help that many suffragists also belonged to the WCTU and loudly expressed their devotion to both causes. Breweries in the state employed hundreds and were owned predominately by persons of German heritage. Writers for German-owned newspapers wanted to support woman's voting rights, but at the same time feared the loss of jobs and an essential part of their culture.

Two forceful Indiana suffragists, Gougar and Sewall, alternately cooperated with and fought against each other on the issue (and others) and national suffrage standout Anthony, who knew them both, grew exasperated with the situation. Anthony believed that nothing was more important than suffrage and while she was a temperance advocate, she realized the damage that mixing the two subjects could do to the national and to the Indiana suffrage movements. Consequently, with all the conflict about prohibition and spats between suffragists, the Indiana suffrage movement drifted. Even when suffragists went to the polls in 1894 and tried to vote, nothing came of it. This chapter also demonstrates that women who wanted to achieve the same goal did not always agree with each other on how to get it.[10]

Chapter 5 brings the state into the twentieth century and the ascendance of a new generation of women who created local suffrage organizations that used the automobile, the telephone, and a more sophisticated use of public relations to present their cause directly to the public. They achieved their first suffrage victory by electing women to the school boards in both Indianapolis and Terre Haute—the only places in the state where school boards were not appointed. Many suffragists involved in this success had learned their campaigning skills not as members of suffrage groups, but as part of the Indiana Federation of Clubs, a group of diverse literary, artistic, and social-reform organizations who pushed legislators to support their goals. Both suffragists and clubwomen knew the state's political system and the state's politicians.

Two major suffrage groups operated in the state, the Equal Suffrage Association and the Woman's Franchise League. The leaders of the ESA resisted all calls by the NAWSA to merge with the WFL into a single organization with an expansive membership that NAWSA believed would be more successful. So, the two worked independently despite repeated attempts by the WFL to follow NAWSA's suggestion to merge the groups. Separately then, both the WFL and the ESA reached out to the Indianapolis African American community to form branch suffrage clubs. Keller, Graham, and Clarke all emerged as suffrage leaders at this time and all worked with African American schoolteachers and with high-school teachers at Indianapolis's integrated high schools to form African American suffrage groups in the capital city. Graham's ESA also reached out to Indianapolis labor and at least one labor union formed its own branch of the ESA. Another sign of the expansion of suffrage work at this time can be seen in the active role that various members of the Council of Jewish Women played in the suffrage movement in Indianapolis and Terre Haute.

The early twentieth century was an exciting time for new groups, new methods, and the embrace of woman suffrage by several politicians. Former vice president Charles W. Fairbanks hosted a suffrage lawn party at his home and Republicans came out in favor of woman suffrage. Suffragists even held a parade through the streets of Indianapolis to welcome Republican presidential candidate Charles Evans Hughes to the city in 1916. Women had entered the political arena in a big way and across the state they took up the fight.

Chapter 6 recounts the highs and lows of the 1917 suffrage victory when two pieces of legislation that gave women suffrage, and one that called for a new state constitution that could lead to the inclusion of a woman suffrage provision, were enacted by the Indiana General Assembly, were challenged in state courts, and only one survived. Before those defeats, however, at least a few women in Warren, Porter, and Delaware Counties had voted and thousands of women across the state, of all ages, economic backgrounds, and races, registered to vote. No one could ever again suggest that women did not want to vote—overwhelmingly large registration numbers proved otherwise. The courtroom defeats did not weaken the suffragists' resolve, but instead inspired them to mount a statewide membership drive to persuade politicians of their constituents' belief in woman suffrage.

Chapter 7 describes victory at home and abroad with the end of World War I and the ratification of the Nineteenth Amendment. After the United States entered World War I, suffragists devoted an amazing amount of time to suffrage work, war work, and to defending suffrage legislation in the courts. Suffragists knitted socks for soldiers, conserved food, gave speeches at every conceivable venue in support of the war, and gave their time and money to Liberty Loan campaigns. Unlike the Civil War, when suffragists abandoned suffrage work for war work, this time they did both to keep their patriotism and their determination to participate in the country's governance on everyone's mind.

After first the U.S. House of Representatives and then the Senate approved the Nineteenth Amendment, Indiana suffragists pushed Governor Goodrich to make Indiana the first state to ratify the new amendment. Thirty-six states were needed for ratification and they felt Indiana should lead the way. Unfortunately, the governor did not want to call a special session of the legislature. Only when two-thirds of the members of the general assembly reassured the governor that they would only vote on the amendment and conduct no other business, did he convene the session. On January 16, 1920, Indiana became the twenty-sixth state to ratify the Nineteenth Amendment (also known as the Susan B. Anthony Amendment).

Each state had approached woman suffrage in its own way. In some states, women won full suffrage long before 1920. In Indiana, sixty-nine years of almost constant agitation did not lead to a change in the state constitution.

Instead, Hoosier women paved the road to suffrage though participation in the political system, persistent lobbying, newspaper stories, meetings, parades, auto tours, and anything they could think of to take the message of woman suffrage directly to the people of Indiana so that, finally, the people themselves persuaded their elected officials to support giving women the vote through a federal amendment.

By the time women got the vote in 1920, political parties had adopted suffrage planks and almost all major Indiana politicians endorsed women as voters. Fairbanks had said suffrage was "a matter of sheer right and common justice." Goodrich, who was probably less of a suffragist than Cora Goodrich, his wife, said the Nineteenth Amendment was "an act of tardy justice." The Indiana WFL noted that President Woodrow Wilson called suffrage "an act of right and justice," but the league probably said it best when they referred to suffrage as "an act of sound common sense."[11]

Chapter 1

"THE POWER TO PROTECT HERSELF"

A perfect storm of temperance, abolition, and a new state constitution led a dedicated group of reformers to call for the 1851 woman's rights convention in Dublin, Indiana. According to the story, earlier that year at an abolitionist meeting in Greensboro, Indiana, Amanda Way, a twenty-three-year-old abolitionist and temperance reformer, stated that since "women of our land are being oppressed and degraded by laws and customs of our country, and are in but little better condition than chattel slaves," the abolitionist group should call for a "Woman's Rights Convention" to discuss the new state constitution. Legislators had failed to include in that document a modified, married women's property law that not only gave women the right to hold their real estate without their husbands' interference, but also to control their personal property. The reformers hoped their meeting might persuade legislators to correct that error. The official call for the convention was signed by "Hannah Hiatt, Amanda M. Way, M. J. Diggs, Henry Hiatt, Fanny Hiatt, T. A. Way, Lydia Davis, Joel P. Davis, and Agnes Cook and others." They met that October.[1]

The call for this meeting, the first such convention in the state, should really come as no surprise to students of history. Reform societies flourished in the United States in the 1830s and 1840s as the relatively new country struggled to define and create its character. Slavery and inebriation were two indicators, for many people, that a lack of individual self-control and sense of responsibility for one's actions created social problems such as violence, crime, and poverty in what many believed should be a land of plenty and prosperity. Reformers created many types of organizations to deal with these social problems with antislavery and temperance societies as the most typical. Accordingly, reform associations such as these had already taken hold of most of Indiana by the time of the Dublin woman's rights meeting. Abolitionists had been hard at work in Indiana since the 1830s. The Decatur County Anti-Slavery Society and an antislavery society composed of students from Hanover College both appeared in 1836. The 1838 formation of a statewide antislavery society led to the creation of thirty-four chapters across the state. While Presbyterians led the earliest abolitionist societies, almost all other Protestant denominations in the state formed similar groups. In some churches, friction arose between congregants who supported antislavery work and those who did not. Those churches suffered ruptures as the membership split and formed separate congregations. Counties with large Quaker populations in the east-central part of the state had the largest antislavery societies although even Quaker churches split over views on slavery. Women as well as men took active roles in antislavery work and formed two women-only abolitionist groups.[2]

Many people believed that slavery was wrong, but it seemed a distant problem unless you lived in a county bordering the Ohio River or participated in the Underground Railroad. For some Hoosiers, temperance reform was more important than abolition. An early temperance group met at Indianapolis in 1829, but it appears the Sons of Temperance meeting in 1845 in Brookville was the real start of the movement. The organization rapidly spread across the state with 336 lodges established by 1850. The Sons of Temperance aimed for abstinence, but the difference between an alcoholic beverage and a nonalcoholic beverage (and therefore what should be abstained from) caused some debate. Auxiliary groups such as the Daughters of Temperance and the Cadets of Temperance and independent groups such as the Washingtonians added to the fervor. Even the Masonic Lodge, while not supporting the call for abstinence, supported moderation in the use of alcohol. Businessmen joined the cause to insure the sobriety and hard work of their employees.[3]

For some people, concerns about excessive drinking were tied to concerns about married women's property rights. In Indiana as across the nation, fathers grew worried that inebriated husbands might sell the property they had previously given or bequeathed to their daughters and send their daughters' families into financial ruin. When Indiana was organized in 1816, a husband had complete control over his wife's real estate and personal property, even if that property was brought into the marriage. That also meant that her property could be sold to satisfy her husband's debts. Similarly, "when a husband absconded with his wife's property or physically abused her, she had no legal recourse" since the wife and even their children were also considered part of the husband's property. Wealth in the relatively new country was usually bound up in land ownership and it became readily apparent to women, and to their fathers, that property laws must change to ensure that a wasteful, spendthrift husband, or perhaps a husband addicted to alcohol, did not squander a daughter's inheritance or gifted land leaving her and her children destitute. To respond to the problem, states began to enact new married women's property laws. Mississippi passed a new law in 1837 in part to protect women's ownership of valuable assets such as slaves. In 1847 Indiana passed a new property law giving married women control over any real estate they had owned before

LIBRARY OF CONGRESS

Elizabeth Cady Stanton (seated) and Susan B. Anthony in 1890. They led the National Woman Suffrage Association until it merged with the American Woman Suffrage Association (led by Lucy Stone) in 1890.

their marriage. The law also said that her "rents and profits" from that land could not be used to pay her husband's debts. She was, however, "responsible for any debts she had incurred before marriage." Many businessmen were critical of this law, stating that husbands could now hide their financial failure behind their wives' petticoats, as the saying went, but the law did in fact protect women who owned land from a husband's unfortunate financial decisions. Indiana was actually quite forward thinking with this law since it was enacted a year before the now famous woman's rights convention at Seneca Falls, New York, that was organized, in part, to argue for just such a law in New York state.[4]

When men in Indiana met in 1850 at a convention to write a new state constitution, married women's property was again an issue. While the 1847 law kept a wife's real estate separate from her husband's holdings and his control, it did not have the same effect on personal property. Further, the 1847 law was not part of the state constitution so its long-term ability to protect women was in doubt. Given these problems, Robert Dale Owen, son of the founder of the New Harmony commune in southern Indiana, argued at the convention for the addition of both the 1847 provisions and a new provision for personal property in the new constitution. Owen maintained that if part of the state constitution, the new law would "not be subject to the action of every demagogue who chanced to have a little, brief legislative authority." The constitutional convention first approved Owen's idea and then had a change of heart. According to famed Hoosier poet and property law reform advocate Sarah T. Bolton, this wavering on whether or not to enact the law happened five or six times. Eventually, the married women's property law was not included in the new constitution. Owen, however, received an engraved, silver pitcher financed by women and men around the state who were grateful for his efforts.[5]

The first meeting of the state legislature under the new constitution did reenact the 1847 law. This left the question of women's personal property open until 1853, when the state finally enacted a law to give women "control of personal property acquired before marriage or by descent, devise, or gift." At this point, reform in property law halted until after the Civil War.[6]

Reformers experienced in abolition and temperance organizations, and who closely followed the debates over property laws, recognized women's disabilities under Indiana law and quickly directed their reform energies toward improving the social, educational, and political status of women. Three crucial steps over the course of the 1850s propelled the woman's rights movement to take its place among the major reform associations that shaped Indiana and the national landscape until 1920. First, advocates directed their energies to the creation of the organization. Women and men with crucial experience in planning, conducting, and following up on committee assignments and resolutions enacted at large temperance and abolition meetings joined the woman's rights association. They knew how to write a constitution and elect officers, understood procedural maneuvers and resolution composition, publicized meetings, and, in general, launched the association on a stable path. Second, the association debated and delineated its objectives until clearly stated goals, essential for any organization's success, emerged and could be tackled. Debates among statewide members, nationally known speakers who related what woman's rights groups in other states were doing to achieve similar goals, and sensitiveness to the opposition's arguments emerged in the 1850s to put the Indiana Woman's Rights Association on a solid footing to approach the state legislature for suffrage and for other legal remedies to restrictions on women's activities. Finally, two important women served as examples of quality leadership for other women in the movement—Doctor Mary Thomas and Amanda Way. As with many women reformers, both Thomas and Way supported other reforms—notably temperance, especially in Way's case—but always kept suffrage as a major focus. Way, who called for a petition to be presented to the state legislature and Thomas, who presented the petition and a short talk on woman's rights to that body, capped the final push for suffrage before the rush to civil war halted their progress.[7]

That first woman's rights meeting convened in Dublin, Indiana, in 1851. That meeting and the next in 1852 served as the formal creation of a woman's rights organization in the state. Personal friendships with nationally recognized woman's rights advocates and abolitionists helped the 1851 meeting organizers persuade well-known antislavery activist Henry C. Wright to attend. His "radical stirring" speeches punctuated both days of the conference. He excoriated existing laws that restricted women's use of their property, unequal wages for work performed, and "the insulting cruelty" of women's lack of access to a high school or college education. The secretary of the meeting noted that Wright gave a "rebuke to men who make the laws that thus degrade their own wives and mothers." His final speech of the meeting "showed how men had made the laws so that women were little better than slaves the husband not only owning all the property but the children and the wife too."[8]

Thomas, who could not attend the meeting, sent a letter of support that Way read to those attending. Thomas, who during the next thirty years became the most well-known and well-respected woman's suffrage advocate from Indiana, was in Fort Wayne studying medicine with her husband, Doctor Owen Thomas. Her letter expressed regret that she could not attend and stressed the importance of a woman's preparation for a profession or trade or what Thomas called "pecuniary independence."[9]

LIBRARY OF CONGRESS

Elizabeth Cady Stanton and her daughter Harriot in 1856. Stanton had seven children, five boys and two girls.

As at all woman's rights meetings across the country at this time period, the delegates debated a series of resolutions and then announced the final product to the public. Their short list of demands stressed the need for women to have access to work and education:

> *Resolved*, That all laws and customs having for their perpetuation the only pleas that they are time-honored, which in any way infringe on woman's equal rights, cramp her energies, cripple her efforts, place her before the eyes of her family or the world as an inferior, are wrong, and should be immediately abolished.
>
> *Resolved*, That the avenues to gain, in all their varieties, should be as freely opened to woman as they now are to man.
>
> *Resolved*, that the rising generation of boys and girls should be educated together in the same schools and colleges, and receive the same kind and degree of education.
>
> *Resolved*, That woman should receive for equal labor, equal pay with man.
>
> *Resolved*, That as the qualification for citizenship in this country is based on capacity and morality, and as the sexes in their mental condition are equal, therefore woman should enjoy the same rights of citizenship with man.[10]

This final resolution implied, of course, but did not state, the demand for suffrage.

These resolutions echoed the resolutions passed by the men and women who attended the Seneca Falls woman's rights convention in July 1848. That now famous meeting of Quaker abolitionists and other reformers is deemed the most prominent opening act of the woman suffrage movement in the United States. Elizabeth Cady Stanton, Lucretia Mott, and others devised the plan in the kitchen of Mott's friends, the McClintocks. The ensuing convention drew an unexpectedly large crowd of approximately 300 and the final product, the Declaration of Sentiments, mostly composed by Stanton and Lizzie McClintock, boldly pronounced, "We hold these truths to be self-evident, that all men *and women* are created equal." The declaration contained a resolution for suffrage that so upset Stanton's husband he refused to attend the meeting and even Mott worried that the suffrage demand "will make us ridiculous." Still, the convention approved the suffrage resolution, though not unanimously, as it had the other resolutions.[11]

The women and men who attended the Seneca Falls meeting had the same concerns as the women and men who met in Winchester, Indiana—temperance, abolition, and changing married women's property laws—and were similar in other ways as well. In 1846, just two years before the Seneca Falls meeting, a group of women from a rural area of New York petitioned that state's constitutional convention for political and property rights. In both states it took the force of a small number of women—in Indiana, Way and the Hiatts, and in New York, Stanton, Mott, and McClintock—to set the wheels in motion. Of all the women at Seneca Falls, Stanton remained the most active and most controversial over the course of the next fifty years. Unlike the Indiana women, she came to reform through her love of ideas and the feeling that her life had too many boundaries. With plenty of education and the support of a wealthy father, her life should have been open to all possibilities, but because she was a woman her role in life was constrained. When she and McClintock wrote the Declaration of Sentiments for the Seneca Falls meeting, it was designed to get rid of boundaries created by a lack of access to education, to professions, to property, and to voting. As the country moved from property ownership to voting status as a sign of citizenship, Stanton understood that women needed both.[12]

While Stanton became the leading philosopher and agitator behind the nineteenth-century woman's rights movement, the woman who worked in the trenches and traveled the nation, often without Stanton, and who became a friend to many Hoosier suffragists was Susan B. Anthony. The dynamic duo of Stanton and Anthony formed in May 1851 just a few months before the Winchester meeting in Indiana. Like Way and Thomas, they were young. Anthony was thirty and Stanton was thirty-six. Anthony, like Way and Thomas, was a Quaker who had been a schoolteacher and had left the profession because of low pay. Like Way and Thomas, Anthony was also much more invested in temperance and abolition than Stanton. Unlike Way and Thomas, who probably did not have a close friendship, the partnership between Anthony and Stanton endured difficult times, sometimes made by others and sometimes by themselves, and gave the woman's rights movement what it needed—a philosopher and a superb organizer and tactician with boundless energy. Much more so than Stanton, Anthony understood the need to focus squarely on suffrage at the expense of all other reforms. This stance later led her into conflict with Hoosier temperance advocates, but Anthony never stopped believing that suffrage came first, and all other reforms had to wait.[13]

In October 1852 the Indiana woman's rights group met again, this time in Richmond at the Warner Building. The delegates focused on the creation of a constitution for the newly named Indiana Woman's Rights Association. The association created four standing committees that reflected the emphases of the new organization: Woman's Labor and Remuneration, Woman's Legal Condition, Woman's Social Position, and Woman's Education. This time the women and men debated a list of twelve resolutions as they continued to refine their purpose and goals. Again, the convention delegates did not explicitly ask for the vote, but instead referred to the idea that "Woman should equally enjoy the rights of citizenship with Man." More resolutions referred to the

HISTORY OF WOMAN SUFFRAGE, VOL. 1 (NEW YORK: FOWLER AND WELLS, 1881)

Lucretia Coffin Mott was one of the most venerated national suffragists in the nineteenth century.

recognition of "natural rights" for both men and women. The most pragmatic resolutions echoed the previous year's call for better employment opportunities, education equal to that which boys received, and "for equal labor equal reward with man." Now that the association had a formal name and a recognized early leadership and members, the members continued to hone their objectives and began to plan public actions to achieve them.[14]

The ever-growing group of women and men dedicated to woman's rights once again assembled in Richmond's Warner Building in 1853. Either the large number of attendees or the small dimensions of the room led them to seek a larger room in the building on that first day, but to no avail. The meeting's secretary felt compelled to note that in spite of the overcrowded conditions, decorum and attention to the speakers ruled the day. Finally, the IWRA acquired a larger room in Temperance Hall. While the previous annual meeting had solidified the creation of the association, this meeting was important for the first bold stance taken on the question of suffrage: "That in a Republic, the greatest dignity is conferred by the elective franchise, bearing in its train all political immunities and rights; therefore, woman for the greater development and preservation of her individuality, demand equality in all of the political rights and functions."[15]

From 1853 to 1859 the IWRA focused on three major goals—employment and compensation for it, education, and, finally, the vote. Demands for expanded employment opportunities for women and equal pay for equal work took center stage at the 1853 conference. At that meeting the IWRA stressed "the necessity, the respectability, and morality of useful occupations" and called for "all trades, professions and employments be laid open to women." The stress on employment options continued across the years with a call for women to be "prepared for lucrative employment." The women at the 1857 meeting declared that women "must burst through the barrier of old established custom of Society, force her way into occupations and offices now wholly monopolized by men, and prepare for the hardships and trials necessarily consequent on business life." In perhaps the most practical and straightforward call for action yet, the association suggested that women only shop at or use the services of women-owned businesses or businesses with women employees. In addition to access to occupations, the IWRA stated again the claim for equal pay. In 1852 it had stated that society should "reward the labor according to the work done without regard to sex" and reiterated in 1857 that women should receive "equal remuneration with man for the same kind of and amount of labor."[16]

Of course, if women were to have access to all occupations, they also needed access to the education required for those occupations. Again, the topic came up repeatedly throughout the 1850s. The association suggested the "institutions of learning may be open to both sexes indiscriminately and that the education of females may be as extensive and thorough as that of the other sex." For some in attendance, the link between education and employment was obvious and a resolution in 1854 condemned the denial of "entrance into colleges or other institutions of learning, the arts and sciences, professions, or other vocations of life, which afford more ample remuneration for services rendered." In other words, women in the IWRA in the 1850s knew women worked outside the home since they themselves did. Thomas completed medical school and began practicing medicine with her physician husband during the 1850s. Way had worked as a schoolteacher and a tailor. Jane Murrow owned a general store. Mary Birdsall published a women's newspaper, *The Lily* (originally published by Amelia Bloomer), a woman's newspaper published in Richmond, Indiana. Sarah Iliff-Davis was a milliner. They also knew that most women, even teachers, made little money and less money than men who did the same work. They not only wanted women to be able to secure employment, but also to find employment that would help them support their families.[17]

Not surprisingly, however, suffrage got the most attention in the years following the 1853 convention. While it took a couple of years for women to specifically demand the vote, once they did, suffrage stayed at the forefront of their cause. This may have been spurred on by Frances Dana Gage, a nationally known and well-respected woman's rights speaker who frequented IWRA meetings. Gage introduced the boldest statement made up to that time at the 1854 IWRA meeting at the Masonic Hall in Indianapolis: "the *right of suffrage* is, in our opinion, the Basis of our enterprise, since we do not seek to place woman under man's protection, but to give her the *power* to *protect herself*." The resolution was accepted by those present and was similar in wording to a resolution that had been offered at an Ohio meeting. By the next year, the question became how to achieve suffrage. Emma Swank suggested the formation of "district societies" throughout the state with the goal of having them act in concert with the IWRA. This led to a discussion about "organized action" which meant gathering signatures on petitions that advocated woman suffrage and submitting those petitions to the state legislature. Birdsall announced that preprinted petitions requesting that the state legislature call a constitutional convention to add woman suffrage, had been printed and were available at the newspaper's office. Mott, a famed and revered national woman's rights leader, one of the organizers of the Seneca Falls convention, and friend of Thomas, attended this convention and applauded this course of "practical action" and recommended asking for suffrage "at once." Ernestine Rose, another nationally known and respected leader of the movement, told the meeting about her experience in New York state when petitions with 13,000 signatures were presented to the New York legislature and given a "respectful hearing."

LIBRARY OF CONGRESS

Prominent women of the nineteenth century, including (clockwise from the top): Lucretia Coffin Mott, Elizabeth Cady Stanton, Mary Livermore, Lydia Maria Child, Susan B. Anthony, Grace Greenwood, and Anna Dickenson in the middle.

Petitioning was again the focus of the 1857 meeting. Although it is not clear if the previous call for petitions had led to their circulation in the state, Way once again mentioned the need to collect signatures from both women and men and to have those petitions submitted to the legislature. Thomas, Sarah Underhill, and Agnes Cook were appointed to present them.[18]

Throughout the 1850s, the IWRA gathered strength. Members organized large meetings, practiced parliamentary skills, consulted with and listened to stirring speeches by national woman's rights leaders, and delivered their own messages to groups of women and men. The Indiana group also drew considerable attention from national reformers and placed itself firmly on the national suffrage scene. The ties they forged in the 1850s led to Indiana women assuming national leadership positions after the Civil War. The final achievement, though, of this first phase of the Indiana woman's rights movement came in 1859 when three of its members—Cook, Thomas, and Birdsall—addressed a joint session of the Indiana legislature in one of the most important events in Indiana women's history.[19]

On January 19, 1859, the usual hubbub of a legislative day intensified until the House chamber dissolved into turmoil. Legislators and the public knew that women were about to address the legislature for the first time. Men and women filled the floor and the galleries of the chamber and some people stood on the furniture to get a better view. Representatives gave up their seats to women visitors leading to "members standing in rows along the aisles among gay bonnets and rich dresses of the ladies like rows of rusty corn stalks in a field of poppies." State senators joined the throng and appeared flummoxed at the disarray. Some senators complained about the lack of seats, half expecting the visiting women to relinquish their places, but nothing could be done to relieve the congestion and confusion.

While a discussion ensued among some of the legislators about whether the scheduled time for the presentation was 2:00 p.m. or 2:30 p.m., other members of the House and Senate took the opportunity to tease unmarried representatives about escorting the women speakers to the platform. No one quite seemed to know how to behave under such unusual circumstances. Finally, Cook, Thomas, and Birdsall appeared. They sat with the Speaker of the House at his usual stand in the front of the chamber. Cook delivered a few remarks "inviting a serious and candid attention to the intrinsic merits of the petition about to be presented." In other words, she wanted the audience to take this momentous occasion as seriously as the women intended it.

Thomas then presented the petition signed by more than 1,000 women and men. She spoke for around thirty minutes on the themes the IWRA had developed since 1851, beginning with property rights and the vote and she stressed that the vote gave women the power to protect themselves. Thomas expanded the usual IWRA call for women's access to the professions by relating how women had worked to support their families during the recent 1858 national financial panic and how women were gainfully employed in such diverse professions as astronomer, author (using Harriet Beecher Stowe and her best-selling *Uncle Tom's Cabin* as an example), and, like herself, as physicians. Her final remarks centered on the injustice of property laws that did not allow a woman to be the "guardian of her own children" when the husband died, and she reassured the audience that women could vote and still be mothers.[20]

Birdsall spoke next, again for about thirty minutes, reiterating Thomas's points—self-protection and the right to vote. At that point the joint session ended, and the senators left the chamber. The House convened to discuss the petition even though the women petitioners and visiting citizens were still present, but after a few minutes decided instead to adjourn and reconvene for a discussion of the petition on Friday. Local newspapers noted that even after the official close of the session, several women and men stayed behind to discuss temperance issues.[21]

Press responses to the joint session were generally negative. The *Lily* emphasized that Thomas spoke "clearly and distinctly." The Indianapolis press agreed, but criticized her for not projecting her voice and therefore not being heard in the "inevitable undertone of bustling and stirring in such a large crowd uneasily situated." An especially vociferous attack leveled against the women found in a letter to the editor of the *Indianapolis Daily Journal* said that instead of women taking such a public stand, "they could tell us of it in our bed chambers. They could argue the case at the breakfast table with their hair in curl papers, they could dun us for rights while going to church or lecture, or when discussing the sweet preliminaries to matrimony." The small temperance discussion that happened after the speeches also rankled the letter writer. Apparently a Mrs. Ferguson threated to "clean up" two taverns in Noblesville, implying the use of "axes and hammers." The disgruntled writer claimed this comment proved that women followed "impulse and feeling" rather than the "cool calculations of statesmanship," apparently ignoring the reality of the often loud and sometimes violent debates heard in both state and national legislative bodies in the first half of the nineteenth century.[22]

His most expansive argument, however, focused on the discomfort men might feel due to a change in their domestic lives should women gain the vote. He ranted, "I know what is the matter with you women's right ladies. You don't rule your husbands by love as the rest of the women of Indiana do; you try to force them into your measures—they turn rebellious on your hands, then you fly to the ballot box and ask to get laws made to suit you. Would you rule the men by fining or imprisoning them? No, no, go home and fold them more closely in your arms; get them up better breakfasts, and dinners, and that will make them good natured; keep the children from squalling, and look well to the shirt buttons and stocking darning, then see if your homes will not be a paradise, and your rights all safe to the true love of your good man." He concluded by claiming that women who participated in politics lost their physical beauty, a comment still used today to denigrate women in politics.[23]

The "reporting" on January 20 and the letter to the editor on January 22 must be examined with great care. Both portray Thomas, Cook, and Birdsall as inexperienced speakers and nothing could have been farther from the truth. Both writers critiqued the speakers' volume and presumed that the women had never spoken before a large crowd. We know, of course, from the minutes of the IWRA meetings, that attendance was large. We know that a meeting in Richmond had to be moved to a larger place to accommodate the large group of women's supporters and that attendees were orderly and attentive despite their discomfort (as opposed to the disorder displayed by their state legislators when confronted with overcrowded conditions on January 19). And we know that all three women were experienced orators. Rather than pointing out the deficiencies of the speakers, these comments in the *Journal* pointed out the lack of attention paid by the writer to the burgeoning women's movement in Indiana.

Who were the women who bore the brunt of such ridiculous insults? Many were quite young for the prominent role they played in the movement. At the time of the 1859 legislative session, Thomas was forty-three and Birdsall and Way were thirty-one. Way had been only twenty-three when she called for the 1851 meeting. Unfortunately, it is difficult to find out much about many of Indiana's other early woman's rights leaders. Names appear briefly in official IWRA documents and sometimes a few, such as Jane Murrow and physiology lecturer Emma Swank, were considered essential enough to the cause at the time to be included in the brief biography section of the standard history of the national woman's movement, *History of Woman Suffrage*. Even these

COURTESY MORRISSON-REEVES LIBRARY, RICHMOND, INDIANA, AND ELAINE GEPFORD AND THE MINCER FAMILY DESCENDANTS

Doctor Mary Thomas, most likely in the 1850s, at the start of the woman suffrage movement in Indiana.

women, however, left no personal papers behind. Luckily, two of the most prominent leaders of this early phase of the struggle for woman's suffrage in Indiana—Way and Thomas—worked in the movement for several decades and left behind enough documentation to piece together both their personal lives and the important work they did for woman's rights in the state and, in their later years, across the country. The similarities between their paths to women's rights included accepting teaching positions as young women and discovering, as in Thomas's case, that she would be paid less than a man. Way found another job—she manufactured women's hats and dresses and men's clothing; Thomas joined with two other women who were also outraged at the discrimination in wages to form, in 1836, a small, local woman's rights organization in Ohio. Their later work with the IWRA stressed women's access to employment, no doubt a result of their own experiences.

More than any other woman reformer prior to the Civil War, Way's bold, vigorous, and persistent work for temperance and suffrage went hand in hand. She dedicated most of her life to reforms within Indiana and across the nation. A birthright Quaker, she was a member of the antislavery Friends and some say she did some work with the Underground Railroad in east-central Indiana. When her father died, she found work as a teacher to help support her mother and a sister's children. While it was not unusual for a woman to teach school during this time, it was usual for women teachers to be paid less than men teachers. Because she needed to earn more money to support her family, she quit teaching and took up millinery, dressmaking, and tailoring. This ability to take charge and to affect change is seen even more forcefully in Way's role in the temperance movement. According to her biography in *History of Woman's Suffrage*, Way organized a "Woman's Temperance Army" in Winchester, Indiana, in April 1854. The women apparently demanded that grocers and drugstore owners, both of whom sold alcohol in their stores, sign a pledge to stop the practice. All except one signed the document. The holdout, William Page, suffered the army's wrath. Armed with axes they broke down his door, broke a window, and split open whiskey barrels in the street. In 1857 Way found herself facing the barrel of a gun when a saloon keeper attempted to prevent her group from breaking up his establishment. Way returned the favor, drawing her own weapon. During the standoff, the rest of the women emptied the saloon of its liquor.

Way held several offices in the Indiana Order of Good Templars and was as well known, perhaps more well known, for her temperance activism as she was for her suffrage work. Surely there was talk among the other woman's rights leaders about Way's daring temperance activism, but there is no indication that it hampered her ability to maintain her leadership position in the IWRA. Still, it was her zeal in reducing the sale of alcohol, possibly brought on by the near death of her brother from alcohol poisoning, that prodded Way to urge the presentation of a petition for woman's rights, including the vote, perhaps to pass temperance legislation, in 1857. Hoosier "liquor interests," as brewers and tavern owners would later be known, eventually campaigned against woman suffrage because they feared women's votes would lead to prohibition. For now, they simply wanted women to not destroy their businesses.[24]

While Way mastered the art of organizing conventions and experienced the results that direct action could bring, the IWRA gained national exposure and prestige through the connections of another woman, Thomas. Like Way, Thomas's life touched on the three big reform movements—temperance, abolition, and suffrage—with Thomas's forays into reform beginning during her childhood. Born in Pennsylvania to Quaker parents, Samuel and Mary Myers, the family relocated to Maryland. Thomas's father worked with nationally recognized abolitionist Benjamin Lundy and, according to Thomas, together they held the first antislavery meeting in the United States. Her father educated his children himself and even took them to nearby Washington, DC, to hear congressional debates. He later moved the family to the Quaker and antislavery stronghold of Salem, Ohio, where Thomas helped her father around the farm and, since her father had also become a physician, she began training with him for a medical career.[25]

Already steeped in reform ideas through her family's abolition work and her own experiment with woman's rights in 1836, the 1840s sent Thomas down the path of more radical reform ideas. She met her husband, Owen

Thomas, and together they lived for a time in one of seven communes devoted to developing an exemplary lifestyle that hopefully would serve as a model for national social reform. The communes failed after just four years due to financial difficulties. Then, at an 1845 Ohio Friends Yearly Meeting, Thomas began her lifelong friendship with Lucretia Mott. National woman's suffrage workers later revered Mott and looked to her for guidance. Most likely, Thomas felt the same.[26]

At the time of Indiana's first woman's rights convention in 1851, Thomas was thirty-five-year-old, the mother of three daughters, and continuing her medical training. After moving to Fort Wayne, Indiana, Thomas joined her husband's medical practice and studied under his direction. Since her father and two of Thomas's sisters already practiced medicine and one sister taught at Penn Medical University in Pennsylvania, her decision was not wholly unexpected. Thomas later explained that her first concern was for her family and after "the most vigorous discipline of my mind and systematic arrangement of time" she sewed six months' worth of clothing for her family and in 1853 left to take her final training where her sister taught in Pennsylvania. This devotion to medical training explains her absence from the earliest IWRA meetings. She sent strong letters of support to Hoosier women, but focused her energies on her family and her medical education. After taking time away from her final coursework because of the death of one of her daughters, Thomas finally received her medical degree in 1856. She also met Lucy Stone, another national woman's rights activist who became Thomas's lifelong friend and was the future leader of the American Woman Suffrage Association. After her family moved from Fort Wayne to Richmond, Indiana, Thomas simultaneously launched her medical practice and spent part of 1857 and 1858 adding newspaper editor to her list of accomplishments. She edited, with Birdsall, the *Lily*. Finally, in 1859, Thomas served as IWRA president and read the petition for suffrage (and delivered some of her own thoughts) to the Indiana legislature.[27]

These two bold, daring, and persistent women were essential to the IWRA's successful first years. It is apparent from their actions—taking an axe to kegs of alcohol and staring down a gun-toting bar owner with a loaded weapon, living in a commune, studying medicine, speaking to the legislature—that they made some, for the time, unconventional life choices. However, a biography about Thomas stressed the "womanly" parts of her life to the point it referred to her as a "womanly woman." Thomas herself emphasized, when recounting her life story, that not only did she meticulously prepare her family for her absence during her medical training, but also that her devotion to putting her family before all other concerns continued after she became a practicing physician. She often rose at 4:00 a.m. to complete her writing (letters and newspaper columns devoted to woman's rights and to temperance) before her family demanded her attention. Thomas even described herself as "unaggressive" and that "she pursued a modest, straightforward method of meeting all difficulties," which evidently was her formula for "victory triumphing over ignorance, mean mindedness, and prejudice" aimed at a woman doctor.

The official history of Wayne County, Indiana, after listing all of Thomas's medical and civic accomplishments, described her as having "easy manners . . . great self-denial . . . a talker rather than an orator . . . kind and benevolent" and possessing "a gentle, motherly tenderness" with her patients. How to reconcile this Thomas with the woman who lived in an experimental commune, toiled long hours to become a physician, sent inspiring letters on women's employment opportunities, edited what was for the time a radical women's newspaper, and braved ridicule by addressing the state legislature? There can be no doubt that the public thought supporters of woman's rights in Indiana in the 1850s stepped outside the norms of acceptable women's behavior. Like Way, Thomas was a birthright Quaker and though both left that faith for the Methodist Episcopal Church (in Way's case she rejoined the Quakers after the Methodist Church no longer allowed women to serve as ministers), they grew up around strong women who, because of the Quaker stress on equality of the sexes, did not believe in any conflict between bold and daring social statements while simultaneously asserting a calm confidence in the justice of their causes.[28]

The IWRA made great strides pursuing ways for women to gain the power to protect themselves. As Thomas noted in her speech to the legislature, by the end of the 1850s it was not unusual to see a woman speak in public and argue for the vote, temperance, improved married women's property laws, or women's access to education or jobs. Women worked at various professions and three women spoke to, and presented a petition with 1,000 signatures to a joint session of the state legislature. Surely, the Indiana woman's rights movement was on a roll. However, the "political excitement that preceded the election of Abraham Lincoln to the Presidency," as Thomas put it, pulled the women into the national political turmoil of 1860 and then into the war itself.[29]

Chapter 2

WAR WORK

Women across the North put aside their suffrage work and shifted their focus to "war work" when the Civil War began on April 12, 1861. They did this out of loyalty to the country; devotion to the soldiers who were often their husbands, sons, or neighbors; and, for many, a firm belief in the immorality of slavery. The Sanitary Commission, a national organization with state branches that coordinated shipments of humanitarian and medical aid to Union soldiers in the field, consumed a great deal of women's time and effort. Women made bandages, canned and pickled vegetables, preserved fruits, and made any other items a soldier might need. The commission forwarded these articles in an organized manner so that Union soldiers and hospitals received the important supplies. Women's groups held bazaars and fairs that stretched over several days to raise money for whatever the soldiers might need. They sold homemade goods, raffled more expensive items, put on theatrical entertainments with themselves and their children as the feature players, hosted notable speakers, and did everything and anything they could think of to get citizens to attend and donate to their cause.[1]

National suffrage leaders such as Susan B. Anthony and Elizabeth Cady Stanton supported the war effort, but also criticized President Abraham Lincoln's slow movement toward emancipation of the Confederacy's slaves. In 1863 they formed the National Woman's Loyal League, a group that pushed Congress toward the passage of the Thirteenth Amendment to end slavery. Women who belonged to the league gathered signatures on petitions and delivered those petitions to Congress to pressure senators and representatives to swiftly pass the amendment and send it for ratification before the war ended. Without the amendment, after the war Lincoln's Emancipation Proclamation, an executive order, could be challenged in the courts and possibly rescinded. Congress enacted the Thirteenth Amendment in January 1865.[2]

When the war concluded in April 1865, many woman's rights activists expected that their service to the country would be rewarded with suffrage. Surely, they thought, the successful implementation of the commission, their participation in the political work of supporting the passage of the Thirteenth Amendment, and the personal war work and sacrifices that a civil war necessarily entailed demonstrated women's important roles as citizens who defended their country. The shock and disappointment they felt when former male slaves were granted suffrage, but women were not, hit many activists hard and inspired the formation or reformation of woman's rights groups across the country. While still agitating for several other important woman's rights, they now made suffrage their major goal.

For the women who belonged to the Indiana Woman's Rights Association, Lincoln's election, followed over the next two months by the secession of seven states from the Union, stalled the momentum and visibility of their cause. Doctor Mary Thomas explained the absence of any woman's rights meetings in Indiana during the war: "The women suffrage workers in common with all other Patriotic Citizens gave themselves to the work of the time, and as duty called followed the soldiers to the camp, the field, and hospitals or engaged with their whole hearts in the Sanitary work at home. . . . during all these years the women suffragists of the state gave their labors, their influence, their money, and in some instances their lives to the cause of freedom for the country, tho ourselves still trammeled with legal and political fetters that we had helped others to cast off."[3]

Hoosier women had flooded the Sanitary Commission with aid by scraping lint, making bandages, canning and pickling produce, and packing boxes with these supplies plus soap, socks, and any other thing they thought a soldier might need. In Indiana the state commission did an admirable job coordinating the delivery of these valuable supplies to the state's regiments, but they also coordinated with the national organization. Some women also worked with the Christian Commission, another humanitarian-aid association.[4]

Local aid groups held fairs and bazaars, often during the late fall/early winter, after harvest but before Christmas, to raise money to give soldiers' families some extra food and/or presents during the holiday. A lavish fair was held in Indianapolis in November 1863. The fair included all the traditional trappings of a community fair—raffles, the sale of homemade goods (food and clothing), an auction, and musical and theatrical performances. It continued over the course of several days. The auction included a 1582 volume titled "A Work on Ecclestical Rhetoric by Bishop Augustine of Verona, Together with His Three Lectures." It seemed that the entire town paid a small admission fee and came out to support the effort. Similar fairs and activities took place across the state. Sometimes towns held community dinners for soldiers' families. In Lafayette a masked ball was held to raise money, but came under criticism for not raising much money beyond its expenses.[5]

Women across the state helped the war effort in other ways as well. In Indianapolis women who did not need paid employment offered to clerk in stores, taking the places of men who had enlisted and, it appears, the women gave their wages to the clerk/soldiers' families. Despite such inventive ways to help, soldiers' families had a rough time during the war. Benevolent societies and concerned neighbors tried to help them, but with so many men in the state enlisting and leaving families behind, many women and their families suffered from the lack of income and absence of labor. Many women needed help to support their families, yet found the time to offer help to others. The state government tried to help by employing hundreds of women at the state arsenal in Indianapolis. From the youngest girls of nine or ten years of age to the oldest at eighty, women filled and packed cartridges and earned a piece-rate wage for the dangerous work. Massive explosions at other places, including the Allegheny Arsenal outside Pittsburgh and at the arsenal in Washington, DC, led to scores of women's deaths. The Allegheny explosion happened on the same day as the Battle of Antietam, leading to the largest loss of life for both men and women on any single day during the war. Fortunately, no explosions took place at the Indiana arsenal. When the arsenal closed in 1864 the state provided soldiers' families (some were former arsenal workers) with bread rations from the bakery at Camp Morton, a prisoner-of-war camp in Indianapolis. Still, both of these efforts helped only a few hundred.[6]

Because of an absence of personal letters or diaries, it is difficult to say what most of the IWRA members did during the war. They probably focused on helping with the war effort and since many members also had ties to

BASS PHOTO COMPANY COLLECTION, INDIANA HISTORICAL SOCIETY

Old City Hospital, Indianapolis, Indiana. The hospital was used to treat both Union soldiers and Confederate prisoners of war (in a separate wing) during the Civil War.

abolition and temperance, it is likely that they continued to focus on those reforms as well as worked for the Sanitary Commission. The public work of the two most prominent reformers, Thomas and Amanda Way, gives us an idea of what was possible for women to do during the war and how those experiences led them to rekindle the woman's movement after the war.

When the fighting began, Way's family became deeply involved in helping the war effort and "four of the five brothers enlisted to serve in the Union Army." Way worked with the Sanitary Commission and also served as a nurse on one of the many hospital steamers that transported wounded soldiers and medical supplies up and down the Mississippi and Ohio Rivers. She was one of seven women aboard the *City Belle* that left for Vicksburg, Mississippi, on June 25, 1863, and arrived just as the siege of that city ended with a Union victory on July 4. The steamer returned to Indiana with fifteen wounded. By this time, Way lived in Kansas to be near her brother and sister-in-law and worked with other women there to help soldiers after a major battle at Mine Creek. Many decades later, in 1897, Way and many other women nurses were awarded nurse's pensions by the federal government—she received twelve dollars each month for her service. Pensions for nurses had become available only five years earlier.[7]

Of the two women, Thomas's war work was more unusual. Early on, she worked with both her local sanitary aid society in Richmond and the Indiana Sanitary Commission. As part of this work, she and other women cared for wounded Hoosier soldiers at Nashville, Tennessee, after the Battle of Stones River in early 1863. Evidently, General William Rosecrans, who oversaw the hospital, at first prevented these Hoosier women from helping the sick and wounded because he did not allow anyone except the sisters of the Catholic Church to care for wounded soldiers. Undaunted, Thomas observed hospital conditions for a day and then wrote a scathing letter to Indiana governor Oliver P. Morton detailing the harm done by both the officers in charge of the ill and those whose job it was to see the dead transported to their homes. Apparently, Morton responded by having those men removed from their work. Later that year, Thomas traveled on a steamer, the *Sunny Side*, along with other women and men, nurses, and doctors among them to escort soldiers wounded at the siege of Vicksburg to Indiana, a mission similar to the one Way had completed. The eventful trip included Thomas calming a patient suffering from delirium and the *Sunny Side* catching fire. Filled with 200 sick and wounded soldiers, the steamship had paused at an island in the Mississippi River and somehow a fire started. Everyone—officers, doctors, and nurses—scrambled to get wounded men off the ship. They insisted, to no avail, that Thomas quickly abandon the burning vessel. She refused to leave the forty-seven men under her direct care, some so immobile that she had to feed them, and insisted on helping evacuate them before leaving the ship herself. Fortunately for all concerned, the ship's crew brought the flames under control and the *Sunny Side* continued its journey.[8]

Later in the war Thomas worked with her husband, a doctor and an army contract surgeon, at a refugee hospital in Nashville, Tennessee (two of their daughters worked as teachers among the refugees). At some point, and the dates are not clear, she also worked in hospitals at Natchez and again at Vicksburg. As a licensed doctor, she did the same work as her husband and still the army only gave her the title of "assistant physician" and she did not receive a pension as was awarded to Way (Thomas died before pensions became available).[9]

The indefatigable Thomas not only traveled across the country to give medical assistance to soldiers and refugees, but she also served as an associate editor of and frequent contributor to the only woman's rights newspaper known to have been published during the Civil War, *The Mayflower*. Edited in Peru, Indiana, the *Mayflower* indirectly descended from *The Lily*, Amelia Bloomer's woman's rights newspaper. Mary Birdsall of Richmond, Indiana, had purchased, and with the help of Thomas, published the *Lily* in the late 1850s. When Birdsall gave up the *Lily*, Thomas probably encouraged Lizzie Bunnell to purchase it. A former typesetter in Fort Wayne, Bunnell had taught typesetting to Thomas's daughter when the family lived there from 1853 to 1854. Bunnell now worked in that capacity for a weekly newspaper in Peru, Indiana, where she lived with her family.[10]

Bunnell's family had moved to Indiana in 1848 and her mother died shortly thereafter. To help support her father and siblings, Bunnell became a teacher, but found that her health suffered from the work, so she took up typesetting. After Thomas apparently approached Bunnell about taking on the *Lily*, Birdsall and Bunnell attempted to negotiate the purchase. In the end, the sale did not happen. Bunnell claimed to have made several different "propositions" to Birdsall, none of which were successful. Bunnell did not receive subscription lists or any material goods that might have made it easier to start her own newspaper. Bunnell offered Birdsall a chance to explain herself in the pages of the *Mayflower*, Birdsall did not, so the details about the difficulty of the purchase remain a mystery. Undaunted, two years later, at the age of twenty-six, Bunnell started her own woman's rights newspaper. Bloomer's letter in the March 1, 1861, issue of the *Mayflower* clearly demonstrates Bloomer's support of and belief in the need for the newspaper. For the next three years, Bunnell tried to support her family, struggling with wartime shortages of paper, problems with deliveries, and a populace whose financial situation, because of wartime inflation, meant few could afford luxuries such as a woman's rights newspaper.[11]

The *Mayflower* commenced business on January 1, 1861, just after the states of the lower South began to secede from the Union. It was an unbelievably difficult time to launch a new periodical of any type, not to mention a paper dedicated to woman's rights. Still, Bunnell produced an eight-page (most of the time) paper, twice monthly.[12]

Despite her usual work as a doctor, her volunteer activity with the local soldiers' aid society, and her work in the field at Union hospitals and aboard hospital ships, Thomas frequently contributed articles in the first two years of the paper's existence. Her first two pieces emphasized her signature con-

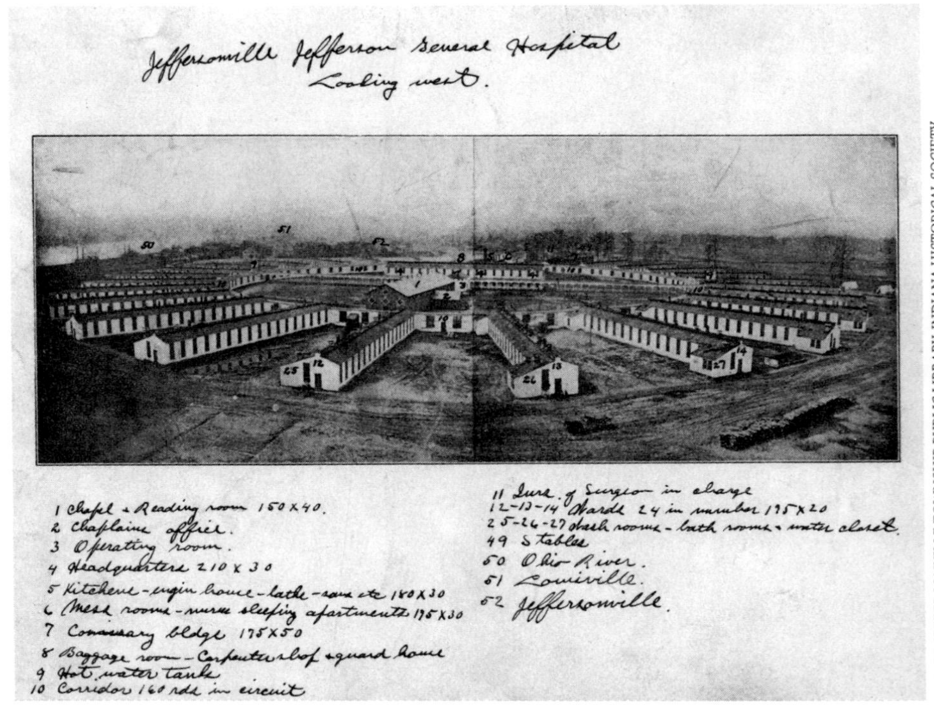

Jefferson General Hospital, Jeffersonville, Indiana, the third largest military hospital in the country during the Civil War.

GIFT OF JEFFERSONVILLE TOWNSHIP PUBLIC LIBRARY, INDIANA HISTORICAL SOCIETY cern—women's employment. She composed an article about women business owners who lived in her hometown of Richmond, beginning with "the oldest businesswoman in the place," Sarah Iliff, a milliner. She also mentioned other milliners, a photographer, boardinghouse keepers, a dry-goods store owner, and two "saloon" owners who sold ice cream and oyster soup, "but keep nothing that will intoxicate." She praised other store owners, presumably men, who hired women clerks and a newspaper owner who employed a woman typesetter. In another article, probably channeling her own frustrations, she opined that women would be more readily accepted into medical schools and women physicians into medical societies after they had proven their skills and value as medical professionals during the war.[13]

Thomas kept the focus of her articles on the question of wartime employment for women, including women (and men) who worked in the medical field. She criticized the employment of "secessionist" doctors (presumably doctors who hailed from the Confederate states) who worked in federally controlled hospitals and praised Dorothy Dix, who established the Union nurse corps and assigned the women to various Union hospitals. In October Thomas heaped praise on an Indiana woman who decided to accompany her husband and son's regiment as a nurse, leaving her two daughters behind in the care of friends. Her duty, the mother felt, demanded the sacrifice. She praised nurses from Wisconsin in the next issue.[14]

Thomas also gave favorable column space to women who served at home, reporting that the Richmond, Indiana, soldiers aid society with between seventy-five and a hundred members, prepared boxes of food and other donations for the soldiers who had just defeated the Confederates at Fort Donelson. She warned that victory should not make women complacent—the war raged on. She also took her pen in hand to urge the government to severely punish any Rebels captured as a means to help quickly end the war.[15]

Thomas also retained her interest in her earlier reform issues—abolition and temperance and mixed them with her vociferous Unionism. She praised women and men who found time in spite of the war to attend the Grand Lodge meeting of the Independent Order of Templars in Fort Wayne. The group supported temperance-inclined military officers who they hoped would decrease the chance that enlisted men might drink or learn to drink during the war. The Templars in Richmond released a set of resolutions in May 1863 in support of the war, President Lincoln, and Governor Morton. Thomas signed this letter, which also asked Templar members to boycott any businesses owned and operated by "rebels or butternuts," probably at Thomas's suggestion. Further, the Templars expressed the hope that no liquor would be found in army camps. Thomas noted that during a visit to Camp Wayne (the Union army mustering site in her home Wayne County), she heard no profanity and did not see signs of drunkenness. The officers, she felt, had set a good example for the men under their charge.[16]

Not surprisingly, most of the strong Unionist sentiment of the *Mayflower* came from Thomas's pen. She called Lincoln "worthy and honored" and the paper printed an article that rebutted criticism of Mary Lincoln. An entire column supported an announced draft of young men into the Union army. She deemed the draft "a good thing as it will take a class of men who have stood aloof from the war. That class of indifferent men who have neither volunteered nor given of their substance to maintain the families of volunteers, will now have to take their full share." She even encouraged the government to require everyone "to take the oath of allegiance and in case of refusal allow them so many days to go to the souther [*sic*] where they belong by right—we should then be rid of a good many *rebels at home*." Thomas wanted Southern rebels punished because "the South inaugurated the rebellion and now should suffer the consequences and pay the expenses." She pushed for the re-election of Indiana's George W. Julian to the U.S. House of Representatives because of his ardent antislavery stand. For "the last fifteen years," she noted, "he has stood in this county as the fearless and undaunted advocate of the great principles of freedom which the Government is now adopting to preserve itself from sinking into inglorious obscurity." She hated the fact that instead of voting for Julian, the most she could do was persuade others to vote for him.[17]

Bunnell's pen was less fierce than Thomas's, but she also cared deeply about the war. One of her most detailed articles about it came when she reported on conditions in Indianapolis after she rushed there to tell her brother good-bye as the Twentieth Indiana Volunteer Infantry Regiment left for the front. She reported on the city, the several military camps scattered throughout the community, and even interviewed a woman cartridge maker at the state arsenal who complained that she made less than a man. Later she printed some of her brother's letters to inform her readers about battlefield conditions. From those letters it was readily apparent that the Twentieth was deep in the fighting in the East so it probably came as no surprise that the black border on the September 1, 1862, issue announced the deaths of her eighteen-year-old brother and one of her cousins.[18]

Both Thomas and Bunnell praised the passage of the Homestead Bill, with Thomas mentioning it first in the June 15, 1862, issue. Congress had attempted to pass the Homestead Bill before the war, but congressmen from many of the states that now formed the Confederacy had blocked its passage. Now, however, the bill easily became law. The bill gave homesteaders 160 acres of public land that they did not have to begin to pay for until five years later—an ingenious way for a still predominately agricultural people to acquire a farm. Since women had proven during the war they could farm without men, Thomas thought homesteading would be a good way for her sex to gain a means of support. Suspicious that the bill excluded women, Bunnell wrote to South Bend's Schuyler Colfax, then Speaker of the House, for verification that women could use the bill to obtain land. He said that yes, women could indeed acquire land through the new law. The *Mayflower* had encouraged women to undertake farm work prior to the passage of the bill and now they pushed farming as a viable woman's career.[19]

The *Mayflower* remained in print until February 1864, but changes were afoot professionally and personally for the editors. Bunnell married Doctor S. G. A. Read in 1863 and at that point probably began the process of giving up the *Mayflower*, which announced its office had moved to Columbia City, Indiana. She and her husband moved to Iowa in 1865, where she published a weekly newspaper called the *Upper Des Moines* and became a well-known Iowa suffragist and speaker. In the last extant issue of the paper, Thomas paused to pay tribute to her recently deceased father, who had continued to speak against slavery until the very end of his life and suffered an apparent heart attack while giving an antislavery speech in Philadelphia. Life had changed for Bunnell and Thomas. They had attempted to prepare women for what they hoped would be a big opportunity after the war to broaden the notion of women's employment, education, and political options.[20]

It was clear to anyone who even glanced at issues of the paper that the war and woman's rights dominated it. Still, after the death of Bunnell's brother, Thomas stated that "while some of our readers may think that our paper savors too much of politics and the war, yet we feel so deeply interested in the success of our country's struggle for liberty, that we confess other considerations are of minor importance compared with this contest."[21]

Perhaps one of the most persistent messages that came out of the *Mayflower* was the belief on the part of the editors and of several contributors that women's war work—nursing, staffing aid societies, taking men's jobs, working the farm, working in arsenals, and publishing Unionist newspapers—would inevitably lead to the passage of woman suffrage legislation after the war. The sacrifices that women made personally, emotionally, and economically proved, once and for all, that women were citizens and that as citizens they should be able to vote. Lecturer and well-known woman's rights advocate Frances Dana Gage expressed this change most succinctly in her article, "What the War is doing for Women." The changes in women, according to Gage, were immense: "Feeble women have grown strong, selfish women philanthropic, giddy women assumed labors and duties unthought of before, ambitious women found opportunities for gratifying aspirations, and good women ample calls upon all the resources of their amiable hearts." In addition to these gains, Gage said that in the long run war affected women by "teaching them the great responsibilities of life; teaching them of their own power; teaching them through suffering to grow strong."[22]

This seemed to be something that others could agree with as well, if for other reasons. Soon after the Civil War ended in 1865, Indiana state representative Charles B. Lasselle, a Democrat, proposed adding woman's suffrage to the state constitution at the legislative session called to deal with end of war business. Why he suggested the change is unknown, although he opposed suffrage for African Americans and perhaps this was his way of adding additional white voters to the rolls. The proposal went nowhere but is just one example of the great anxiety that was about to overwhelm the country over the question of African American male suffrage. At the national level, after the war ended, former abolitionists and woman suffrage advocates had formed the American Equal Rights Association to push for suffrage for African Americans and for women. Then, first the Fourteenth and then the Fifteenth Amendment to the Constitution attempted to give only African American men the right to vote. Women did not understand why they were excluded at what seemed to be a perfect time to extend the vote to those who had just proven themselves to be loyal, patriotic citizens through their war work.[23]

The 1869 IWRA meeting came on the heels of four years of this intense national debate about suffrage for African Americans. The Fourteenth and Fifteenth Amendments had grown out of Congress's dealings with President Andrew Johnson, who had attempted to thwart Congress's ability to ensure that former slaves had basic citizenship rights by vetoing the Civil Rights Acts of 1866. Congress overrode his veto (the first case of an override in American history) and saw the need to embed citizenship rights for former slaves in the

Constitution to prevent any future veto from interfering with African American suffrage. On June 18, 1866, the Fourteenth Amendment made it through Congress, went to the states for ratification, and became part of the Constitution on July 28, 1868.

The wording of the new amendment had caught woman suffrage activists by surprise. For the first time in the Constitution, citizens were defined as male. Prior to the Fourteenth Amendment, gender was not designated in reference to citizenship—the Constitution was gender neutral. Women had assumed they were citizens, but now the Fourteenth Amendment called that assumption into question. If the word male was included, did that mean that women were not citizens? The amendment did not explicitly say that African American males could vote, but, if they were to enjoy all rights of citizenship, it would logically include the vote. The wording of the Fourteenth Amendment dismayed the three undisputed leaders of the national woman's movement—Elizabeth Cady Stanton, Susan B. Anthony, and Lucy Stone. They and other suffrage leaders struggled with how to respond to what many women believed to be a slap in the face after all they had done for the country during the war. Stanton was beside herself with anger. She railed against any man, no matter his race or nationality—with little to no education—voting, and women, who had attained the highest level of education possible for women in the country and who had supported the nation in a time of dire emergency, could not vote. It seemed an impossible thing had just happened. The national woman's right movement leapt back to life, this time with an almost singular focus on suffrage.[24]

Instead of excluding women, suffrage leaders thought, why not include women? This amendment seemed to be the perfect opportunity to guarantee voting rights for both African Americans and women. The need to protect the gains of the Civil War for former slaves was clear (voting rights would help in that regard), but woman's rights and African American rights did not need to be mutually exclusive. Once the states ratified the Fourteenth Amendment, it would take a separate amendment for women to also gain suffrage. Stanton feared that it would take another hundred years before that happened. The American Equal Rights Association had promoted the cause of both African Americans and women and now women had been left behind.[25]

Woman's rights advocates did have friends in Congress. U.S. Senator Samuel C. Pomeroy of Kansas introduced a woman suffrage amendment on December 8, 1868, just a few months after the passage of the Fourteenth Amendment, but it went nowhere. African American rights remained Congress's focus when, on February 25, 1869, the Fifteenth Amendment, which explicitly stated that race, color, or previous condition of servitude could not be used to deny someone the vote, went to the states for ratification. Again, woman's rights advocates were outraged. It would seem easy enough to add "sex" to the wording—race, color, previous condition of servitude, or sex—and therefore ensure that women had the vote. Echoing Pomeroy's earlier attempt, Indiana congressman George W. Julian introduced another woman suffrage amendment in March 1869, but again it went nowhere. The first states ratified the popular Fifteenth Amendment in March.[26]

The American Equal Rights Association met in May 1869 while the ratification process of the newest amendment was still in progress and, of course, the group focused its debates on the new amendments. The tumultuous meeting split woman suffrage proponents into two camps. The background here is important. While the Fourteenth Amendment proceeded through the ratification stage in 1867, woman's rights advocates flocked to Kansas to campaign in support of referenda there—one for African American voting and one for women voting. Stanton, Anthony, and Stone, along with her husband, Henry Blackwell, crisscrossed the state promoting the referenda, enduring terrible weather and housing to no avail. The measures failed. While in Kansas, Stanton and Anthony accepted financial help from the racist, eccentric Democrat George Trainor. He also funded their new woman's suffrage newspaper, *The Revolution*. With Stanton as the editor and frequent contributor, the newspaper covered suffrage, marriage laws, unions, women's employment, and a variety of other subjects that were important to women. Accepting the help of the disreputable Trainor and debating personal topics such as divorce and marriage in speeches and in the *Revolution*, brought Stanton and Anthony into conflict with other members of the American Equal Rights Association who wanted to sharpen their focus on gaining suffrage and thought Trainor repugnant. By the time of the May 1869 meeting, many suffrage advocates in attendance were disgruntled with other suffrage advocates. The atmosphere could not have been worse. Stanton and Anthony remained uncompromising in their opposition to the Fifteenth Amendment despite incredibly persuasive arguments on the part of leading African American abolitionist and woman suffrage supporter Frederick Douglass that the dire situation of African Americans demanded the vote to protect them. He noted:

> When women, because they are women, are hunted down through the cities of New York and New Orleans; when they are dragged from their

> houses and hung upon lamp-posts; when their children are torn from their arms, and their brains dashed out upon the pavement; when they are objects of insult and outrage at every turn; when they are in danger of having their homes burnt down over their heads; when their children are not allowed to enter school; then they will have an urgency to obtain the ballot equal to our own.

Douglass's argument of course echoed that same theme that women had argued for years—suffrage gave African Americans the power to protect themselves.[27]

The Fifteenth Amendment did not go as far as many, including Douglass, would have liked. Defining who could and who could not vote was a tricky business and weakened the amendment. Republicans in the North wanted to retain their own state's suffrage qualifications. For example, "in the West, the Chinese could not vote . . . Pennsylvania demanded the payment of state taxes to vote; Rhode Island required foreign-born citizens to own $134 worth of real estate; Massachusetts and Connecticut wanted literacy." The amendment left the door wide open for not allowing voting for a myriad of reasons. Still, adding the word sex to the amendment would have been easy to do. During this debate, Indiana ratified the Fifteenth Amendment on May 14, 1869.[28]

The national Equal Rights Association dissolved after the May meeting, dividing its members between those who supported, even if reluctantly, and those who did not support the Fifteenth Amendment. Stanton and Anthony, who did not support the amendment, formed the National Woman Suffrage Association almost immediately. Stone and Blackwell, disappointed that the Fifteenth Amendment did not include women, but willing to back it anyway, formed the American Woman Suffrage Association in November 1869. On January 8, 1870, they published the first edition of their newspaper, the *Woman's Journal*, just as Stanton and Anthony's *Revolution* breathed its last breath. Although Stanton and Anthony and Stone and Blackwell tried to remain cordial, the rift grew acrimonious and former friends, while not enemies, could see no grounds for working together. The split in the national woman suffrage movement lasted until 1890.[29]

When the IWRA met for the first time since 1859, a decade of war, postwar political chaos, and the very recent dissolution of the national woman's rights organization into factions were not far from anyone's thoughts. On June 9 and 10, 1869, at the Masonic Hall in Indianapolis, a large mass of women and men heard Way call the meeting of the association to order. She announced that this meeting continued the pre-Civil War IWRA. Its goals included pressuring the Indiana legislature to pass suffrage legislation and to enact new laws regarding woman's education, woman's labor and wages, and even marital relationships. The chair, according to the *Indianapolis Daily State Sentinel*, then urged that attendees to work as quickly as possible toward their goals.[30]

While it is safe to assume that woman suffrage advocates rejoiced at the successful restoration of the Union, we do not know exactly how Indiana's suffrage leaders felt about the controversial Fourteenth and Fifteenth Amendments. Surely, they felt as upset and befuddled as the national leaders with whom they had long been allied. Way, according to the *Indianapolis Journal*, stated, "that it was time that woman was again asserting her right and demanding to be admitted to her just relation to the world."[31]

The official call for the IWRA convention did not appear to stress topics other than had been discussed over the course of the 1850s. It once again emphasized "the right of a larger range of employments, juster wages, and more efficient education of women." Still, it became obvious beginning with the opening prayer offered by Reverend C. H. Marshall of the Fourth Presbyterian Church that suffrage would be the convention's focus when he stated, "as we have now the influence of women in so many departments of life, the time might be speeded when the ballot should be given into her hands, so that in this we might also receive and enjoy the benefit of her moral influence."[32]

Despite similar goals, the IWRA that met in June 1869 was in many ways a different organization from the 1850s group and the meeting attracted different types of people. Some familiar people issued the call for the convention—Way, Thomas, and Emma Swank—but new faces joined them, including Professors A. C. Shortridge and R. T. Brown of Indianapolis. Both men had pushed for the acceptance of women into the teaching profession. Doctor William Hannaman, the director of the Indiana Sanitary Commission during the war and someone who had to know both Way and Thomas, also signed the call. Other new names included Doctor Mary H. Wilhite and Lizzie Boynton (later known as Elizabeth Boynton Harbert) of Crawfordsville. In the coming years both held important roles in the suffrage movement—Wilhite in Indiana and Boynton in Iowa and Illinois.[33]

The Indiana group had also moved beyond the dominate Quaker influence of its early years. Ministers representing a wide variety of Protestant denominations attended the two-day convention. Joining Marshall of the Fourth

Presbyterian Church were Reverend E. P. Ingersoll of the Plymouth Church (Congregational); Reverend M. H. Mendenhall of Grace Church (Methodist); Reverend Blanchard of the new, for Indianapolis, Unitarian Church; and Reverend J. B. Criley of the English Lutheran Church. Military officers and various politicians attended, including Colonel H. B. Carrington, General James C. Veatch, General John Coburn, and Major Isaac Kinley. The government officials—some former Whigs and all now Republicans—included Coburn and Kinley, along with U.S. District Judge David McDonald, State Senator John Greene from Tipton County, State Representative Thomas Vater of Marion County, E. M. Ninde, and Judge Charles Martindale.[34]

Both the *Indianapolis Journal* (the major Republican newspaper in the state) and the *Indianapolis Sentinel* (the major Democratic newspaper in the state) extensively covered the proceedings and both reported that the crowd in Masonic Hall consisted of about an even number of women and men. Way noted that "we are here for that purpose [the vote], not to wage a warfare by one half of humanity against the other half but recognize that husbands, brothers, and sons have a common interest with us." This seemingly unimportant statement probably referenced the split of the Equal Rights Association just a few weeks earlier. The new NWSA wanted only women involved in their group (Stanton clearly distrusted men after the seeming betrayal of the Fourteenth and Fifteenth Amendments); the AWSA welcomed men as members and as officers.[35]

The first debate at the convention probably angered IWRA president Way, who wanted to run a tight convention. The owner of a woman's rights newspaper in Dayton, Ohio, a Mr. Belleville, rose to speak with the evident intent of boosting his paper's circulation by arguing two points that he thought might do the trick—women were educated "too much as women," and, he raised for one of the first, but definitely not the last time in the decades long debate of suffrage that was about to follow, that nine out of ten women did not want the vote. His newspaper, apparently, could help women out of both difficulties. This was audacious—the hucksterism, the apparent denigration of women's education, and the assertion that women did not want the vote. Thomas could not let the comments go unanswered. She refuted the assertion that many women did not want the vote. Her experience over the last two decades proved otherwise. Next to enter the fray was an 1868 arrival to Indianapolis—the minister of the new Unitarian Church. He brought what he referred to as his "East Coast" observations into the conversation and agreed with

Belleville. Women did not realize the importance of suffrage and needed to be enlightened about the importance of the vote for the completion of successful temperance and antiwar work. At that point, Way displayed her ability to tamp down what the *Journal* called a "spiced up" conversation. She offered to clarify Belleville's obtuse comments and suggested he meant that women needed to be educated to be something other than "well-dressed ornaments" or "kitchen drudges." The meeting then adjourned.[36]

The evening session of the first day featured the famous Mary Livermore as the speaker. Livermore rose from editing a relatively obscure newspaper with her husband to becoming the master organizer of delivering sanitary aid to Union soldiers during the Civil War. In her travels for the Sanitary Commission, she had seen women assume men's work and now traveled the country speaking in support of woman's suffrage. A tall woman with a clear voice, Livermore was a popular speaker, with women and men flocking to hear her. While the *Sentinel* simply referred to the Masonic Hall as "densely packed," the *Journal* described a standing room only situation in which even women stood in the aisles, behind the final row of chairs, and close to the door. It was so packed that one man asked to have the windows opened. Much to the chagrin of the IWRA, Livermore arrived late. When she finally appeared, she kept her remarks short and the audience in her hands—the *Sentinel* called her "an eloquent advocate of woman's rights." She emphasized women's access to education and good-paying jobs so they would have a real choice about what to do with their lives. She stated that women too often had a choice between a husband and nothing "and in most cases it was simply a choice between two nothings." She left her audience wanting more.[37]

The agenda for the next day included the possible adoption of several resolutions. Most of the discussion centered on suffrage. The group chose to fully recognize suffrage as its goal by changing the name of the group to the Indiana Woman's Suffrage Association. While national political debates on the Fifteenth Amendment were part of the convention, the possible Sixteenth Amendment that would codify woman suffrage and had been introduced by Julian in May was the first concern the attendees discussed. A resolution praised his efforts, but caused unexpected debate. The resolution (the fifth of the meeting) read:

> *Resolved*, That we feel justly proud of the actions of our representative in Congress, Hon. George W. Julian, for his bold position in favor of the Sixteenth Amendment: for we feel that while our laws are being reconsidered

> so as to give the elective franchise to colored men, they should not forget the women of the country who are surely as competent to use that power judiciously as those who have so recently been in the degradation of chattel slavery.

Swank vociferously objected to praising Julian. He had not given his name in support of the call for this convention. Therefore, she believed he did not support their cause and should not be praised for introducing the amendment. Livermore objected to Swank's objection. As a member of Congress, Julian must be a busy man. He did, after all, introduce the Sixteenth Amendment to the House of Representatives and for that lone fact he deserved their praise. Amazingly enough, Thomas agreed with Swank. After praising Julian for his abolition work and recommending his re-election to Congress a few years earlier, Thomas had changed her mind about him. The convention altered the resolution to "we feel justly proud of the action of our representatives in Congress" with Julian's name omitted. The entire discussion must have been incredibly uncomfortable for Laura Giddings Julian (George's wife) who, by the end of the convention, was named an IWSA vice president.[38]

Having dispensed with Julian, the fallout from the national Equal Rights Association meeting finally came up at the Indiana convention when Thomas and a Mrs. Burns from Dayton, Ohio, introduced a resolution about the IWSA's stance on the Fifteenth Amendment. Douglass's comments on the importance of African American enfranchisement caused, she said, "a great conflict of sentiments and words." They wanted the IWSA to "steer clear of this rock." In all likelihood this was a reference to the rift that was about to lead to the formation of the two new suffrage groups—the NWSA and the AWSA. The resolution recognized that the Fifteenth Amendment would probably be ratified and that "the true interests of society demand the education and enfranchisement of every citizen." It also recognized that the Republican Party must work for African American suffrage. Although "the framers of it [Fifteenth Amendment] refused to recognize the equal rights of women in that amendment" the IWSA thought it "unworthy of the philanthropic character of women" to stand in the way of its ratification. The resolution was quickly adopted, and Thomas immediately followed with another that "urge[d] all true patriots and lovers of temperance and moral purity to unite on woman suffrage as represented in the Sixteenth Amendment, as the rallying cry of the next political canvas." In other words, Republicans had proven they could get a suffrage amendment passed and now it was time to work for woman suffrage.

Thomas wanted the entire convention to vote on this resolution and Way ordered a standing vote.[39]

This was a big moment. The IWSA was about to endorse a constitutional amendment. It would be beyond belief to think that at least one person would not object. Of course, someone did. Martindale wanted some discussion. Early in her resolution, Thomas had noted that 200,000 women had signed a petition asking Congress for a woman suffrage amendment. Martindale did not believe that was a very large number out of the total U.S. population. He also critiqued the number in attendance at the Indianapolis meeting, even though the *Journal* reported that about 400 people, both men and women, were there. These numbers, he believed, indicated a lack of real interest in suffrage on the part of the women of the nation and the state. Therefore, woman suffrage did not address what women really wanted. Besides, he continued, the sincerity of Republican politicians was in question. Corrupt politicians would do anything, including giving women the vote, just to get elected.[40]

Livermore countered Martindale's arguments. She declared that 200,000 women who dared to sign a petition was a large number given that many women still, after all these years, had to fight public and private opposition to woman's suffrage. As to the present meeting, the hard rain in Indianapolis that day, she insisted, had held back more women from attending this important session (even though both newspapers reported the Masonic Hall was packed). In a phrase similar to one that Stone had uttered at the Equal Rights Association meeting just a few weeks before, Livermore noted, "You have lifted the negro out of the pit, and women intend to hold on to the ladder until you bring her out of the pit, too." Martindale made a few more remarks, but knew he was defeated. When the vote was taken, he, along with everyone else in the hall, stood in favor of woman suffrage.[41]

At some point during the debate over suffrage, and when is not made clear in the local newspapers, the first mention of African American women's participation in Indiana suffrage meetings appears. The *Sentinel* indicated that a note had been passed to Livermore during the debate from an African American woman wanting to know if she would be included in woman suffrage. Livermore reportedly replied, "Certainly, madam. We are all on the same footing." This is the first time any African American is specifically mentioned attending an IWRA/IWSA meeting. Given that the earliest suffragists in Indiana were also abolitionists, it is possible that they attended from the beginning. We also do not know the identity of this woman.

Indianapolis had always had an African American population and the Civil War brought more free blacks and former slaves into the city. The woman in question also could have attended the convention with members of the IWSA from the Quaker centers of Wayne County, which had at one time had the largest African American population in the state. Regardless of the residence of this woman, and any other women who attended the convention with her, unlike many other states Indiana had a presence of African Americans at suffrage meetings from the earliest days and continued to work with African American women through 1920.[42]

The 1869 meeting ended with strong speeches by Swank and Livermore. Both forcefully supported suffrage as the only means by which women could take control of their lives. Swank, after stating that women needed "better education," "better work," and suffrage, spent most of her talk on suffrage. Swank's biting remarks blamed men for a government that "for eighty years had left it a mass of corruption, and the women ought to have a chance to clean it out." Not content with chastising men, she also took aim at women who focused on fashion more than suffrage. While Swank's comments reportedly drew rapt attention and laughter from the crowd, they had attended to hear Livermore's speech and she did not disappoint them.[43]

Livermore assured her audience that prosuffrage women were not anti-domestic. Women realized, she argued, that families were "the great matter of their lives" and a belief in suffrage in no way changed that attitude. She then launched into the main point of her talk—to dismantle the objections to woman suffrage. One of her central points was to argue against taxation without representation. According to the *Journal*, Livermore argued "there were $500,000,000 of property in the half dozen largest cities of the Union, owned by women, and taxes paid upon it by them; and yet not one of them had a vote." That voting women would bring more justice to the world was another topic and she illustrated her point with the case of a woman from Chicago. A mother of five children, including an infant, the woman's husband had joined an Illinois regiment during the war. With the difficulties that existed in sending his pay to Illinois, his wife, who needed to feed her children, had no funds to do so. She decided to steal some money, with the intention of paying it back once her husband's pay reached her. She was caught and arrested. According to Livermore, the poor woman's shame and the fact that only men surrounded her in the courtroom left her mute and unable to defend her actions. Only when Livermore stumbled upon and intervened in the proceedings, did the true story come out and she was released.

Livermore forcefully argued that women who could vote would feel more comfortable in a courtroom and more important that women jurors would be able to offer more justice for cases such as this because they understood the difficulty a woman alone might have in feeding her children. Instances such as this, and the difficulties women faced with laws involving a husband's death, proved to Livermore that women needed to be heard when laws were made, and suffrage would allow that to happen. She demolished the notion that women did not want the vote by stating "it is a right, and a right cannot be withheld because many or few who may possess it choose not to exercise it." She similarly took on objections to "bad" women and Catholic women voting saying that men in those categories also voted. As to the possible exposure to "vulgar, drunken fellows" that women might face at the polls, she noted that women associated with such men already since "women do ride in the cars, walk in crowds." A polling place would be no different. She also related her own run-in with "vulgar, drunken fellows" in this case Illinois politicians who had argued with her earlier in the day that women would "debase" politics. These same men created a ruckus in a hotel (where Livermore was staying) that night by breaking whiskey bottles and furniture and vomiting in the hallway. Women, her point was, could not possibly be any "baser" than that. Her concluding remarks pivoted back to the war which, she stated, "had raised women to the stature of men" and as such, they should have the vote.[44]

Livermore's last remark was really the essence of this first woman's suffrage meeting after the Civil War. Women in Indiana had proven their value as citizens through war work. They had taken risks in the arsenal and at hospitals both away from and at the front, some nurses had died, wives of soldiers had carried on the work at home, grieved fallen husbands, sons, and fathers, and in every way accomplished their war work. The presence of many Civil War officers and ministers from a variety of Protestant denominations surely meant that even more men agreed with the women that war work had proven their worth as citizens who should enjoy the full rights of citizenship, including the vote. At the end of the tumultuous 1860s, it appeared that woman suffrage was in the not too distant future.

Chapter 3

VICTORY AND DEFEAT

How could a piece of legislation be pending and at the same time not exist? That was the question that confounded suffragists and temperance advocates in 1883. Woman suffrage and prohibition laws approved by the Indiana General Assembly in 1881 had apparently vanished. Intensive lobbying by the Indiana Woman's Suffrage Association and a new group, the Woman's Christian Temperance Union, along with a Republican majority in the legislature had led to those laws. Where had they gone?

Woman suffrage and temperance organizations became the two largest women's political groups in the United States in the late nineteenth century. In Indiana they took the form of the IWSA and a few other, smaller suffrage groups, and a state chapter of the WCTU. The IWSA and the WCTU tried to work together, in part, because many women belonged to both groups, but there were problems. Women who favored temperance or prohibition legislation did not always favor women voting. Women who wanted the vote did not always believe in regulating alcohol consumption. Prohibition agitation unnecessarily complicated the suffrage issue and kept many people—in Indiana that often meant people who lived in German immigrant communities—from supporting woman suffrage. Suffrage groups and the WCTU consistently held state and local meetings and lobbied state legislators.

That persistence led to the astonishing victories of 1881 during a special legislative session. The Indiana General Assembly, however, met only every other year and any changes to the state constitution had to pass two separate legislative sessions—in this case that would be in 1883. In spite of woman's suffrage advocates' massive efforts in 1882 to ensure that newly elected officials favored their cause, the suffrage bill and the prohibition bill went down to defeat in a clear case of political chicanery. Whether it was that defeat, or the distraction of the WCTU, or the rocky transition of suffrage work to the next generation of activists, suffrage activity was less robust by the late 1880s.

National luminaries in the field of woman's suffrage rallied Indiana suffrage workers at the IWSA meeting at Masonic Hall in Indianapolis in June 1870. Susan B. Anthony, Lucy Stone, and Henry Blackwell represented the two new national suffrage groups. Anthony and Elizabeth Cady Stanton had formed the National Woman Suffrage Association to push for a federal woman's suffrage amendment and to focus on other woman's rights issues including divorce reform and other personal reforms. Stone and Blackwell led the American Woman Suffrage Association, which pushed for state-level suffrage reform and for the most part stayed out of controversial personal issues. Both groups pushed Indiana women to get better organized at the county level so they could more easily lobby their local and state representatives.

The convention ran true to standard IWSA form with the introduction of resolutions and some debate about them, but the most important event occurred after the public portion of the meeting during an executive session. The IWSA voted 15 to 14 to become an affiliate of the AWSA, but also urged the competing national groups to "unite" as soon as possible. The IWSA remained aligned with AWSA until the two national groups merged in 1890 to form the National American Woman Suffrage Association. At one point the IWSA almost disassociated itself from both national associations, but instead formed both AWSA (IWSA) and NWSA (an Indianapolis suffrage group) affiliated groups and did so with less acrimony than national suffragists had done.[1]

Amanda Way and Emma Swank presented another suffrage petition to the state legislature in 1871. One historian has called the ensuing discussion "the most serious debate on the subject which had yet been heard in the legislative halls of Indiana." The importance came from the fact that the legislators debated at all and not from the quality of the comments. The arguments in favor emphasized fairness and equality. State Senator Othniel Beeson of Wayne County, home to many suffragists, defended a constitutional amendment. He thought the time had come to "lift the burden from the shoulders of these petitioners asking for the rights and equalities that belong to them as citizens of our common country" and reminded the legislators of women's recent Civil War relief work. In his opinion, that work proved women's devotion to the country and confirmed they should have access to the vote. Another legislator frankly stated that any man who did not want to give "either man or woman equal chances with him in the race of life . . . is a moral coward."

Arguments against suffrage ranged widely. One man argued that women would not want "to be brought in right behind the negroes. . . . They would feel less humiliated to wait a little while until these XVth Amendment tracks are somewhat obliterated." Another feared that women voting would "revolutionize society, array the sexes against each other and against themselves, and that can not possibly promise us any good result." One legislator based his arguments on men's anatomy. Man was "the strongest, is given the greatest stature, the broadest shoulders, the largest arms, the hardest muscles, the largest

COURTESY TIPPECANOE COUNTY HISTORICAL ASSOCIATION, LAFAYETTE, INDIANA

Suffragist and prohibitionist Helen Gougar of Lafayette helped guide the woman suffrage movement in Indiana through the 1880s and 1890s.

feet, the coarsest voice, the strongest limbs, the greatest endurance" and apparently that was reason enough for only men to have the vote. One legislator gave a fictional example of a woman who served on a jury (juries were selected from voter rolls) whose husband had to periodically bring a breastfeeding child to the courthouse. In the legislator's mind that maternal duty proved that women should not vote. What, another legislator asked, if a woman wanted to run for and hold a political office? She would have to "throw off the mantle of her modesty, banish all her female graces" and campaign everywhere at all hours of the day and night. In the end, even the bill's supporters chose to vote against it. An amendment that had inserted the word "white" before the word "woman," and thus eliminated the chance for suffrage for African American women, had turned the bill into something woman suffrage supporters could not defend, so they voted no. One disappointed lawmaker remarked, "I believe that the time has passed in this country when distinctions should be made in law on account of color in every thing either civil or political."[2]

While the IWSA petitioned the state legislature to no avail, women in other states decided to try to vote. These test cases, today referred to as the New Departure, were meant to challenge whether the Fourteenth and Fifteenth Amendments to the U.S. Constitution included women or not, based on the use of the word citizen in the documents. Women asserted that citizen referred to them as well and therefore they should be allowed to vote. According to one account, about 150 women attempted to vote in several states and in the District of Columbia, where two African American advocates, Frederick Douglass and Mary Ann Shad Cary, and approximately seventy women, white and African American, tried to vote. The most famous of these was the attempt by Susan B. Anthony and sixteen other women to vote in her home town of Rochester, New York, in 1872. The most consequential was the attempt to vote by Virginia Minor, also in 1872. In all the cases the NWSA, which spearheaded this New Departure, hoped that women would attempt to register, be denied or arrested, and would challenge the denial or arrest in the courts and argue that the Fourteenth and Fifteenth Amendments already gave women the vote.[3]

When Anthony attempted to register to vote she was allowed to do so, and she voted. Local authorities subsequently arrested her for illegal voting. Before her trial began, the judge had already decided to find her guilty, but did not want to jail Anthony or take the case any further through the court system and give her the opportunity to argue at a higher court. When Anthony refused to pay her fine, Rochester officials declined to pursue the case and she never had to pay. Minor's case, on the other hand, went all the way to the U.S. Supreme Court. Minor attempted to vote in Missouri and when officials denied her the opportunity, she sued. The 1874 case, *Minor v. Happersett*, gave the Court the opportunity to state that the Constitution did "not confer the right of suffrage upon any one." The decision in *Minor* unexpectedly led states to devise ways to disenfranchise African American males. Suffragists were dismayed at the unexpected consequences of their actions.[4]

Indiana women relied on older methods to advance the suffrage cause and did not make the bold move to attempt to vote until the 1890s. Instead, the IWSA praised a Michigan woman for voting and encouraged Indiana women to also make the attempt, although no records exist to suggest that anyone did. The IWSA also offered its support to Anthony after her arrest for voting, but again, no one in Indiana attempted to vote. The defeat in the state legislature in 1871 was a harbinger of things to come for the 1870s. The IWSA was broke and confused. While the group agreed that "agitation" was needed to advance the cause of suffrage, no one knew just what agitation meant. Perhaps, someone suggested, working with a political party? Could suffragists "nominate our candidates" for the major political parties and "cooperate with the party that promises us the best prospect of Success to our cause"? That idea appealed to some suffragists because at a meeting in Fort Wayne in 1874 they debated whether to "recommend the friends of impartial suffrage to meet in a mass state convention at as early a day as possible and put in nomination a ticket that all women suffragists and temperance men can heartily support." Many women in the IWSA, including Way and Doctor Mary Thomas had always firmly believed in temperance reform. The possible enactment of temperance or outright prohibition legislation as a reason for suffrage had come up frequently at IWSA meetings over the years. Joining forces with "temperance men" must have been tempting. A statewide Prohibition Party ticket in 1872 coincided with this first strong mention of the IWSA's need to "agitate." Given that not all suffragists agreed with interfering with a person's right to drink alcohol, the IWSA kept its distance from the issue for the time being.[5]

Women in other midwestern states also found themselves caught in this volatile mixture of suffrage and temperance. The WCTU grew out of the 1873–74 Woman's Crusade in Ohio. Women gathered on street corners and outside drugstores and saloons (both sold liquor) and prayed until the owner agreed to sign a pledge not to sell alcohol. Many proprietors signed just to keep the women away and went back to selling alcohol a few months later. Still, the crusade spread to other states and in November 1874 the WCTU was formed. Excessive consumption of alcohol was an issue for women everywhere because women in many states still did not have complete control over their property, wages, salaries, or children. A husband who drank to excess caused untold damage to everyone involved. Despite the obvious advantage of aligning with suffragists, the WCTU was slow to adopt suffrage in its official platform and did not do so until 1881.[6]

The WCTU came to Indiana in 1874 as supposedly the first state WCTU chapter in the country, with Zerelda Wallace as its president. Wallace, the widow of former Indiana governor David Wallace, was well known and well liked throughout the state, and, at that time, she was no suffragist. Her work squarely focused on the elimination of alcohol. Her conversion to suffrage came in 1875 after presenting the Indiana legislature with a prohibition petition containing 10,000 signatures and addressing the men on the topic of prohibition legislation. The story goes that "one senator told her that the prohibition petition 'might as well have been signed by 10,000 mice'" since he represented the will of his constituents—men only. At that moment, Wallace realized that to be heard, she needed to be a constituent, too, and that meant she had to be able to vote. She thanked the senator for converting her to the suffrage cause and after serving as president of the state WCTU for many years (1874–77 and 1879–83), she then led the national WCTU's committee on suffrage (1883–88) and served as an officer in Indiana suffrage groups.[7]

After her own conversion, Wallace attempted to convince other women in the WCTU to adopt the suffrage cause. She reportedly met with a cool reception. Some temperance women in Indiana did not want to see the two questions connected. The *Indianapolis News* interviewed one WCTU member about the matter. She stated that "I have been compelled to withdraw from the WCTU ranks in Indiana during the last two years because I was not willing to be used to forward woman's suffrage at the expense of the temperance work." She insisted that suffrage had "driven off or kept away many of the best women. We have been forced to endure the situation, because ladies who do not desire to take up suffrage are, as a rule, quiet and retiring, and prefer to yield the field to the suffragists rather than fight for what they think right."[8]

While the contretemps with temperance did not help the advancement of the suffrage cause in Indiana in the 1870s, another innovation, the creation of local suffrage clubs, probably did. It is difficult to know how suffrage clubs formed in other parts of the state, but Indianapolis women left behind some fascinating records. Martha McKay and her husband, Horace McKay, along with highly respected public high school teacher Laura Donnan, formed the Indianapolis Suffrage Society in 1872. McKay was a member of the IWSA and by extension the AWSA. Born into a Quaker family, she married Civil War captain Horace McKay, who she credited for bringing her into the suffrage fold because he "was an ardent supporter of woman suffrage." Donnan taught at Indianapolis High School, subsequently Shortridge High School, and later served a vital role in connecting African American suffrage organizations in the city with groups dominated by white women. In an interview given many years later, McKay stated that no church let the Indianapolis group meet in its building, so they met at the Masonic Hall. Martha attended legislative sessions to hear arguments about suffrage and other legislation. Legislators who knew her socially ignored her when they passed in the statehouse. Donnan agreed with McKay that suffragists were not socially accepted in Indianapolis in 1872.[9]

INDIANA HISTORICAL SOCIETY

Home of Horace and Martha McKay at 1241 Broadway Street in Indianapolis. Horace McKay was instrumental in persuading his wife to embrace woman suffrage.

Another Indianapolis suffrage group formed later in the decade—the Indianapolis Equal Suffrage Society. Indianapolis educator May Wright Thompson Sewall's description of a secretive meeting, where nine women and one man organized the new society, might have been exaggerated by her tendency to drama. She stated that "had we convened consciously to plot the ruin of our domestic life, which opponents predict as the result of woman's enfranchisement, we could not have looked more guilty or have moved about with more unnatural stealth." By 1878 when the group first met, woman's suffrage had been in the air for decades and the McKays had a society up and running. Perhaps what McKay and Sewall both alluded to was that although there had been suffragist activity in the state for almost thirty years, Indianapolis society in general, or the well-to-do middle classes specifically, might not have been as accepting of the topic as women who lived elsewhere in the state. By the next meeting of Sewall's new group, twenty-six persons, including staunch temperance advocate and now suffragist Wallace, attended. Sewall's suffrage society accepted new members only by a vote of the existing membership. In an elitist view of its members, Sewall reported that by 1885 the group had "a membership of 175, including many representatives of whatever in Indianapolis is best in character, culture, and social place."[10]

Unlike the IWSA, which depended on yearly or sometimes twice-yearly conventions to discuss and organize their work, Sewall's group worked through women's existing social networks and hosted festive events to draw everyone's attention to the suffrage question. Through the sheer force of her personality; her popular, respected, and academically rigorous Indianapolis school for girls; and her association with the nationally known and respected Wallace, Sewall soon became known in national suffrage circles and most closely identified with Stanton and Anthony's NWSA. As with any small town, and Indianapolis was still like a small town at this time in spite of its size, conflicts arose even among people who worked toward the same goal. In this case, the dispute started because of a letter Lucy Stone sent to Martha McKay. Stone wanted to hold the 1878 annual meeting of the AWSA at Indianapolis to encourage women from the Midwest and the West to attend the meeting and join the group. McKay, as a member of the national AWSA board of directors, was the logical person for Stone to appoint to make local arrangements. McKay excitedly told her friend Sewall about the event. The women knew each other well. They lived near each other in the College Corner area of Indianapolis close to Northwestern Christian University (which later moved to other sites and was renamed Butler University after its founder) and with other women created the then new (1875) Indianapolis Woman's Club. (The IWC did not and still does not participate in political work, but there was no ban on individual members pursing such work away from the club.) Sewall eagerly responded that "I should feel like taking hold of the matter of 'ways and means if it is thought desireable' that the Com. do so," indicating a commitment to have the two Indianapolis suffrage groups—one affiliated with the AWSA and led by McKay and one affiliated with the NWSA and led by Sewall—work together to organize the meeting.

By September, however, Sewall had made local arrangements for the meeting without consulting with McKay who had also made arrangements. A very confused Stone wrote to McKay and pointedly directed her to take charge of the event. Stone blamed herself for the confusion as to who was in charge, but the blame clearly lay with Sewall. For all her positive traits—her energy, her organizational abilities, and her speaking and writing skills—Sewall also seemed supremely confident (and she was often right) that only she could organize meetings and other suffrage events in the correct way. When the AWSA met in Indianapolis that November, neither McKay nor Sewall hosted the convention—Thomas of the IWSA introduced her old friend Stone.[11]

The tension between Sewall and McKay is a striking example of another problem for Hoosier suffragists that began in the 1870s and lingered throughout the entire campaign for suffrage—personal conflicts between intelligent, energetic, and highly motivated women who wanted to improve women's lot in life but disagreed on the ways to accomplish that goal. Barred from official party politics because they could not vote, suffragists formed close alliances with other like-minded women and distanced themselves from those whose tactics differed from their own. What began as a misunderstanding between McKay and Sewall over local arrangements for a national meeting blew up into a long-lasting disagreement. Mary Livermore, who made frequent visits to Indianapolis for speaking engagements and to visit friends, found herself drawn into the fray, siding with her longtime friend McKay and distancing herself from Sewall. Similar battles took place at the national level. The NWSA and AWSA disagreed, sometimes vehemently and often with a distinct sense of sadness and even betrayal, about how to achieve suffrage. While it can be theorized that women who wanted the vote should always have closely cooperated with each other, ambitious, dedicated women, and men, often take their own paths. To McKay and Sewall's credit, their disagreement evidently did

GIFT OF THOMAS CREVELING, INDIANA HISTORICAL SOCIETY

Martha Nicholson McKay in the 1880s.

not carry over into the IWC, where both remained active members.[12]

The IWSA drifted throughout the 1870s. On February 2, 1877, Thomas, Wallace, and Livermore attended a special session of the Indiana House of Representatives. Livermore spoke on behalf of a resolution that stated the Indiana legislature thought that the Fourteenth and Fifteenth Amendments to the Constitution gave women the vote—a technique of the New Departure that had been used earlier in the decade by Anthony and Minor, but for some reason just now surfaced in Indiana. The *Indianapolis State Sentinel*, at one time no friend to the woman suffrage movement, thought her argument "eloquent and logical, and was by far the best speech that has been made in the house during the present session." The resolution lost by a vote of 22 to 51, but some men apparently said they voted against the resolution not because they thought women should not vote but because they believed a Sixteenth Amendment to the Constitution that gave women the vote was the best way to go. Other men across the country agreed with that strategy. The next year, U.S. Senator A. A. Sargent of California introduced what became known as the Susan B. Anthony Amendment, which stated, "The right of citizens of the United States to vote shall not be denied or abridged by the United States or by any state on account of sex." This proposal, with the same wording, was the amendment that Congress approved decades later.[13]

The Indiana suffrage movement finally made real progress in the early 1880s because women more directly and consistently moved suffrage into the political arena and adopted political lobbying techniques to get their message to their representatives. Their achievement is one more indication that the path to success for suffrage was persistence and continuous pressure. One of the places to see that is in the early 1880s meetings of the IWSA with Thomas presiding at all three meetings. The first, in 1880, included remarks by Wallace, now vice president of the IWSA despite also belonging to an NWSA affiliated group, and Helen Gougar of Lafayette, whose speaking abilities made her enormously popular even as her adherence to temperance reform caused problems for other suffragists. Thomas suggested that IWSA members "take some active measures toward moving in numbers and force upon the next Legislature in the matter of securing their enfranchisement." Members urged men who favored woman suffrage to nominate and vote into office other men who supported suffrage. The group encouraged women to write to their local representatives about the topic. Since national political conventions were about to convene, the IWSA hoped to send one woman to each convention to directly lobby politicians. The Indianapolis Equal Suffrage Society, led by Wallace as president and Sewall as secretary, did just that. These techniques applied constant pressure on the men who could change the laws—a technique that was initially successful but was then dropped for decades.[14]

The 1880 Indiana general elections had been brutal with mudslinging and personal animosities leading some politicians to abandon one party for the other. When the votes were counted, Republicans had taken the governor's office and both houses of the state legislature. This gave the new governor, Albert G. Porter, the opportunity to promote legislation that he thought particularly important. He urged legislators to enact woman-suffrage legislation. In addition, Marion, Bartholomew, Blackford, Boone, Brown, Clinton, Decatur, Franklin, Fulton, Gibson, Grant, Hamilton, Hancock, Henry, Howard, Huntington, Marshall, Monroe, Parke, Perry, Riley, Saint Joseph, Shelby, Spencer, Starke, Tippecanoe, Vermillion, Wayne, and Wells Counties had all sent petitions to the governor asking for women's enfranchisement.

Both the Indiana Senate and House created committees specifically to deal with woman's suffrage with John H. Furnas in charge in the House and Simon P. Yancey in the Senate. Suffrage supporters wanted both an immediate presidential suffrage bill (meaning women could vote for the United States president through presidential electors) and a bill that amended the state constitution so that women could vote in all matters. Asking for two suffrage bills at once—one for immediate (limited) suffrage and one to guarantee it in the state constitution—remained a strategy in the following decades. Suffrage lecturer and Indianapolis resident Mary Haggart, along with Gougar, addressed the House on February 15. While they argued for suffrage based on no taxation without representation and the natural rights of citizens, they also countered the often-repeated argument that women did not want the vote. Both cited statistics from other states where hundreds of thousands of women had signed petitions asking for the vote. Haggart, Gougar, and Thomas also addressed the Senate on February 17. From the brief summary of Haggart's remarks, it appears that she reminded the senators that more men than women were found in reformatories and penitentiaries and that more women than men worked in some factories, perhaps trying to make the point that women contributed to society in positive ways and therefore deserved the vote. Gougar's remarks were not mentioned, but Thomas, appealing to the legislators' vanity, noted "the fact of the women having their petitions for the ballot before the Legislatures of eleven States this winter, the Indiana General Assembly had a great and glorious opportunity to be the first in the field for the recognition of the rights of women." In addition to these speeches, Wallace and Gougar lobbied for two weeks at the statehouse, as did Paulina T. Merritt of Indianapolis, a suffragist and philanthropist who funded housing for soldiers' orphans and projects operated by the Indianapolis Colored Women's Mutual Society.[15]

An early argument against suffrage raised in the state senate acknowledged women were intelligent enough to vote and were equal to men, but worried that voting would "degrade" women. The speaker was "willing to give to woman all the legal rights enjoyed by man, placing her upon an equal footing with him before the law in respect to her person and property," but he wanted to "save" woman from the "evil tendencies and debasing influences of political strife." The Senate subsequently denied women the vote and some legislators went on record to explain their final decision. One noted that giving women the vote was "a simple act of justice." Another thought that "the true test of qualification for a voter is intelligence, virtue and patriotism" and stated that "the women of the State of Indiana possess these qualifications in an equal degree with men" so voted in favor of the bill. Another voted no because he thought it unconstitutional. Representative James Hinton of Marion County, the first African American elected to the state legislature and a Republican, voted against woman suffrage without offering a reason. He and a legislator of Irish descent who also voted no came under fire in a Bloomington newspaper. The paper excoriated them for voting against enfranchising "intelligent and cultivated ladies" implying perhaps that the men lacked those qualities. At the close of the regular legislative session, it appeared that women had lost this round. At least one paper rejoiced at their loss, stating that the decision would harm only "a few women whom misfortune or mental bias, or what not, has made dissatisfied with the duties and responsibilities of women, have left the fireside and pushed into public places."[16]

Other issues confronting the state led the governor to call a special session of the legislature not long after the first had gaveled out of session. In an amazing turn of fortune, this time both houses voted in favor of both a suffrage bill and a prohibition bill. Legislators gave only the slightest hints for their changes of heart and the resulting 62–24 vote in the House and 27–18 vote in the Senate. One legislator noted that he voted in favor of the suffrage bill because women were "persistent" and that, unlike his colleagues, he was "not afraid of their [women's] voice." Another suggested that men "might as well accept the inevitable, for the women of this country have become a part of the machinery of this great Government. They have become a part of the commercial and manufacturing interests. We cannot do without them." He further noted that "as long as you tax the female's property—as long as you make her amenable to the law—she has a right of representation at the ballot-box." For his part, Hinton changed his vote to aye, he said, because the wording of the resolution in the special session was different from the wording he voted against in the regular session. Victory had sidled up to suffragists, but one last hurdle remained. Indiana's legislature met only every other year and any amendment to the constitution had to pass in two separate sessions—for this bill that meant 1883. Although a year's wait might cause opponents of suffrage, and prohibition, the time needed to mount a strong challenge, Hoosier women decided to rejoice in the victory in hand. To celebrate, the two major suffrage groups in the state, the IWSA and Sewall's Equal Suffrage Society, quickly put together a party to thank the women and men, including state legislators, who made the bill's passage possible.[17]

Suffragists' foes quickly realized the gravity of what had just occurred and the opposition to prohibition and to woman's suffrage became intertwined. Prior to the passage of both the prohibition law and the suffrage law, the *Indiana Tribüne*, the leading German-language newspaper in Indianapolis, came out staunchly in support of woman's suffrage. It gave a favorable report on the speeches that Haggart and Gougar gave to the House and Senate. The reporter noted the repeated applause both women received throughout their talks and ended with the hope the legislature would "make this bill into law." Another article on women's education stressed the need for girls to receive for an education equal to what boys received with the end result that "an independent woman with acquired skills which she can use to drive her accomplishments does not need to be afraid of providing for herself if certain circumstances force her to stand on her own two feet, as her independence will provide her the ability to better protect herself from exploitation." The paper further supported suffrage by stating, "women are subjected to all of these laws just the same as men, yet they are not allowed to participate in writing them. . . . though women bear the burdens of war, they are excluded from all possible glory of victory."[18]

At the same time, the German press abhorred the idea of temperance and chastised women who tried to accomplish both goals. It railed against suffrage leaders "struck with pious piety and silly temperance quirks." In one case, the editor claimed that an interview with an Evansville temperance advocate "brought us to the realization that after listening to such nonsense one becomes endlessly thirsty and then a glass of beer is absolutely necessary."[19]

Once both prohibition and suffrage laws passed the special session, the newspaper came out swinging. "Our legislature has decided to offer the people a vote on two constitutional amendments," the article began. "One would give women the right to vote and the other would prohibit making and selling alcoholic beverages. One amendment gives rights, while the other takes away rights; one amendment expands freedom, while the other limits it." After stating that "not all women's rights activists are prohibitionists and not all prohibitionists are women's rights activists," the editor declared that "it cannot be denied that many Americans only support women's suffrage because they hope that with the help of women, the temperance ideas will be more easily and securely implemented." Regretfully then, "we cannot decide to recommend the practice of women's suffrage as long as temperance fanaticism is being played with . . . we must at least push off the implementation of the principle of women's suffrage until American women learn that it does not agree with the principles of freedom to give rights in one direction and trample the other under foot." Clearly the problem for some was not with suffrage, but with prohibition.[20]

Indiana had a thriving German immigrant population and breweries located in Indianapolis, Fort Wayne, and Evansville. A strict prohibition bill would strike a severe blow to both state and local economies and undermine the prosperity of German American communities. In response to this very real threat of a loss of income for hundreds of people and a loss of a distinctive part of German culture, brewers and distillers created the Indiana Liquor League to fight the prohibition bill by funding and campaigning for Democratic candidates in the 1882 elections. While both Republicans and Democrats had voted in favor of the prohibition amendment, the league blamed the Republicans since they had controlled the executive and legislative branches in

Autographed photograph of Zerelda Wallace sent by her to Susan B. Anthony.

1881. The Democratic Party rewarded the league's support by condemning the prohibition amendment. Democrats subsequently swept into state offices by almost 11,000 votes and took back the legislative branch.[21]

Unaware of the trouble ahead following the victory in the 1881 special session, the IWSA laid out an ambitious plan for the next year and a half before the 1883 legislative session. Meeting in June 1881 suffragists devoted most of their time to devising a plan of action and the meeting's minutes have a sense of urgency not found in earlier reports. They implemented, really for the first time, a scaffold for the organization that closely resembled that of a political party. It started with a Central Committee and reached down to every town in the state. That Central Committee, composed of Haggart, Wallace, Sewall, and the state IWSA president, coordinated all suffrage efforts from a base in Indianapolis to facilitate oversight of legislative sessions. One IWSA member from each congressional district in the state worked with that committee to ensure that a suffrage group formed in each district or preferably in each town. Crawfordsville, Indianapolis, and Kokomo already had such clubs, and they had proved to be effective in creating public interest in favor of suffrage. The representatives from the congressional districts plus the Central Committee formed the State Executive Committee that coordinated mass meetings, lectures, conventions, and the distribution of suffrage literature throughout the state. A speakers' bureau to staff those proposed meetings also originated in Indianapolis. The association hoped to publish a suffrage newspaper and expected to receive funding for all these activities from "individual contributions, personal solicitations and annual dues from suffrage societies." The convention approved these plans with debate found only over the idea of the suffrage newspaper which was in the end narrowly approved.[22]

The energy and optimism from the meeting seems to have spilled over into the local press. The *Kokomo Weekly Dispatch* summed up the meeting with a prediction that indicated the paper might have had a seer on staff:

> The fact is plainly apparent that before a decade of years shall have passed, the State of Indiana will have to meet the matter fairly and squarely at the ballot-box. Without endorsing the cause of woman suffrage we are frank to confess that there is more merit in it than its opponents are willing to grant. We take it that prohibition and equal suffrage will be the great questions of the immediate future. The conflict is irrepressible so long as the march of intellectual progress grows apace. We had as well trim our sails for the coming storm which is even now gathering all over this country.[23]

The formation of this grand strategy to secure passage of the suffrage bill at the 1883 legislative session did not overshadow other important business. The previous year, Haggart had attended both the national Democratic convention at Cincinnati and the Greenback Party convention. She reported on both including that, as a delegate, she had been allowed to vote at the Greenback convention. Elizabeth Boynton Harbert (from Crawfordsville, Indiana, and now married and living in Illinois) relayed her experiences at the Republican convention in Chicago. Not only had Indiana women adopted lobbying techniques in the state but they made their first rather tentative steps toward working with national political parties.[24]

One of the more touching moments at the 1881 meeting had to have been when Thomas held the convention's attention with what became her last presidential speech in front of an IWSA annual meeting (she subsequently spoke at the thirtieth anniversary celebration in October). She praised Haggart and Gougar for their speeches at the 1881 legislative session. She praised the "continued agitation" of the IWSA as a major reason for the passage of the suffrage amendment. She even praised the press, which she said had "dealt very liberally with this subject: fair argument and reason . . . has taken the place of the jeers and jests with which it was formerly coupled." She praised employed women who set an example of what women could do beyond the home. After all this uplift, Thomas also warned suffragists that a big part of the work ahead would be to reach women—defined by Thomas as women of financial means—who thought they did not need the vote. She told these women that "there are large numbers of women as worthy by nature as themselves who have not the blessing of home comforts laid at their feet" and who needed the vote "to carry on successfully the life-work that has been assigned to them, the duties that have come to them unsought." In other words, women with fewer financial means needed the vote to successfully support themselves and their families.[25]

The final meeting of the IWSA for which minutes exist was a celebration more than a meeting. Held in October 1881, thirty years after the first meeting of the Indiana Woman Rights Association, Lucy Stone and Henry Blackwell joined Thomas for a retrospective of the movement in Indiana and an optimistic look at the future. The organization's first president, Hannah Hiatt, "now quite infirm and blind," could not attend the meeting, but sent a letter of congratulations for the continued work, as did Way, who now lived in Kansas. Stone and Blackwell spoke about the progress of the last thirty years and

COURTESY DREXEL UNIVERSITY, COLLEGE OF MEDICINE, PHILADELPHIA, PENNSYLVANIA

Doctor Mary Thomas in later life. Thomas worked tirelessly with wounded soldiers during the Civil War, edited The Mayflower *also during the war, and kept the Indiana Woman Suffrage Association together until just before her death in 1888.*

Thomas read from IWRA/IWSA minutes to demonstrate that progress. In spite of the optimistic atmosphere, the final statement in the meetings' minutes, which seems to be written in Thomas's hand recognized that more work might need to be done: "Altogether the anniversary was a grand success and the old and new workers join hands for another 30 years conflict if need be for the triumph of the principles of universal justice for man and woman."[26]

The grand plan from the June 1881 meeting led to a large meeting the next year. Petitions had been signed, local groups organized, and "all women within the boundaries of the State who believed in equal suffrage, or were interested in the fate of the pending amendment" had been asked to attend a mass meeting in Indianapolis scheduled for May 19, 1882. On opening day approximately 350 women appeared. Included in the group were some African American women. Wallace made sure that they could "participate in the deliberations." Women from around the state reported to the assembled group about their local suffrage clubs' activities. Thomas read letters from supporters including one from Laura Giddings Julian whose husband, George, had introduced a woman suffrage amendment in Congress. Three different women stressed that if women could vote, they would "vote the liquor seller out of existence." Given the extensive organizing done by the liquor interests at this time against the suffrage and prohibition bills, those were probably not the speeches some suffragists wanted reported in their local press. The IWSA had received three thousand letters from across the state in support of the cause. Porter was supposed to attend the meeting but could not. The paper ended the generally positive report of the evening with an odd story: "During the evening a rat was seen to run across the stage, and although fifty ladies were seated there, not one of them so much as moved. It was taken as the most convincing evidence of the evening that women are becoming developed in strength of mind and better fortified mentally and physically, to meet the perils of life."[27]

To get the suffrage and prohibition bills of 1881 out of the second session of the state legislature in 1883 and thus into law, suffrage and temperance supporters campaigned for politicians who supported both goals. The Republican Party in particular wanted to work with women and asked Gougar and Haggart to speak on behalf of Republican candidates. They spent part of the summer traveling across the state speaking at "Sunday-school conventions, teachers' associations, agricultural fairs, picnics and assemblies of every name" to keep suffrage in the minds of the public and the politicians. Part of this work appears to have been carried out under the auspices of the IWSA, but the rest was sponsored by the Republican Party.[28]

In Gougar's home county, Tippecanoe, she and Haggart campaigned for DeWitt Wallace, a Republican. The Wallaces and Gougars were close friends and Gougar gladly took to the stump for him, giving fifteen speeches and Haggart eleven. Having the popular temperance/prohibition speaker campaign for Wallace was too much for Tippecanoe County Democrats to bear. They spread the rumor that Gougar and Wallace were more than friends and noted a specific place, Wallace's law office, and time when at least one assignation allegedly took place. Whether this rumor alone cost Wallace the election is unknown, but he lost and Gougar was now "infamous." Democrats made the loss even more miserable for Wallace and Gougar when they "paraded the streets of Lafayette with a huge painted cartoon in which Wallace lay prostrate, Francis Johnson [the Democratic victor] stood with his foot on Wallace's throat and Helen Gougar, half-dressed, pointed to Wallace and said, 'I did it!'" Rather than cower in embarrassment about the rumors, Gougar boldly brought a $10,000 lawsuit for slander against Police Chief Henry Mandler, the man behind the rumors. While Gougar's dilemma probably garnered her some sympathy among many women, others, who knew more about the story, had less compassion. Hoosier suffragist Ida Husted Harper addressed the lawsuit in her column in the *Terre Haute Saturday Evening Mail* with a "what goes around comes around" lesson. Gougar had openly accused "bolters," Republicans who did not want to vote for fellow Republican Wallace, "of infidelity to their wives, of being drunkards, of not paying their debts and of mistreating their families and she even reminds one of them that his wife 'neglects her children and house duties to such an extent as to be a matter of notorious comment.'" In other words, the rumor of Gougar's infidelity might have been payback for her own slanderous comments. Harper concluded that "women must be exceedingly circumspect in political matters, since all they have in this direction, at present, is theirs by favor only, and they should be very careful not to abuse the rights they already possess if they hope to have more in the future."[29]

Neither Gougar nor Wallace handled the extreme stress of the slander trial well. Gougar hissed at a witness; exclaimed, "I can't stay in the courtroom;" left; and then screamed in the hallway, where she broke down and had to be attended to by a doctor. Wallace engaged in his own courtroom hysterics and at one point threatened a witness in the hallway shouting "I'll shoot you! I'll shoot you!" The jury, despite these outbursts, unanimously found in favor of Gougar and awarded her $5,000. Mandler, however, never paid the judgement and the Gougars had been forced to spend about $2,000 in lawyer's fees.[30]

Suffragists had mixed reactions to the courtroom drama and to the verdict. Susan B. Anthony, while most likely embarrassed by the rumors and the unwanted association of possible immoral behavior with a suffragist, offered her support. Harper welcomed the verdict, but then once again placed some of the blame on Gougar. Gougar's own combative editorials and speeches brought on some of the problem because according to Harper, "when Mrs. Gougar attacked the character of the most prominent citizens, she might have known they would turn upon her. She showed no mercy, she received none." She also reminded her readers that "there are certain rules of propriety which we must observe. At times they seem despotic and we are tempted to rebel but a little reflection will convince any sensible person that some restrictions of this kind are necessary." Harper did not condone the slanderous comments from either side.[31]

Most important, attention on the sensational trial diverted everyone's attention away from the dramatic events taking place in the Indiana legislature. A spectacle of a trial that included outbursts by a well-known suffragist and prohibitionist could not have made for better propaganda for antisuffragists about what could happen when women became involved in politics.

The 1883 legislative session must go down in history as one of the most bizarre displays of political gamesmanship in Indiana history. The newly Democratic-controlled legislature punished Republican governor Porter by taking away his power to appoint some state officials. Then they refused to bring up and vote on the 1881 suffrage and prohibition amendments. Someone had found an old legislative rule that stated that any pending legislation had to be recorded in full in the House and Senate journals for the legislation to be considered at the next session. Whether unwittingly forgotten in the excitement, or more likely an intentional political maneuver, neither the woman suffrage amendment nor the prohibition amendment could be found in either journal. William Dudley Foulke, a lawyer, state senator, future civil-service reformer, and future president of the AWSA, repeatedly attempted to get a new amendment introduced, which led to some doubletalk on the floor as to whether the 1881 bill was still "pending." If the 1881 bill was pending, no new bill could be introduced. In Foulke's mind it had been decided, however, that the bill could not be pending since it was not found in the Senate journal. As an understandably frustrated Foulke argued: "According to the position of the Senator for Jackson (Mr. [Jason B.] Brown) we cannot submit to the people the present proposed amendments to the Constitution because they are not pending before us, and we cannot introduce any new amendments because the present amendments are pending before us. Those two statements cannot stand together." Foulke might have saved his breath. All was lost. Despite some politicians' loud complaints about the cumbersome Indiana Constitution, these sorts of arcane rules and measures remained in place and continued to bedevil women's suffrage advocates into the twentieth century.[32]

The loss of the suffrage bill took the wind out of the newly energized, politically savvy IWSA. Members met again in 1884, 1885, 1886, and 1887, although no association minutes can be found for those meetings. Early Indiana suffrage proponents were aging or had moved out of the state. Perennial favorite guest speaker, Frances Dana Gage, died as did Laura Giddings Julian. Thomas and Haggart served as officers for the national AWSA in 1884 and Foulke became its president the next year, taking all three away from more active participation in the state. It really was Thomas's last national event—she had to decrease the amount of time she devoted to suffrage work. When Hoosier suffragists at the IWSA Warsaw meeting in 1885 elected Thomas as their president, she declined to serve because of her age.[33]

While the IWSA slowed down, the Indianapolis suffrage group that had been organized by Sewall and Wallace became more active with the NWSA. Gougar, recovered from her trial and reentered the fray, and Sewall and Haggart spoke at the NWSA meeting in Washington, DC, in 1884. All three women also presented their arguments at either U.S. Senate or House Congressional Hearings on Woman Suffrage. In 1886 Wallace and Gougar served as vice presidents for NWSA and the next year they reconstituted the old suffrage group in Indianapolis as an official branch of NWSA, the Indiana National Woman Suffrage Association. Both Anthony and Gougar spoke at its inaugural meeting. The *Indiana Tribüne* noted that Gougar was "an excellent speaker. Her improvised speaking is fluent and captivating . . . sadly this woman is not using her great speaking talent for a better cause. By this we naturally do not mean her agitation for women's suffrage, but for the agitation of this temperance humbug. Mrs. Gougar is a prohibitionist through and through."[34]

Thomas died in August 1888 at the age of seventy-two. Actively practicing medicine up until her end, Thomas's last house call happened after midnight. The patient lived three miles out of town and Thomas did not let time of day or distance keep her from her duties. Three days later she died. Friends and neighbors, members of the reform societies to which she belonged, and several doctors attended her large and lengthy funeral. The pallbearers, all women, represented her life's work and also, not coincidentally, the three major pillars of the early Indiana woman's suffrage movement. One pallbearer represented the suffrage movement, two represented the temperance movement, one represented the Home for Friendless Women, and two African American women—Mrs. Kizzie Johnson and Mrs. M. A. Mason—represented both the abolition movement and Thomas's continual work within the African American community.[35]

Thomas's death marked the end of the first productive phase of the suffrage movement in Indiana. Her steady leadership in the IWRA/IWSA could not be replaced. She had attended almost all the statewide meetings, spoke at them, served as president or other officer for most of those years, served as the national AWSA president, and published the only woman's rights newspaper printed during the Civil War. When her health prevented her from moving around the state, the IWSA faltered. It cannot be a coincidence that as she moved away from active involvement, the organization ceased to keep its records up to date and eventually faded into near irrelevancy.

One year before her death, Thomas had made plans for what was most likely her last venture in public speaking for suffrage. The Indiana branch of the NWSA had arranged for suffragists to speak in all thirteen Indiana congressional districts in November 1887. Thomas, evidently, had been assumed to be one of those speakers. In a letter to Sewall about the upcoming speaking engagements, Thomas alluded to some past difficulty between them and noted, "I think we need all our combined thought to fight the enemy, *not* each other." It seems that Thomas was supposed to speak at Muncie and La Porte, but she hinted that while she knew she would be needed at La Porte, she might not make it to Muncie because she felt she needed to give up "some of my public work, I cannot do it much longer." Her husband's health and her duties at home were going to keep her "from the field." She acknowledged the presence of "younger and more active hands" in the suffrage movement and said she had "a great objection to continuing in a place after I feel I cannot be as useful as I used to be." Thomas was ready to pass the work to others, but was anyone ready to take it up?[36]

Chapter 4

"SO SLIGHT AN ORGANIZATION"

After the suffrage excitement of the 1880s, the Indiana woman suffrage movement stagnated in the 1890s. Despite a flurry of activity in 1894, when Hoosier women across the state attempted to vote, little suffrage work was done on a consistent basis. In contrast to Indiana, exciting events took place in the West. When the Wyoming Territory became a state in 1890, it granted suffrage to women. Utah followed suit when it became a state in 1896 and Colorado and Idaho men voted for woman suffrage in 1893 and 1896, respectively.

Exciting events such as these might have inspired Hoosier suffragists to dedicate more time and effort to suffrage work. However, Hoosier women were preoccupied by other matters. The Woman's Christian Temperance Union within the state and women's groups outside the state, distracted two of the best Hoosier minds of the time—Helen Gougar and May Wright Sewall. Indiana's lack of attention to suffrage worried Susan B. Anthony, although it is not clear why she fussed so much about the Hoosier State. Was it because she closely worked with three Hoosier women—Sewall, Ida Husted Harper, and Grace Julian Clarke? Was it because of Indiana's national political importance? As a swing state, Indiana drew a great deal of national attention—Indiana's Benjamin Harrison was president when Wyoming became a state. Did she hope that Indiana's suffragists could persuade Hoosier politicians to enact sweeping suffrage laws that other states might model? Was it that Indiana's state suffrage organization was one of the oldest in the nation and its near death might be an omen for the movement in general? Anthony had good reason to worry if she looked only at Indiana's suffrage movement. However, Indiana's woman's club movement was training the next generation of suffragists in organization, politics, public speaking, and publicity. Anthony most likely did not see what was bubbling underneath the surface and before she died in 1906 she had every reason to doubt that Indiana would ever again enter the suffrage fray. Fortunately, she was wrong.[1]

In 1890 the National Woman Suffrage Association and the American Woman Suffrage Association merged to become the National American Woman Suffrage Association. The move came as no surprise. Younger suffragists had entered the picture and the old arguments that Elizabeth Cady Stanton and Anthony had with Lucy Stone and her husband over the means to attain suffrage seemed less relevant and surely, the thought went, one group working with intense focus was better than divided efforts. Talks about blending the two groups began in late 1887 and continued for two years. Hoosier suffragists negotiated the merger as members of both the NWSA and the AWSA. For the AWSA, William Dudley Foulke and Doctor Mary Thomas, both former AWSA presidents, served, although it is not clear how much time Thomas gave to the merger before her death. For the NWSA, both Gougar and Sewall negotiated the merger. That these two women both served in that role in spite of increasing personal and professional tensions between them is a testament to their commitment to the suffrage cause.[2]

Few Hoosiers today know about Gougar's and Sewall's national and international influence at the close of the nineteenth century. Hoosier politicians such as Harrison and Senator Albert Beveridge capture our attention, but not these forceful women who used the same political skills as men to accomplish their goals. Gougar and Sewall had much in common. Born one year apart (Gougar the elder of the two), like many Hoosier suffragists before them they started their careers as teachers. Gougar taught for a short time in Lafayette; Sewall taught in Wisconsin and Michigan, served as the principal of the Franklin, Indiana, high school, and then moved on to Indianapolis High School, where she taught German and English. Both women also had strong working relationships with their husbands. Gougar's husband, a lawyer, had an apparent medical issue with his eyes, so she often read his legal papers to him and became so well acquainted with the law that she was eventually admitted to the bar. Sewall's first husband, Edwin Thompson, who battled tuberculosis and died in 1875, taught with her at Franklin and Indianapolis. Her second husband, Theodore Sewall, operated a private boy's school, the Indianapolis Classical School, and she taught with him there before opening her own private school for girls. Neither couple had any children. Gougar and Sewall both wrote for their local newspapers. The *Indianapolis Times* supported woman suffrage and Sewall's column, "Woman's Work," appeared in its pages from 1881 to 1885. She discussed suffrage, equal pay for equal work, and women's access to higher education. Gougar composed "Bric a Brac" for the *Lafayette Daily Courier* from 1878 to 1880. Gougar eventually branched out into her own short-lived newspaper, *Our Herald*.[3]

For all they had in common, they differed in their approaches to gaining woman suffrage. Gougar embraced the WCTU and third-party politics, while Sewall steered clear of such affiliations. Sewall instead inadvertently paved the way for the creation, both in Indiana and the nation, of one of the largest training grounds for future suffragists, the General Federation of Women's Clubs. Women who were not quite ready to embrace suffrage but wanted an outlet for their intellectual and creative endeavors, joined women's clubs. Over the course of the 1800s, most women's clubs started with a focus on cultural studies and then shifted to political action in what is known today as progressive reform. In Indiana women who participated in their local women's clubs learned how to organize, how to identify local problems, how to suggest solutions to those problems, and in some cases how to petition and directly lobby state legislators for the desired changes. When the national and state suffrage movements regained their momentum around 1910, suffragists tapped into this existing network of clubwomen to quickly and efficiently spread their message.

LIBRARY OF CONGRESS

Mary Garret Hay about 1921. Hay was born in Charlestown, Indiana, where her father was active in Republican politics. She became involved with the Woman's Christian Temperance Union and with suffrage. She served as the chair of the Republican Women's National Executive Committee in 1919.

When people described Gougar they stressed her lecturing skills. She made straightforward arguments in a clear, strong voice and spared no one from her biting criticism or sarcasm if she thought it appropriate to launch an attack. Born in Michigan, she moved to Lafayette, Indiana, as a teenager, taught school for a while, and lived there for the rest of her life. Beginning in 1878, the thirty-five-year old gifted orator began her career as a temperance lecturer in Lafayette and other towns in the northern part of the state. She had been involved with local temperance work prior to 1878, but according to Gougar in that year she witnessed firsthand the devastation caused by a man who drank too much. She witnessed his wife's death and their children's suffering. This experience changed her mind about how to tackle temperance because, "when I first became a temperance worker, I believed in praying away the evil. But I became convinced that the best way was to vote it away! After I really investigated the matter of woman suffrage, I became a fanatic on both subjects. And I am proud to say I am a fanatic." Anthony happened to attend an Indianapolis suffrage meeting that year, met and talked with the impressive young speaker, and Gougar then more seriously adopted the suffrage cause. Gougar also met another powerful orator, Mary Haggart of Indianapolis, and together they lobbied the 1881 Indiana General Assembly to encourage the enactment of both woman suffrage and prohibition legislation. Their efforts proved unsuccessful in the regular session, but both bills passed a special session convened immediately after the close of the first.[4]

As much as Gougar lectured about and believed in the benefits of woman suffrage, her heart belonged to the prohibition movement. She continuously lectured for the cause. In the summer of 1881 her lecture at a temperance picnic drew 7,000 people, many traveling by excursion train from Kokomo and Frankfort to the village of Michigantown. She even started her own newspaper, *Our Herald*, and rooted it firmly in temperance and prohibition. Still, when called upon to speak for suffrage, she did. After all, she and Haggart had crisscrossed the state at the behest of both the Republican Party and the Indiana Woman's Suffrage Association to encourage Hoosiers to vote for politicians who would support woman suffrage legislation in the 1883 legislature. The scandalous rumor that dogged her after that speaking tour led to the infamous slander trial after which Gougar took a little time away from speaking engagements. Then, not to be stopped by rumors and innuendo, she courageously returned to the stump, speaking for both prohibition and suffrage and paused just long enough to become the president of the Indiana National Woman Suffrage Association. Her bold and continuous activity drew the attention of the Redpath Bureau, an agency that booked national lecture tours for well-known speakers, including Anthony, and Gougar signed on to do a series of speaking engagements. At the INWSA annual meeting that May, Sewall and Anthony asked Gougar to postpone her work with the bureau for a year. They needed her to speak in the state on behalf of suffrage. Gougar delayed her lecture series and helped with suffrage work.[5]

In 1887 Gougar joined other suffragists on a tour of all thirteen Indiana congressional districts to rekindle interest in a cause that had not recovered from the 1883 legislative defeats. Anthony joined the tour and, with her remarkable stamina on full display, spoke in every corner of the state with the INWSA for the full thirty-four days of district meetings. Under the guidance of INWSA secretary Harper (who had earlier criticized Gougar over her public remarks about political parties), a public-relations blitz announced the upcoming meetings. Posters, handbills, and more than 300 letters sent by Harper alerted the public and the press of the coming crusade.[6]

The official report of the meetings, as found in the INWSA records, reflect Gougar's personality and what she wanted to believe about the meetings, more than the reality. While they all probably drew reasonable crowds, the Terre Haute meeting, by all accounts the largest meeting, spread over two days, exacerbated tensions between Gougar and Anthony, as well as between Gougar and other suffragists who were still upset about her actions during the slander trial. Gougar used the Terre Haute suffrage meeting to stump for prohibition and for the Prohibition Party, which went against Anthony's personal beliefs (Anthony believed in temperance, but not at the expense of woman suffrage) as well as against the NWSA's policy of giving no endorsement to any political party. Gougar spoke for such an extended period that Zerelda Wallace, a popular speaker not only in Indiana but also in suffrage circles throughout the country (and a prohibitionist in agreement with NWSA policy on the issue), did not have time to deliver her address. As the *Wabash Express* headline described it, "How Mrs. Gougar, the State President, Monopolized the Time and the Topics." Harper issued a press release distancing the NWSA from Gougar's remarks

> The strong advocacy of prohibition by Mrs. Gougar in her address was in the nature of a surprise to the members of the association, as it is in direct contradiction to the customs and principles of the order. So careful is the Suffrage association of any alliance, that when the WCTU of any city offer to arrange for a suffrage convention their assistance as a body is declined although as individuals they are gladly welcomed as coworkers. Miss Susan B. Anthony and Mrs. May Wright Sewall are pronounced anti-prohibitionists. Mrs. Gougar must be held personally responsible for her remarks on prohibition as they were not sanctioned by the association. They were especially unexpected Wednesday evening as she had been particularly requested not to advocate prohibition in the Terre Haute.[7]

Since reports of the district meetings are limited in content, it is impossible to know why Gougar unleashed her support of the Prohibition Party and blocked Wallace from speaking. It was not the first time that she had talked about political parties during the district tour. In Bloomington a week earlier, a Major Mulky asked Gougar why she criticized Republicans when in his mind the party had always favored woman suffrage. She stated that she blamed "whiskey Republicans" for the suffrage and prohibition defeats in Indiana in 1883. Anthony jumped into the conversation to neutralize Gougar and emphasized that nonpartisan tactics helped suffrage more than aligning with a party. At her next speech in Bloomington, Gougar tried to make up for her gaffe and praised Kansas Republicans for their support of municipal suffrage (the ability to vote in local elections for specific offices) for women in that state. Perhaps Gougar, who was never known to shy away from controversy, simply believed that she must speak about politics, but it did not help her standing with the NWSA or with Anthony.[8]

Despite these glitches, the 1887 tour increased women's interest in suffrage. In May 1888, when the INWSA met at the Plymouth Church in Indianapolis, all thirteen state districts reported progress in suffrage work, but the most important events that year happened away from the convention. The suffragists presented resolutions to each major political party in Indiana—Prohibition, Democratic, Republican—to request that it add a suffrage plank to its platform. Harkening back to the antebellum IWSA, the INWSA emphasized the rights of women who worked stating, "taking into consideration their work in the homes, women form one half of the industrial population;

LIBRARY OF CONGRESS

Ida Husted Harper of Terre Haute, Indiana, worked for suffrage both in Indiana and at the national level. A trained journalist and newspaper columnist, Harper led the NAWSA publications bureau prior to women gaining the vote in 1920.

but even conceding that their interest in the home is properly represented and protected by the votes of men, it must be remembered that the women of this country to the number of many millions, and the women of this State to the number of many thousands, are also engaged in various trades, professions and other non-domestic occupations, and they need the ballot to protect their interests as wage-earners." Because of this lobbying, the Prohibition Party unanimously adopted a woman suffrage plank. The Democrats did not allow the suffragists to present their memorial in person, so they never knew if the politicians discussed or simply tabled the petition. Republicans allowed Gougar and Harper to speak to the resolutions committee. Gougar had high hopes for the Republicans because some of the men in the party had worked for suffrage in the past, but she later stated, "We were courteously heard, and, as was the case with the Democrats, completely ignored."[9]

With renewed interest in suffrage appearing around the state because of the 1887 speaking tour, the IWSA and Sewall's and Wallace's group, the INWSA, who knew about the impending combination of the national suffrage groups, completed their own merger in October 1889. Anthony attended the convention at Rushville to offer her support. It must have been embarrassing for local leaders that very few suffragists attended. It must also have been an awkward meeting. All the officers of the INWSA—Gougar, Wallace, Harper, and Sewall—had been involved in the affair at the Terre Haute district meeting with everyone upset with Gougar. Still, by a unanimous vote, the two suffrage groups became one, adopting the name of the original group—the Indiana Woman Suffrage Association—and agreed to be an auxiliary of the NWSA. They also partially absorbed the INWSA's $100 debt by contributing the twenty-five cents from the IWSA treasury (all the money they had), collecting fifty-seven dollars in donations from the members present, and the generosity of Harper, who gave up her secretary's salary to restore the group's solvency.[10]

More problematic was the selection of officers. An argument arose over whether to have a nominating committee put forth names to the convention or to take nominations from the floor. A carefully chosen nominating committee could opt for women who followed a specific point of view and quash any diversity of opinion. They decided on Gougar's choice, a nominating committee. Sewall received the highest number of votes but refused to take any office because of duties elsewhere or because, as the *Indianapolis Journal* put it, the "extreme partisan spirit" of the election. To what must have been Anthony's dismay, the paper reported that "the third-party women [such as Gougar] . . . want suffrage but they want it for the one and only purpose of downing the 'demon rum,'" which was, of course, a policy that Sewall and Anthony opposed. Mary Cardwell, who attended the meeting as the press agent for the INWSA, had to defend what happened in an official press report. The paper had declared the "Woman Suffragists combine in Harmony and at Once Split Up in a Grand Row" in what would be the first but not the last time the Indiana press highlighted and exaggerated differences of opinion between suffragists. Cardwell denied the split and denied an argument although she did admit to "warmest protests" over how to take the vote, but the results of the meeting spoke louder than Cardwell's public explanation. When the dust cleared, Sewall, Harper, and even Cardwell declined to serve in their elected offices for "personal reasons," which may have included the conflict with Gougar in Terre Haute and the machinations (where Gougar played a leading role) over who could vote in the convention. Former IWSA treasurer Georgia Wright became the only IWSA officer to serve on the new board. She became the "superintendent of the press." Other officers included Gougar as president, Wallace as vice president, Caroline C. Hodgin as secretary, and Hattie E. Merrill as treasurer. Cardwell reported that the members of the reconstituted IWSA tabled a resolution to endorse a political party, presumably the Prohibitionist, but clearly pro-prohibition forces were at work in the association.[11]

By 1890 Gougar had been lecturing for the Redpath speaker's bureau for two years with most of her focus on prohibition. She spent part of 1888 purposely shadowing famed orator Anna Dickinson around the state as Dickinson stumped for the Republican Party for the November election. Gougar booked her own talks to take place immediately after Dickinson spoke and at each stop extolled the advantages of the Prohibition Party over the Republican Party. Once again, Gougar's overt political activity brought ridicule from men. She complained to the *Lafayette Morning Journal* that on November 12 "five wagons filled with men halted immediately in front of my house. They threw red calcium lights and in the full glare hoisted beer and whisky bottles, drinking or pretending to drink therefore. Another wagon was filled with men, dressed like women; upon this they had a figure dressed to impersonate myself, while the mob hurrahed for 'Helen Gougar.'"[12]

A strong contingent of WCTU members in the new version of the IWSA meant that from now on the two groups worked together. Beginning in 1890, IWSA membership grew based on the interrelationship between the two groups and meeting minutes proudly noted that a national convention of brewers declared themselves "unalterably opposed to woman suffrage for when women get the ballot they will vote solidly against our business." WCTU groups around the state sent messages or delegates to IWSA meetings and prohibition became one of the suffragists' primary objectives as did "Scientific Instruction of Alcohol and Narcotics." The group offered statistics to support its stand on prohibition stating, "Indiana has three and one-half times as many saloonkeepers as teachers, eleven saloons for every school house, and fourteen saloonkeepers for every minister of the gospel and one boy in every five is doomed according to statistics to be a drunkard." At its 1891 meeting the WCTU said it would support the political party that supported a prohibition law (in addition to municipal suffrage). This negated everything that national suffragists asked state suffrage groups to do.[13]

Gougar's adoption of third-party politics and the WCTU led to her final break with Sewall, who turned much of her attention away from state suffrage activities and focused instead on her work with national and international suffrage groups and her local nonsuffrage affiliated Indianapolis Woman's Club. Through her national work, Sewall became part of the organizing committee for the World's Congress of Women that met at the Chicago Columbian Exposition in 1893. She scheduled famous women lecturers for the event (she did not include Gougar). The insulted Gougar went to Chicago to publicly confront Sewall. The *Indianapolis Journal* ran a front-page headline proclaiming, "Quarrels of the Fair Sex" and "Mrs. Helen Gougar Raises a Disturbance at the World's Congress of Women." Newspapers played up the horrible event stating that "the Indiana public which is acquainted with Mrs. Helen Gougar's aggressive methods will not be surprised to hear that she was instigator and leading participant. Mrs. Gougar is a professional agitator, and when she is temporarily without a great moral cause to labor for she delights to agitate her fellow woman." Exactly how the public embarrassment, for both women, happened is not clear. Whether or not Sewall wanted to purposely omit Gougar from the list of speakers (and there is no way to know), Gougar heard rumors that was the case, so she attacked. She announced to newspaper reporters, "May Wright Sewall and I are bitter personal enemies, and have been for some time. The trouble arose over prohibition work in Indiana." At Gougar's insistence, Sewall, NAWSA officer Rachel Foster Avery, Gougar, and the vice president of the fair's women's group, Ellen Henrotin, presented themselves and the conflict to the president of the exposition.

Henrotin had a prior conflict with Sewall about the Congress of Women and she was not inclined to see Sewall's point of view. Just as Sewall had attempted to take control of the AWSA meeting from Martha McKay in the 1870s, Henrotin and Bertha Palmer (president of the Board of Lady Managers at the fair) believed Sewall attempted to take control of the Congress from them. So, when Gougar accused Sewall of engaging in "spite work," they unfortunately had a predisposition to side with Gougar. The exposition's president decided that Gougar could speak and Sewall acquiesced. A local reporter clearly blamed Gougar for the disturbance and noted that she "attained the notoriety she sought." The final break with Anthony followed in 1894, when Gougar, who now also lectured with Mary Lease for the Populist Party (not the Prohibition Party), called Anthony a failure as an organizer and blamed her and the Republicans of "moral cowardice."[14]

Gougar also found more positive ways to remain in the spotlight in Indiana as she tried to advance woman suffrage. She managed to be reelected president at the 1894 IWSA meeting—even though it was not for the seventeenth or eighteenth time as newspapers reported—and to garner support for her plan for women across the state to vote in the November elections, similar to what had been done in other states and by Anthony in the early 1870s. The timing was purposeful. In 1894 Colorado women voted legally for the first time in a general election and the juxtaposition of their right to vote and the absence of the vote for Hoosier women presented a great opportunity for public discussion. For her own voting attempt, Gougar met with Lafayette election officials to arrange everything in advance. On election day, she proceeded to the Fifth Precinct and attempted to vote. Election officials denied her access to three ballots—state, county, and township—because of her sex. She tried to swear to her citizenship and again could not because of her sex. She then left the polling station.[15]

As part of the plan, other women across Indiana also attempted to vote. In Marion, twenty-nine women went to the polls in the southern part of the town and one in the north. Twenty-five women made the attempt in Fairmount. In Anderson the local WCTU sent women to the polls. In Portland about twelve women tried to vote. Election officials in Crawfordsville turned away women. Doctor Martha Griffith decided to sue the Crawfordsville election board as a result. In Kokomo a joint meeting between the WCTU and the Kokomo Equal Suffrage Club led to the largest number of women who attempted to vote in the state. All members of both clubs, wearing yellow ribbons for suffrage, rode in carriages (also decorated with yellow) visited all fifteen polling places in town, attempted to vote, and everywhere voting officials turned them away. The Kokomo suffragists even carried tax receipts with them to show they paid taxes and should therefore be able to vote.[16]

Under their prior agreement, Gougar sued the election officials who denied her a ballot. Just before the local court heard the case, *Gougar v. Timberlake*, in January 1895, Gougar arranged to be admitted to the Tippecanoe County bar so she could participate in her own defense. The defendant's attorney agreed to this novelty. She argued her case for about two hours, followed by her attorney's arguments. The attorney for the election board went last. As expected, the Tippecanoe County Superior Court found against her in April 1895, and Gougar took the case to the Indiana Supreme Court. Following the pattern set in 1895, Gougar arranged to be admitted to the bar of the Supreme Court moments before she argued her case in 1897. The argument is published as, "Constitutional Rights of the Women of Indiana." In spite of receiving praise from the court for her logic and her argument, the court ruled against her and in the decision stated, "Whatever the personal views of the justices upon the

LIBRARY OF CONGRESS

May Wright Sewall (middle front row) and National Council of Women officers Rachel Foster Avery, Isabella Charles Davis, Frances E. Bagley, and an unidentified officer.

advisability of extending the franchise to women, all are agreed that under the present [state] Constitution it cannot be extended to them."[17]

While Gougar involved herself with Prohibition and the WCTU and tried to vote in Indiana, Sewall stayed close to the suffrage movement by working with national suffragists. Her views on prohibition and suffrage put her in agreement with the leadership of the NWSA and the respected teacher from Indianapolis served on the NWSA executive committee from 1882 to 1890. According to Harper, Sewall and Anthony worked closely together on the 1890 merger with the AWSA—no easy feat with the differences of opinion on the matter than existed within the NWSA.

Sewall opened her Girls' Classical School in 1882. The school offered the same sort of training for future collegiate careers as her husband's boy's school. It must have been exhausting to manage and teach at the school, write a newspaper column, steer the nascent Art Association of Indianapolis into a thriving entity (the creation of the association was another one of her ideas), and serve on the NWSA executive committee. Still, Sewall had big plans outside of Indiana. Stanton and Anthony had dreamed of convening an international women's council and Sewall wanted to create a national woman's council. With the fortieth anniversary of the Seneca Falls convention about to take place, Sewall quickly moved to create both councils. Anthony, Rachel Foster Avery, and Sewall organized the first meeting of the International Council of Women in 1888 with forty-nine women representing eight countries and fifty-three different organizations in attendance. From that meeting came the creation of a larger committee to create the National Council of Women of the United States. Both councils welcomed all types of women's groups, not just those groups associated with suffrage, to join them—this was Sewall's idea and while Anthony did not wholeheartedly agree, she acquiesced. Sewall did not then, nor does she today receive as much credit as she is due for the creation of the councils. She is most often mentioned as a member of the organizing committee when in fact she was the driving force behind it. As Harper told Sewall years later, "I remember distinctly a long talk I had with you in the library of your home in Indianapolis in 1887. You then outlined to me in full detail the plan of a National and an International Council of Women, which should be formed at the International Council that was to meet in Washington in March, 1888, and you said they would far exceed in scope any organization of women in existence." The councils led to Sewall's work with the World's Congress of Representative

Women at the Columbian Exposition in Chicago in 1893 where she had the dustup with Gougar.[18]

Sewall inadvertently contributed to the creation of another national umbrella organization for women's clubs. Her National Council of Women convention included women from nonsuffrage-oriented women's clubs, most important, the president of one of the oldest women's club in the country, Sorosis. The group's president, Jane Cunningham Croly, then took Sewall's idea and created a similar group, hosting the first meeting of the national General Federation of Women's Clubs in 1890 to unite all women's literary/study clubs in their work. Sewall helped with the organization of the new group that she thought might join her National Council (it, for some unknown reason, did not). States then formed their own federations of women's clubs and sent representatives to biennial GFWC meetings.[19]

This proved to be an opportune time to form the GFWC because women's clubs had grown with great rapidity across the United States. Most clubs did not have men as members (although some in Indiana did), but all clubs grew from the same sort of factors, including an increase in the number of college-educated women who desired an outlet for their intellectual abilities and an outlet for their interest in improving their communities. The clubs often started as "culture" clubs or study groups that focused on literature, art, music, or similar endeavors and moved into supporting the development of public libraries and improving local schools, including ways to expand art and music lessons for all children and establishing free kindergartens. From here, their work later expanded into other areas and what today is known as municipal housekeeping or an interest in improving the health and welfare of their communities through lobbying for improved food-safety laws, housing reforms, sanitary conditions, and other improvements to their towns even if they had to become politically active to achieve them. An African American women's club movement developed at the same time, the National Association of Colored Women. Although it remained separate from the GFWC in spite of attempts to at least have NACW members attend the GFWC biennial meetings, the NACW served the same purposes as the GFWC. In all these women's clubs, women honed political skills and established organizational structures that allowed for quick transfer of information on important topics of legislation. Sewall had inadvertently created the training ground and the organizational structure later used by suffragists. In Indiana that proved to be an essential part of revitalizing the suffrage movement after 1910. The same proved to be true in Illinois and Wisconsin. Antebellum suffragists had trained for their work by starting with issues aside from suffrage. At the end of the nineteenth century, the next generation of suffragists received their training through women's clubs and worrying about local concerns.[20]

Women's clubs flourished in towns throughout Indiana, often taking the form of a "literary club" that focused on studying specific authors or producing and reading their own works. Sometimes the clubs resembled a study group that focused on art, music, perhaps another country, a current event, or even the best way to care for their children. Sometimes a club did all these things—there was no set formula. Suffragists joined women's clubs, such as the College Corner Club that Martha McKay and Sewall organized and included men as members. For women who thought that joining a suffrage group was too "bold," a literary, art, music, or study club was an acceptable way to meet with other women and exchange ideas.[21]

For example, the Woman's Club of Greencastle was one of the earliest and continuous clubs in the state. Like many Hoosier clubs, it started as a literary club, but then slowly moved into community work. Greencastle politicians saw the advantage of asking a group of civic-minded women, who already met

The Propylaeum in Indianapolis in 1917. The idea to construct a building for women's club activities in Indianapolis originated with May Wright Sewall.

BASS PHOTO COMPANY COLLECTION, INDIANA HISTORICAL SOCIETY

on a regular basis, to take part in community affairs and approached them for their assistance. Another long-term club, the IWC, had been organized by suffragists McKay, Laura Giddings Julian (wife of abolitionist/woman suffrage supporter George Julian), and Sewall (who was May Thompson at the time) in 1875. Although individual members embraced suffrage, politics and religion could not be discussed at IWC meetings. Women's clubs became so popular in Indianapolis that in 1888, even while forming an international woman's council, Sewall decided that all women's clubs in the city needed a place to meet—not a room of their own, but an entire building. She found other women who agreed with her plan and they formed a corporation to erect a building for that use. The building, the Propylaeum, served its purpose until it had to be razed for the building of the World War I Memorial; it is now located in a house once owned by an Indianapolis brewer and is still known as the Propylaeum. That same year in Milwaukee, Wisconsin, clubwomen opened their new building, calling it the Athenaeum. Club women in Cleveland, Ohio, built and opened their building, also called the Propylaeum, soon after. The expansion of and increased interest in club activities led women across the Midwest to expand the space where they could work.[22]

McKay's sister, Elizabeth Nicholson, formed a large organization to unite Indiana's women's clubs for a yearly meeting. In 1890 the Indiana Club Union, later renamed the Indiana Union of Literary Clubs, met for the first time. This group gave Indiana clubwomen a chance to compare activities with other clubs, to get ideas for meetings, and to meet other women. Not surprisingly, it did not take long for clubwomen to get involved in investigating social problems. Virginia Claypool Meredith, president of the Union of Literary Clubs, noted in her presidential address of 1895 that clubwomen should lead an "investigation of subjects that concerned the welfare of people in the every-day walk of life. . . . clubs are potent to create public sentiments . . . potent to enter the unexplored regions of truth near us. Public sentiment is the great force that accentuates and accelerates human advancement" and in the end, she noted that public sentiment shapes laws: "Let the club make public sentiment and just laws will easily follow."[23]

Everyone did not agree with Meredith's idea. Evans Woollen of Indianapolis (men belonged to the literary unions) "urged concentration on the literary features rather than the social." In a move that blended both Woollen's concerns and Meredith's, Harriet Noble, a professor of English at Butler University and a suffragist, suggested that the group send a resolution to the state regarding an upcoming tax levy for libraries she believed would harm small libraries across the state. Both Meredith and Woollen supported the suggestion. In 1896 the union sent its first resolution to the Indiana General Assembly. It urged the lawmakers to fund libraries across the state in commemoration of the upcoming centennial of the creation of the Indiana Territory.[24]

There was no turning back. The next year the union looked at possible school reform measures and continued its work on greater access to libraries, since many Indiana counties had no public library at all. The union also branched out into concerns about access to kindergartens and access to art and music instruction in public schools. These topics combined both the social and literary/cultural group aims and served for many as a gateway to look at larger social issues in Indiana. The 1899 state union meeting featured three-minute talks on a variety of topics that constituted a running conversation about what literary clubs should do. Some people still thought that only literary topics should be discussed at meetings and any social issues left to boards of charities. Others thought that literary clubs had become too "aristocratic" and needed to be sure to welcome members from all walks of life. Another mentioned that for those who had not attended college, giving papers and practicing public speaking at club meetings served as a form of education. Another thought that clubs provided practice at "discussion of vital questions and learn to think on our feet." Other remarks noted work with local schools and for the first, but not the last time, the importance of conservation when the Bloomington clubs reported they had planted four hundred trees.[25]

The Literary Union remained separate from the Indiana Federation of Clubs (the state branch of the GFWC) for as long as it could, but by 1906 the time had come to consolidate. The Union of Literary Clubs had lost membership and many remaining members wanted to be involved in the federation's community work. The Indiana Federation had formed in 1897 with the Indianapolis Woman's Club and Clarke, who had attended club meetings with her mother when she was a child and knew the ins and outs of clubs, led the way. The Union of Literary Clubs had feared a loss of autonomy and, the point that McKay stressed, men belonged to the literary clubs and there did not seem to be a place for men in the federation. Still, in 1906, the two groups met separately but simultaneously and sent telegrams to each other about their consolidation votes. In both cases, they voted in the affirmative and the groups held their first joint meeting later that year.[26]

Women's clubs throughout the state served as a place for women to learn how to work with other women, to speak in public, to organize a vast group of people who might not have that much in common, to devise and achieve goals, and how to work with the state legislature. While these skills had long been practiced by suffragists and WCTU members, women who did not embrace suffrage or prohibition developed the same sort of skills through the clubs. Women learned to feel comfortable asking for funding and working with the state on issues such as libraries, schools, housing, conservation efforts (the Indiana Dunes and the development of a state park system were high priorities), and any other efforts that might improve the lives of Hoosiers. They enjoyed meeting women who worked at similar tasks in other states at national General Federation meetings. Even though many suffragists belonged to a variety of these women's clubs, and, Luella McWhirter, Vida Newsom, and Grace Clarke, three of the most prominent suffragists in the state beginning in the 1910s, served as presidents of the federation, it was difficult to get the body as a whole to endorse suffrage. It finally did in 1913 after the creation of new, active, energetic suffrage groups that were already hard at work in the state. Still, when the time came to move suffrage back onto the stage of Indiana politics, the vast organization of women's clubs in Indiana skillfully promoted the cause at their annual meetings. It was through their work with the federation that many women came to realize that lobbying and petitioning the state could take their efforts only so far and that the vote was a surer route to create change.[27]

After years under Gougar's control and her unhelpful debates about temperance and third parties, Sewall's successful time and effort spent on national and international women's organizations, and the competition from the women's club movement, the 1889 version of the IWSA almost ceased to exist after its attempts to vote in 1894. There just did not seem to be much reason to keep the group engaged and working closely with the WCTU most likely drove away some potential members. Someone had to try to breathe new life into the Indiana suffrage movement and that someone was Anthony. On February 5, 1897, she arrived in Indianapolis to speak to a joint session of the Indiana General Assembly about the need for Hoosier women to get the vote. Sewall and most of the state's elected officials attended as did the members of the Indiana Supreme and Appellate Courts. Men as well as women filled the gallery and applauded her arrival. Her talk started as a historical review of voting rights in the United States highlighting the broadening of the voter base over the years. She even mentioned her own attempt to vote in 1872 and the fine that she still had not paid. She stressed that women in Colorado, Idaho, Wyoming, and Utah could vote, so why not women in Indiana? She ended her talk on a humorous note stating, "I want the politicians of Indiana to see that there are women as well as men in this state, and they never will see it until they give them the right to vote. Make the brain under the bonnet count for as much as the brain under the hat."[28]

When nothing happened to invigorate the movement after her visit to Indianapolis, a clearly exasperated Anthony wrote to Sewall about the state of affairs in Indiana and about the upcoming IWSA 1898 meeting. Anthony's analysis concluded that it was the IWSA constitution's method of picking delegates for state conventions, using a nominating committee that left Gougar in power and therefore without, in her view, an effective state leader. Anthony encouraged Sewall to prod Kokomo and Tipton suffragists and all other suffragists who disagreed with Gougar's leadership to send large numbers of delegates to the annual meeting and force through constitutional changes or, as Anthony put it, to "rescue the society from her grasp but if all stay home of course she will have everything her own way." Carrie Chapman Catt, the national organizer for NAWSA, wanted a replay of the 1887 canvass of Indiana congressional districts to inspire new life into the state, but, as usual, no money was available.[29]

Sewall's busy schedule outside of Indiana did not let her call a meeting that would effectively remove Gougar from the presidency of the IWSA, so Clarke stepped into the fray. The thirty-four-year-old daughter of Indianapolis Woman's Club cofounder Laura Giddings Julian and her abolitionist husband George Julian, and granddaughter of abolitionist Joshua Giddings, came to the work with the natural organizational and political skills that within the next two decades moved woman suffrage to the forefront of Indiana politics. She had followed her mother into club work and knew the procedures to get things done. When the NAWSA decide to revive the Hoosier group, Clarke, who knew Anthony, put the wheels in motion.

The NAWSA purposely chose Indianapolis as the site for its annual business committee meeting on December 7 and 8, 1899, to encourage Hoosier women to whole-heartedly jump back into the work. In conjunction with that meeting, Clarke and Alice Wheeler Peirce organized two days of suffrage sessions at the Plymouth Church. In a notice to women's clubs and the state's few suffrage organizations, they emphasized "the hope of Miss Anthony and her associate officers that at the conclusion of the conference steps may be taken for the reorganization of suffrage work in Indiana." They knew that not all club women were suffragists, but also knew "almost every woman's club included leading women who are suffragists." They offered reduced rates at the Denison Hotel for the duration of the meeting to spark interest in the IWSA revival.[30]

Anthony arrived in Indianapolis the day before the meeting. In an interview with the *Indianapolis Journal*, she chastised the IWSA, "While Dr. Mary F. Thomas was the president it [the IWSA] flourished, but in the last few years there has been little heard of it." Anthony thought that Hoosier women had become "occupied with other things and did not have the time to go into the philosophy of the cause, and if they did, they would undoubtedly be on the womens' side." In another interview, this one with the *Bloomington Progress*, Anthony revealed that she did not believe that women should affiliate with a political party and while voters would have an impact on local liquor laws, "women have made no open fight against the saloon" in Colorado (where women voted). Gougar, who clearly did not agree with Anthony, did not appear at the preconvention meetings and reception. She was, however, acutely aware of the meeting. In a letter to WCTU member and clubwoman McWhirter, Gougar excoriated Anthony for being an "agitator, not an organizer." She bluntly stated that Anthony wanted her out of the IWSA (Anthony did) and that she wanted to put Sewall in charge (that is debatable). Gougar hinted that she was biding her time before she reappeared with the IWSA stating, "When we women get ready to work for suffrage in Indiana we will pay no attention to them." The reality was that Gougar's lecturing had slowed and she was now interested in the Democratic Party and with her personal finances. Before she suddenly died in 1907, she no longer made woman suffrage a priority and never called another IWSA meeting.[31]

At the first session of the reorganization meeting, Catt announced from the podium that "in 1851, Indiana organized the first suffrage association in this country [this was incorrect, there is no way to know if that is true], but today she is the only State in the Union without one; we are going to have a meeting tomorrow morning, and I want the women of this city to come out and redeem their state." Anthony continued the theme of Indiana's long history with suffrage. She noted that George Julian presented a petition for woman suffrage to the U.S. House of Representatives the same year she first visited Indianapolis (1869).[32]

Anthony's desire to get the Kokomo and Tipton clubs involved came true. Officers for the new Indiana State Suffrage Association included: Mary Jameson Judah of Indianapolis, president; Mary S. Armstrong of Kokomo, vice president; corresponding secretary Albertina A. Forrest of Irvington; recording secretary Bertha G. Wade of Indianapolis; and Alice Waugh of Tipton as treasurer. Two Indianapolis women, Lila M. D. Ketcham (Mrs. John L.) and Virginia S. Patterson, served as auditors (a position similar to a board member). Indianapolis suffragists created a local branch with Ketcham as president; Clarke, vice president; Catherine Boyd (Mrs. James A.) Mount (Governor James A. Mount's wife), corresponding secretary; Mrs. Ada B. Leck recording secretary; and Louise (Mrs. J. Cumming) Smith and Mrs. George Philip Meier as auditors.[33]

At this point the resurrection of suffrage in Indiana appeared to be complete, but problems erupted almost immediately. The morning after her election, Judah declared that she could not be president and Wade assumed that office. The corresponding secretary also immediately resigned (did the governor interfere?), so Peirce filled the post. Since Wade was now president, Hester Moore Hart filled in as recording secretary. Both auditors also resigned, and Clarke and Forrest replaced them. Finances from the meeting needed to be sorted out. Then of course there was the matter of affiliating with the national organizaton. All three local suffrage groups—Kokomo, Tipton, and Indianapolis—had to become part of the state organization and then the state had to pay dues to the national. Anthony wrote a letter to Clarke suggesting that she and Peirce and one other person attend the national NAWSA meeting in February.[34]

Unaware that Judah had resigned as state president, the NAWSA sent petitions to her to be signed and forwarded to Congress asking for woman suffrage. She apparently did not pass those forms on to the new president. The treasurer did not pay the state's membership dues to NAWSA. Anthony paid them herself so that the state's delegation could vote at the February national meeting. Even Clarke seemed to be on the verge of backing out of the national convention. All this left Anthony in distress. "It would be very funny indeed," she wrote to Clarke, "if all that hard work in December should bring about nothing but letting the whole state fall back into the hands of Mrs. Gougar, as everything will of course do unless there can be found two or three women sufficiently alive to the situation to pull themselves together as a state society . . . and make it a real organization and not merely a paper one."[35]

Unfortunately, Anthony's concern about a "paper" organization proved to be based on the reality of the situation in the state. Many women and men wanted women to have the vote, but as the *History of Woman Suffrage* later explained, in Indiana at that time there was "so slight an organization that little opportunity is afforded for public expression or action."[36]

Chapter 5

"WOMEN TO THE LEFT OF THEM, WOMEN TO THE RIGHT OF THEM"

After years in the doldrums, by 1912 suffragists across the Midwest and in Indiana seized on new ways to call attention to their cause. Petitioning and speaking to state legislators was not enough. As Virginia Claypool Meredith had noted in 1895 at the Indiana Union of Literary Clubs meeting, women needed to sway public opinion to make politicians take them seriously. To do that, they learned to take advantage of new technology. The most obvious new technology—the automobile—enabled women to reach towns and villages that were almost inaccessible when trains provided the major form of rapid transportation. They also began to use the telephone and by the time suffrage was won a few years later had come to rely on its ability to move events along quickly with just a few moments of dialing and conversation. Suffragists also embraced a new, positive relationship with the press. Women reporters and photographers (as newspapers embraced photography), joined suffragists in the field. Reporters' lengthy articles about suffrage events and the publication of suffragists' photos immeasurably aided the cause. Suffragists adopted street meetings as a publicity tactic, a strategy as old as the American Revolution but recently used most effectively by the Woman's Christian Temperance Union to maintain its public presence. Sometimes the street meeting followed an automobile tour as suffragists stood in cars brightly decorated with yellow suffrage banners and delivered their messages to the assembled crowds. Suffrage parades also caught everyone's attention and made for great newspaper stories.[1]

The Woman's Franchise League, created in 1911, injected new life into the Hoosier woman's suffrage movement in part by its skillful use of these techniques. Automobile tours to various towns, street meetings in downtown Indianapolis and other towns across the state, a suffrage tent at the state fair, and a large party on the lawn of former vice president Charles Fairbanks's home, all covered by the press, were just some of the new strategies that suffragists used to draw attention to women's quest for the vote. Another Indiana suffrage society, the Equal Suffrage Association, developed a skill for hosting mass meetings that involved local labor unions, socialists, and the African American community in Indianapolis. The city's African American suffrage groups' solo activities were also covered, but less intensively, in the local press. So, no matter which suffrage group you examine, suffragists in Indiana suddenly and boldly reappeared and this time kept up the persistent pressure until suffrage was won.

Of the two major Indiana suffrage groups active in this period, the ESA was the oldest. After her final attempt to get an energetic suffrage group up and running ended in 1900, Susan B. Anthony left Indiana to chart its own course, which meant that Indiana for all intents and purposes had no suffrage group. The National American Woman Suffrage Association experienced problems of its own at the same time and all in all not much was accomplished nationally or locally. Anthony died in 1906 just a few months before the last vestiges of the Kokomo suffrage group called an Indiana suffrage convention. Sarah Davis became president of the new group, the ESA, but then she had to leave the state. One of the vice presidents, Anna Dunn Noland, answered the NAWSA's request to revive the organization in 1909 and called a meeting for her hometown of Logansport. Noland later reported for the *History of Woman Suffrage* about several ESA meetings in Logansport. The most lavish appears to have been the 1912 meeting, complete with a parade and announcements "dropped over the city from an air ship." The group became masters of publicity that summer with billboards, fences, barns, and any other stationary object covered with handbills and signs that read "Votes for Women." After this impressive display, little is known about other state-level ESA work.[2]

The WFL, the other major suffrage group in the state, arose from the local victories of placing women on the Indianapolis and Terre Haute school boards. Women in other states served on school boards or at least voted on ballot questions concerning local schools and, in some cases, had done so for decades. Suffragist and clubwoman Grace Julian Clarke and suffragist, member of the Indiana University Medical School, and practicing physician Doctor Amelia Keller set out to do the same in Indiana. Clarke reached out to women in school suffrage states to get advice on how to proceed. One of her correspondents, Harriet Taylor Upton, also happened to be the NAWSA treasurer. Upton had been a salaried member of her local school board in Ohio for twelve years. At one point, Upton had opposed school suffrage because she felt partial suffrage of any type was a bad idea. She had changed her mind and decided that women working in a professional manner with men on one issue might persuade men that women should have a voice in all matters. Kentucky also had school suffrage and while Mrs. M. D. Breckinridge did not have much solid advice to offer Clarke, she did point out that once women had school suffrage, they should more readily see the advantage of fighting for full suffrage. Women in twenty-

Carrie Barnes Ross was the first president of Branch No. 7 of the Equal Suffrage Association of Indianapolis. Branch No. 7 was the first African American woman suffrage organization in the city. She was also the president of the First Colored Woman's Suffrage Club. She moved to Boston after her marriage in 1916.

nine states already voted on school issues so this foot in the door by Hoosier suffragists should be easily achieved.[3]

In 1909, the same year as the revival of the ESA, the Woman's School Commission Organization, as it came to be known, worked to place a woman on school boards in Terre Haute and Indianapolis, the only two cities in the state that elected school board members. In Indianapolis the WSCO asked Martha McKay's sister, Mary Nicholson, to run for the board. Nicholson led the Teacher's Training School in the city and was therefore a perfect candidate. Local labor unions, in a first display of cooperation in the state between labor and suffragists, supported her and encouraged union members to vote for her (since women could not vote) in part because she expressed a firm belief in public education. Her campaign staff visited party precinct meetings and reported cordial welcomes from men of both political parties. "Whenever we entered a room where twenty, or thirty, or forty men were crowded together discussing campaign plans all hats came off and profuse apologies were tendered for the tobacco smoke," Keller recalled. "In a few instances elaborate apologies were made for the use of beer at the meeting." Most important, the men listened to what the women had to say. Nicholson won in Indianapolis and in Terre Haute Stella Stimson, suffragist and WCTU member, won a school board seat. One Indianapolis newspaper reporter had the audacity to speculate that the highly qualified Nicholson won only because "she had the ardent support of a number of the hustling women of the city, who promoted her candidacy from the start. Undoubtedly there was many a voter who followed the instruction of his wife when he voted for Miss Nicholson." Nicholson received the second highest number of votes cast for the school board in Indianapolis (10,351).[4]

Not everyone rejoiced that women won seats on local school boards. First Lady of Indiana Lois Marshall came out forcefully against women voting or even holding an elected position on a school board:

> I don't believe in woman's suffrage. I have always felt that the men are more capable to take care of these affairs and I am still of that opinion. If there is any place, however, in which a woman's voice should be heard, it is in school matters. Still, I am inclined to believe that men are just as competent there as anywhere else. A man has better foresight; he weights all questions before acting on them. A woman is liable to act on an impulse without the careful consideration a man would give the questions. It is for this reason that I think men who are really good men should have charge of these affairs.[5]

Many women obviously did not agree with Marshall. The school board victories and "a membership of more than six hundred" led the WSCO to change its name to the Woman's School League. Members decided to work for what was known as municipal or partial suffrage. In other words, they wanted women to vote in a variety of specified local elections; they would not be fully enfranchised, but they could vote for some local offices. Perhaps Clarke's earlier correspondence with Upton and Breckinridge had inspired this use of partial suffrage to "soften" or "warm up" Hoosiers to eventually accept women as voters in all elections. The WSL geared up for the 1911 state legislative session to lobby elected officials to enact a partial suffrage bill. In the fall of 1910 the WSL sent notices to women's groups around the state explaining partial suffrage and it canvassed politicians to find out where they stood on the issue. Keller explained the plan simply: since most school boards were appointed and not elected, if women wanted to have a say on school issues they needed to put men in office who would do right by the schools. Therefore, partial suffrage was a necessity. Clarke, as president of the Indiana Federation of Clubs, supported the bill, as did Edgar A. Perkins, the president of the Indiana Federation of Labor. Clarke's support for the idea came from her concern for women's reform work and Perkins wanted to aid the "15,000 employed women in Indianapolis" who, if they could vote, might put into office men who could improve working conditions and living conditions for women and children across the state. One historian has theorized that another aspect of this bill was perhaps to appeal to the clubwomen in the state led by Clarke, some who might be reluctant to favor full suffrage. Teachers favored the plan

INDIANAPOLIS STAR/USA TODAY

Doctor Hannah Graham led the Indianapolis branch of the Equal Suffrage Association for many years and was instrumental in the formation of the first suffrage association composed of male and female union members.

as did temperance, housing, and child and women labor reformers.[6]

The WSL asked for permission to place desks in the corridors of the statehouse from which they could directly lobby politicians and visitors during the legislative session. They were not allowed to do so. Even so, state representatives John J. Keegan of Marion County and James W. Hedrick of Sullivan County gave suffragists a chance to participate in the legislative session. A public hearing for the partial-suffrage bill, known as the Keegan Bill, and for an unexpected piece of legislation, the Hedrick Bill, which would amend the state constitution so that women could vote in all elections, was held on February 3, 1911. A reported crowd of more than two hundred women attended the hearing in the House chamber. Those speaking in favor of the Keegan Bill (partial suffrage) included Keller, Clarke, and Belle O'Hair of the Teacher's Federation. Keller, as president of the WSL, spoke first, explaining that this bill extended suffrage for school-board elections throughout the state and arguing that women's votes would improve local schools. Clarke appealed to politicians' need to be elected and told them that by supporting the bill they would gain friends (women) across the state. Mrs. W. T. Barnes of the Indianapolis Council of Women (a local women's club) and Lenore (Mrs. Lewis J.) Cox from Terre Haute, representing the Indiana Federation of Clubs, echoed Clarke's statements.

Perhaps the most unexpected person to take the floor at the hearing was famed Indianapolis author Meredith Nicholson. According to local newspapers, Nicholson asked "why woman should be educated up to the point where she asks questions and then is told that she was educated merely out of compliment to the public schools and that the men, in their superior wisdom, shall take care of things." Nicholson had apparently seen his mother vote in Colorado and reported that the state suffered no ill effects when women voted. Eugenie Nicholson, a suffragist and his wife, also spoke in favor. Other men who spoke stated that only men who "prefer the company of a weak-minded woman to that of the strong-minded one" would be against partial suffrage and that "women have as much right to vote as the negroes of this country." It was probably surprising to the cadre who supported the bill when famed Indiana lawyer and Sullivan County native Antoinette D. Leach, representing the ESA, spoke in favor of the Hedrick constitution bill, but warned that the Keegan partial-suffrage bill might be unconstitutional. The Hedrick bill would, she also noted, place Indiana's women "on the same plane" as a male immigrant who could vote in Indiana after living in the state for one year and declaring his intent to become a citizen. She thought that women, who knew the history and institutions of the state and country, should hold as much power as new voters from other countries. (This would not be the first time that Hoosier women or other women across the country made this point about what came to be known as "alien suffrage.") This public splitting of views by the two major suffrage groups in the state was most likely not the tone that Keller, Clarke, O'Hair, and Nicholson wanted to set for the rest of the legislative session. For what remains to this day some unknown reason, the two groups entered the legislative chamber arguing for different things. Not surprisingly, by the end of the session, neither bill had moved out of the legislature.[7]

Clarke explained the results of the session in a letter to Ida Husted Harper. Indiana governor Thomas R. Marshall had let it be known that he did not support the partial suffrage bill (like his wife he opposed woman's suffrage), therefore, many legislators may have voted against it at Marshall's bidding. Still, the bill had failed in the House "by only a few votes." Unfortunately, the Senate did not even pick it up for consideration. So, women decided they needed to once again change the name of their organization and modify their purpose—the Woman's Franchise League was born. Clarke said women wanted "to be free to ask for full suffrage next time if that seems best, as it probably will; for our women are gradually coming to it." Obviously excited about the change, she told Harper, "I feel that no finer work has been done for the cause of woman's enfranchisement in years than has been accomplished here during the past 18 months, and it has been done so quietly and skillfully that it hardly seemed to be going on at all!" But even Clarke had to realize that one of the things that held up the bill was a lack of public attention to

CARRYING SUFFRAGE DOCTRINE TO INDIANA CITIES AND TOWNS

MRS. N. O. STANBROUGH AND MRS. ANNA D. STEPHENS, PRES. AND VICE-PRES. OF NEWLY ORGANIZED WESTFIELD BRANCH.

MISS MAUDE MOORE OF WESTFIELD, A SUFFRAGIST IN CALIFORNIA, WHO LOST HER VOTE BY MOVING.

MRS. GRACE JULIAN CLARKE DISTRIBUTING WOMAN'S SUFFRAGE HANDBILLS AT NOBLESVILLE.

The members of the organizing committee of the Woman's Franchise League of Indiana, who made a flying trip through Hamilton county yesterday to stir up interest in the suffrage cause and prepare for the formation of branch leagues, are well pleased with the results of the trip, the first of a series of automobile expeditions into territory where women are not actively demanding the right to vote.

"The success at Westfield, where a branch league was organized yesterday, was very encouraging," said Mrs. Grace Julian Clarke, who was a member of the suffragist campaigning party. "We are not disappointed at all with the visit to Noblesville. Our arrival was on short notice and the fact that two prominent clubs were holding open meetings the same afternoon explains why the attendance at our meeting was not large. Preparations for the club meetings had been made far in advance of the announcement of our coming."

The women, believing that Noblesville in the future will develop into a strong ally of the suffrage cause, planned another visit to that city in the near future.

A committee of Noblesville women, consisting of Mrs. Harry Alexander, Mrs. Walter Sanders and Mrs. Charles Neal, was named at the meeting at the First Presbyterian church, to make arrangements for another gathering at Noblesville, at which the suffrage question will be discussed. The Indianapolis seekers for suffrage were firm in their belief that the Noblesville meeting, although it had not been the same unqualified success that the one at Westfield had been, will be productive of much good.

The establishment of a strong and healthy branch league at Westfield on the first visit to that town by a campaigning party is regarded by the suffragists as being in itself a "good day's work." While it had been planned that the party would stop over at Carmel and spread the gospel of equal suffrage, the visit on the return trip to Indianapolis became unnecessary, as the enthusiastic women of the newly organized Westfield branch at once volunteered to organize Carmel, which is only three or four miles distant. Mrs. N. O. Stanbrough, president; Mrs. Anna D. Stephens, vice-president, and Mrs. Lizzie [illegible], secretary of the new branch, expect to begin work at Carmel at once.

To Visit Sheridan Later.

The organizing committee expected to go into Sheridan, but it was later decided to wait for that until the trip to Frankfort, which will be made within a short time. Allisonville, on the return trip to Indianapolis late yesterday afternoon, received a liberal supply of handbills, setting forth numerous arguments in favor of giving the ballot to women.

At Noblesville, although no branch league was organized yesterday, with the handbills it was a case of "everybody's reading 'em." Mrs. Clarke and Miss Sara Lauter distributed the leaflets among all the business houses around the courthouse square, and to people in the streets. The loafers in the courthouse yard having received only a limited allotment, asked for more.

Just prior to the arrival of the suffragist party, there had been a distribution of "dodgers" by a tent show company, which was producing "From Rags to Riches," but the show "dodgers" were cast into the gutters and the suffrage bills became the topics of interest. Sex equality supplanted theatricals as the topic of conversation and debate in the Noblesville square.

League's Plans Explained.

How the franchise league hopes to make its activities coextensive with the limits of Indiana within a few months was explained by Mrs. R. Harry Miller, Mrs. M. Henderson, Mrs. W. T. Barnes and Mrs. Clarke and Miss Lauter, at Westfield and at Noblesville. Mrs. Miller pointed out that it was hoped that every part of the state would have organizations by counties and by congressional districts by the time the Republican state convention meets this summer. The women plan to make a strong appeal to that convention to indorse suffrage.

By the time the legislature meets in January, the suffragist leaders hope to have an organization that will win favorable action from Indiana's lawmakers. Mrs. Clarke explained that it had not yet been determined whether women would ask for an entirely new Constitution or for a constitutional amendment.

That the Indiana women hope to win by persuasion and not by such methods as have been adopted by the English suffragettes was evident throughout the campaign. At Westfield, Miss Frances Doan, who temporarily presided, said:

"In England, and in some parts of America, it is unfortunate that this movement is in the hands of some who are indiscreet. We are proud, however, that we, in Indiana, are represented by a different class. We call ourselves suffragists instead of suffragettes."

Enrolled at Westfield.

Among those enrolled in the new branch league at Westfield is Miss Maude Morris, who has just returned to that town after two years in California. Miss Morris is a very energetic suffragist, and was one in California. She was heart and soul in the movement of women in California to obtain the ballot. After that privilege was granted, however, Miss Morris lost her chance to the distinction of being the only feminine resident of Westfield who had ever voted at a real political election. She was living at Los Angeles, and registered there for the municipal election, but lost her vote by moving from one precinct to another within thirty days of the election.

"I don't like to tell about that," said Miss Morris, when she learned that some of the other women had given her "secret" away.

"SUFFRAGE FUN FEST."

Franchise League to Have Fete at C. W. Fairbanks Home.

The Woman's Franchise League of Indiana is to hold a suffrage "fun fest" at the home of Charles Warren Fairbanks, in North Meridian street, the afternoon and evening of June 13. The affair is to be a lawn fete given for the benefit of the league.

Those in charge of the entertainment have arranged for fancy dancing, stump speaking, music and a suffrage parade. Mrs. J. H. Hyers is chairman of the committee in charge and Mrs. William Allen Moore is assistant chairman.

This is the first of the open air benefit entertainments the league has planned for this summer. The members of the league are arranging for a number of such meetings in order that interest in the movement for woman suffrage will not lag during the summer months.

Dr. Mary E. Spink, 1140 East Market street, will entertain the members of the Woman's Franchise League and of the Equal Suffrage Association at her home, Monday afternoon at 3 o'clock. Mrs. Grace Julian Clarke will deliver an address on woman suffrage.

Automobile tours became part of the publicity strategy of Indiana suffragists. The first tour by the Woman's Franchise League to Hamilton County garnered favorable publicity and interest in the cause.

it despite the significance of having the renowned Nicholsons speak at the hearing. Sylvia Pankhurst, famed English suffragette, visited Indianapolis in March. Clarke and other members of the soon-to-be WFL questioned her at a private luncheon for ways to both work with the legislature and gain publicity. The time had come for a more sustained public-relations campaign, so why not ask someone with a vast range of experience, even if some of that experience included time in jail, for some advice? Following the consultation, the WFL ramped up its presence. The group acquired an impressive office on the twelfth floor of the Odd Fellows Building in downtown Indianapolis and hired a secretary to answer questions, to send out suffrage literature, and to coordinate statewide activities. The WFL's plans for more continuous publicity came just in time as woman suffrage came under assault from the governor. Marshall, like almost all politicians (including suffragists) in Indiana, felt constrained by the state's constitution and he had just proposed a new one that, among other provisions, included the word "male" under voter qualifications. Clarke asked Harper, and by extension NAWSA since Harper served in its publicity office, to give the new group any assistance she thought they might need to fight against this proposed new constitution.[8]

The officers of the WFL included Keller, president; Luella (Mrs. Felix) McWhirter (known throughout the state for her temperance work with the WCTU and as a board member of her husband's bank, People's State Bank) and Eugenie Nicholson as vice presidents; Julia C. (Mrs. G. H.) Henderson, secretary; Celeste (Mrs. J. F.) Barnhill, treasurer; and twenty-five directors (board members), including Grace Julian Clarke, Indianapolis schoolteacher Charity Dye, former Butler professor Harriet Noble (who had participated in suffrage demonstrations in England with Pankhurst), and the wife of the president of the Indianapolis Central Labor Union, Mrs. Edgar A. Perkins. All the officers lived in Indianapolis and while this later became a source of contention, for now, for a new organization, having all the officers in one place made sense. Doctor Hannah Graham of the Indianapolis branch of the ESA, in a tentative move toward cooperation, attended the first WFL meeting in April. She spoke about the new child-labor law just enacted by the state and Keller supported her statements and the cause. The WFL hired well-known publicity agent and newsman Lannes McPhetridge to get out the word about the organization. He spent the summer of 1911 sending information about the WFL to women's groups across the state. The league's stated goal was "primarily to forward the welfare of Indiana communities and to promote the interest of women." The

WFL's message assured women that "the old and strong point of suffrage—giving women the privilege of going to the polls and vote on equal terms with men—has not been lost sight of by the Woman's Franchise League, but it's no longer the dominating note." In a nod to Indianapolis ESA president Graham, and probably also to the Indiana Federation of Clubs, the WFL wanted to also focus on "cleaner cities, better schools, taking politics out of affairs which have in many instances entangled and engulfed public movements." Another circular noted that clubwomen in Indiana, estimated to now be 10,000 strong, worked hard for new legislation concerning "play grounds for children in towns and cities, the formation of parent-teacher clubs, abolishing the public drinking cup, fighting tuberculosis, and other public health movements" and that the same women who belonged to the Indiana Federation of Clubs could join the WFL because while suffrage was implied in the name, the WFL did not intend to sit idle and wait for the vote, but rather to demonstrate that women

CARRY SUFFRAGE GOSPEL TO INDIANA CITIES.

LEFT TO RIGHT—MISS SARA LAUTER, MRS. R. HARRY MILLER, MRS. GRACE JULIAN CLARKE AND MRS. W. T. BARNES.

INDIANAPOLIS STAR/USA TODAY

The Hamilton County tour heralded the start of a close working relationship between the press, the Woman's Franchise League, and other suffrage organizations in Indiana.

were already active citizens who needed the vote to continue this important work. Another circular pointed out that three states around Indiana already gave women the vote in school board elections and that the WFL would work with the IFC and the groups known as Mother's Clubs to bring that to Indiana as well. They even leveled criticism at the 1911 legislators handling of the partial-suffrage bill stating the "legislature declined to take the suffragist bill seriously although pretending to listen to the advocates attentively."[9]

Despite the emphasis in 1911 that suffrage was only one WFL goal, in 1912 that facade gave way to a strong push for suffrage. The United States was at the beginning of one of the most interesting presidential elections to date. With four prominent candidates— incumbent Republican William Howard Taft, former president Theodore Roosevelt with his new Progressive Party, Democrat Woodrow Wilson, and frequent Socialist Party candidate and Terre

FRANCHISE LEAGUE AUTO CAMPAIGNERS.

MISS MARY WINTER, MRS G M. HENDERSON, MRS JOHN F BARNHILL.

Campaigners for the Woman's Franchise League were much encouraged by the success of their automobile trip yesterday to Lebanon and Zionsville, where women agreed to organize league branches soon. Other similar trips have been planned by the organization.

INDIANAPOLIS STAR/USA TODAY

The second automobile tour took place in Boone County with considerable press coverage, but less success in organizing any suffrage clubs.

Haute native son Eugene V. Debs—there was a candidate for everyone and it must have been difficult for the WFL and the ESA to remain nonpartisan. Still, the groups did. What could have pushed them to focus on suffrage with such determination that year? The new constitution introduced by Marshall did the trick. It had not gone away as some political proposals did—it was a serious threat and it was promoted widely in this election year since its passage had national implications (a possible nomination for the presidency) for the ambitious Marshall. Suffragists did not like the current Indiana Constitution any more than anyone else did. The bizarre rules and the amendment process prevented any sort of meaningful change in the state. Marshall's ideas, however, did not help. Suffragists applauded the provisions that made the document easier to amend, but his new, rigid, voter requirements negated any advantages. Marshall wanted "literate male citizens of the United States who were registered in the state and had paid a poll tax for two years" to be the state's voters—specifically excluding women, the poor, and male immigrants and who currently voted with what was known as "first papers" or a declared intent to become a citizen. Women admittedly agreed with excluding men who voted on "first papers," but in their view the other provisions had to be stopped. Marshall pushed back and hoped to ride his plan to a spot on a national ticket.[10]

Of the two suffrage associations in Indiana, the first out of the gate with a convention in 1912 was the WFL. Clarke warmed up public interest in the event with a column in the *Indianapolis Star* the day prior. After giving a history of the suffrage movement in Indiana, she explained what had improved for Hoosier women since that first 1851 convention. For example, she noted that "130 women in the ministry, 195 doctors, seventy-nine journalists, forty lawyers, thirty-four dentists, forty-four commercial travelers" all women, now worked in the state. Doctor Mary F. Thomas's focus on improved employment opportunities for women had come to pass. The ministry also had developed favorable attitudes toward suffrage and many ministers openly supported the cause. The press no longer ridiculed suffragists on a regular basis and the days of describing suffragists as masculine women appeared to be over. On the negative side, she noted the "almost impossibility of amending the [state] constitution" and that "the entangling alliance that existed at one time between the suffrage and temperance forces" had delayed suffrage. When the WFL convention officially opened for business, two well-known Hoosier politicians offered their support and drew even more attention to the cause. Former vice president Charles W. Fairbanks addressed the crowd of an estimated two hundred women and men, and popular former state senator William Dudley Foulke sent a message of support from Richmond. The attendees unanimously called for votes for women. The press gave extensive coverage to invited speaker Virginia Brooks of West Hammond, Illinois, who easily held the suffrage supporter's attention as she told of her efforts to fight corruption among politicians and the police in that city. At one point she needed to be hospitalized because, she stated, of the rough physical handling she had endured at their hands. Voting and not direct confrontation, it was implied, would be a safer way to stop corrupt politicians. Local newspapers emphasized the convention and the *Indianapolis News* ran a series of front-page editorial cartoons about suffrage.[11]

While the WFL tried to extend its organization throughout the state and worked its publicity machine to do so, the Indianapolis ESA met with organized labor. On April 3 the ESA met first in the afternoon with workers at the U.S. Encaustic Tile Works. Graham and others addressed the group of about three hundred men and women workers. The Union and the ESA organized a new ESA group, Branch Number 6. That evening, Graham and state ESA vice president Mrs. A. M. Noe met with approximately three hundred members of the Stove Plate Molders' Union. Its union members endorsed woman suffrage but did not form an ESA branch. Graham and the Indianapolis ESA continued to court other labor unions over the next few weeks.[12]

As the WFL had done earlier, this appears to have been a calculated part of the ESA's campaign to garner support among local laborers. In February Graham had told members of the Salvation Army that "working girls and the families of poor people" should be interested in gaining woman suffrage because, she stated, too many "wealthy women" were interested in other things. After its success at these smaller union meetings, the ESA held a mass meeting in conjunction with the Central Labor Union at Tomlinson Hall on April 23. A reported two thousand people attended the affair and Indianapolis mayor Samuel Shank presided. Graham noted that the state ESA "had received the indorsement of the United Mine Workers of American, and sixteen other labor organizations, including the Central Labor Union." Fairbanks did not appear at this meeting but sent a letter in support of woman suffrage thus showing no favoritism between the suffrage groups. Brooks reappeared and again related her story much as she had at the WFL meeting. After her talk, the *Indianapolis News* reported that "one of the most applauded speeches of the evening was

INDIANAPOLIS STAR/USA TODAY

MISS ELDENA LAUTER, TACKING UP "VOTES FOR WOMEN" PENNANT

Eldena Lauter hangs bunting at the home of former vice president Charles W. Fairbanks on Meridian Street in Indianapolis in preparation for the "funfest" in June 1912.

made by F. B. Ransom," an African American attorney and community activist. Ransom argued that women, because they could not vote, were taxed without representation and this needed to be changed. He also felt that women voters could help end prostitution in what he called "immoral resorts." After Ransom's speech, the ESA mass meeting then degenerated into an argument among male members of the Democratic, Republican, and Socialist Parties who left the woman suffrage debate by the wayside. Graham essentially lost control of the meeting and later said she had no idea that so many Socialists would attend. A local reporter stated that those Socialists in attendance "only smiled when asked if their demonstration had been prearranged." Suffragists again made the news, but this time not the type of attention they wanted.[13]

Once the political season began to heat up in August, the WFL tried to arrange times and locations for the candidates for governor and other state offices from each of the parties to speak at a WFL public meeting. It seems that despite all their efforts, only Albert Beveridge, the Progressive candidate for governor, managed to find time to speak. Undeterred, the WFL urged members across the state to invite their local candidates to attend their suffrage meetings. They also created flyers for statewide distribution—one flyer for farmer's wives explained why they should want the vote and the other was simply titled, "Why Indiana Women Should Vote."[14]

In addition to these rather traditional forms of publicity, from the very first meeting for which minutes are recorded, May 25, 1912, it becomes obvious that the WFL also wanted to pursue more creative and very public means to keep the idea of suffrage on everyone's mind. Lucy (Mrs. Henry C.) Riesenberg, WFL board member and member of the local Council of Jewish Women, wanted to put together a "ball game" for suffrage and Clarke suggested an automobile tour as she had heard had been done in Wisconsin. A "fete" on the lawn of the Fairbanks home had already been scheduled for June.[15]

Riesenberg's novel idea for a suffrage baseball game had to be approved by city bureaucracy to become a reality. First, the WFL wrote a letter to the Board of Control to request a facility. Then, the board referred that request to the Indianapolis Athletic Association. The association agreed to grant the use of its field for the game as long as the WFL agreed to sell three thousand tickets at fifty cents each. These "unreasonable" terms permanently quashed the idea.[16]

Clarke's idea for the automobile tour was as much a success as the baseball game idea had been an unfortunate failure. Sara Lauter offered the use of her car and just a few days later, on June 5, 1912, five members of the

WFL—Clarke, Mrs. R. Harry Miller, Julia Henderson, Mrs. W. T. Barnes, and Sara Lauter—along with local reporters and photographers, "made a flying trip through Hamilton County" to Westfield and Noblesville for the first such tour in the state. The goal, depending on which newspaper you read, was to venture "into territory where women are not actively demanding the right to vote" or, to put it another way, the women were "tilting with oratorical lances, against the enemy of indifference in towns of Hamilton County." After leaving Indianapolis at around 9:30 a.m., the suffragists held meetings and distributed suffrage literature throughout the area. Their meeting at the Westfield public library included a crowd of men and women, a luncheon, and rousing speeches by the suffragists. Announcing "a good day's work," three women—Mrs. N. O. Stanbrough, Mrs. Anna D. Stephens, and Mrs. Lizzie Tresmire—organized a Westfield WFL branch and offered to organize one in the neighboring town of Carmel as well. Things in Noblesville did not go as planned. Due to a scheduling mix up, women's clubs in that town were in the midst of meetings when WFL members arrived. So, still determined to make an impact, Clarke and the others handed out suffrage literature to people on the street and in businesses around the courthouse square and arranged with three townswomen to meet later. On the way back to Indianapolis, the group motored through Allisonville and distributed more handbills.[17]

This successful tour led to another, this time focused on Boone County. Suffragists stopped first at Zionsville, where League members Mary Winter and Celeste Barnhill, accompanied by reporter Betty Blythe, addressed a group at the Christian Church. Even the pastor, Reverend G. W. Nutter, joined the proceedings and, according to the *Indianapolis Star*, was an "emphatic" supporter who gave an "unqualified and ardent endorsement" of woman suffrage. Zionsville's women did not immediately form a branch as had happened in Westfield, but the reporter noted that those in attendance took the suffrage literature and the talk given by Winter and Barnhill "very seriously." Blythe noted that much of the opposition to suffrage seemed to come not from men, but from "commercialized vice" and from the apathy of women themselves. After spending time in Zionsville, Winter and Barnhill motored in a car adorned with a "Votes for Women" banner to Lebanon for another meeting, this one at the county courthouse. Here, they emphasized three important issues for women—"labor, vice, and the liquor traffic." Winter railed against "starvation wages" and said that women with the vote could help enact improved laws regarding women, children, and health. They noted that they presented this information as volun-

Interesting Suffrage Champion Here.

MISS GERDA SEBBELOV.

One of the interesting speakers at the Woman's Franchise League dinner Thursday evening was Miss Gerda Sebbelov of Laporte. Miss Sebbelov is a Danish girl who is much interested in the suffrage cause through her wide experiences among the Eskimos and the Canadian Indians. She is acting as the county chairman for the league in Laporte and is arousing much interest through her enthusiasm and by her clever addresses in a quaint but interesting accent.

INDIANAPOLIS STAR/USA TODAY

Danish immigrant Gerda Sebbelov worked with the Woman's Franchise League branch in La Porte, Indiana.

teers, not as paid speakers. Lebanon women also did not create a WFL branch on the spot, but did arrange for a future meeting.[18]

The energetic League members continued the fast pace through June. Whether it was the summer weather when everyone would be outside or the idea of hitting the ground running that appealed to them, soon after the Boone County auto tour, they hosted a "fete" or "funfest" on the lawn of the Fairbanks' Meridian Street home. A "dancing pavilion," American flags, suffrage banners, and festival booths filled the lawn in preparation for a parade, dancing, and even a debate. The event would have lasted all day and into the night, but cool weather brought the evening part of the program to an early end. Still, an estimated one thousand people attended in spite of a noon shower and the cool temperatures that followed.[19]

Men, women, and children participated in the lawn parade bearing "Votes for Women" banners with many wearing the "'suffrage sunflower,' the big yellow cockade, in whose center nestled the suffrage button." Several women performed a musical titled "The Blue Lady," which included songs that presented "sharp and pointed sarcasm in the direction of the arguments and attitude of the anti-suffragist, were keen and humorous enough to bring out hearty laughter from even the few anti-suffragists present." High school students, one girl and one boy on each team, debated suffrage for the crowd. One of the anti-team declared that only "unmarried women" wanted the vote and they wanted it only so that they could meet male politicians. The crowd voted in favor of the prosuffrage debaters.

Festive booths included a stand for hot roasted peanuts, a psychic, suffrage literature, banners, badges, and other items to make money for the League. After this great success, the WFL repeated the fete the next year at Clarke's Irvington home.[20]

Although the woman suffrage movement in Indiana had always included African American women at its meetings, African American women are not mentioned in newspaper reports about the funfest. Early in its life, the WFL had pondered how to join forces with African American suffragists. Sara Messing Stern, an Indianapolis native and now a Terre Haute resident, member, and officer of the Indiana Federation of Clubs and of the Council of Jewish Women (her father had been the longest serving rabbi in nineteenth-century Indianapolis), sent a message through WFL board member Julia Henderson asking about "the advisability of organization among the colored women of the city [presumably Terre Haute] and what on the Board's judgement should be the manner of procedure." The board agreed that "all women must be interested regardless of race," but offered no plan, or at least no plan was recorded in the meeting's minutes, for representation of African American women on the board or really any plan at all for how Stern should proceed.[21]

The Indianapolis ESA, however, moved quickly to organize a branch of its organization within the African American community. Ransom helped Graham with the endeavor. He then stepped back from his leadership role after a woman had been elected to lead the branch, which included both women and men as members. The public announcement of what became known as Branch Number 7 met with a sharp, decidedly negative response from at least one person. Graham received a letter from a supposed woman's suffrage supporter who declared she would pull her support if the plan went through: "You will find that this move to secure more numbers by bringing in a negro contingent will deter hundreds of self-respecting white people from supporting the cause and will disgust many that are already active in it." Graham had her own sharp retort, "Is the suffrage movement to be placed on the pink tea basis? The suffrage movement is not a stepping stone to social distinction. It is a stepping stone to political emancipation, and since the negroes are permitted to vote by our constitution, then they should be considered in this suffrage movement."[22]

Local African American businesswoman Madam C. J. Walker hosted the first meeting of Branch Number 7 at her home on June 24 with Ransom temporarily presiding. Carrie Barnes, a young local public-school teacher who had also taught at the Tuskegee Institute and lived in Colorado and had worked in woman's suffrage clubs there, became president of the group. Other officers included Lucy Flint as secretary, Mrs. Hudson as assistant secretary, and Elizabeth Mays as treasurer. Five or six men in a crowd estimated to be between thirty and forty also attended the organizational meeting. Barnes reported, "We all feel that colored women have need for the ballot that white women have, and a great many needs that they have not."[23]

ESA officers spoke at the next Branch Number 7 meeting held at Flanner House (a local settlement house) and spoke on the history of the suffrage organization and its goals. The branch met several times throughout the summer and Barnes spoke at a July 8 ESA meeting along with male representatives from various trade unions. They planned a large meeting of the branch for August 12 at the Second Christian Church, where Barnes, Graham, and "S.C. Garrison of Montpelier, Ind., a well-known colored socialist" all spoke. Garrison, a minister who was running for state geologist, had been speaking at Socialist meetings across the state and was apparently well received. The rest of the program for that night included discussions about "the platforms of the four leading political parties." Other local churches, such as the Mount Zion Church, also hosted meetings.[24]

In the November 1912 state and federal elections, the Democrats defeated the other parties by capitalizing on a split in the Republican Party into the Progressive and the Republican Parties. That meant that Woodrow Wilson and his vice presidential running mate, Thomas Marshall, occupied the White House. Samuel Ralston won the governor's race and Democrats captured control of the Indiana General Assembly. If suffragists could get Democrats to favor suffrage when they controlled both the legislative and executive branches, woman suffrage legislation had a real chance to become law.[25]

In spite of the vigorous and spirited suffrage activities of 1912 and the ability to work with one party, the 1913 Indiana legislators did nothing for woman suffrage and the disorganized suffragists did not help their cause. The WFL and the ESA were once again on opposing sides of a suffrage bill and, amazingly enough, their positions were the opposite of what they had been two years earlier. What the press termed "the most sensational public hearing that thus far has marked the session" stemmed from Senator Evan B. Stotsenburg's bill for school suffrage for women, in other words, a partial- suffrage bill. Approximately two hundred women representing both sides of the question appeared at the public hearing on the bill, held on January 27, 1913.

They were up in arms even after Stotsenburg withdrew the bill and replaced it with another and even after a minor fire broke out on the statehouse's lower floor. The WFL railed against the "dinky school suffrage" bill that granted suffrage to Indianapolis and Terre Haute women, but to no other women. The new bill also extended the right to serve on school boards to women across the state but did not give women the ability to vote for their own school

THE INDIANAPOLIS NEWS, SATURDAY, MARCH 1, 1913.

WOMAN'S FRANCHISE LEAGUE WILL GO TO STATEHOUSE MONDAY AND ASK SUFFRAGE AMENDMENT TO CONSTITUTION

Suffragists Say, However, That Demonstration Will Be Devoid of Spectacular Features, and Not of the Militant Variety—Many Workers of the Indiana Organization Are Not in Sympathy With Methods Adopted by the English Women—Views on Present Situation and Outlook for the Future Given by Leaders of the Organization.

Of High Character.

No Right to Criticise.

Faith in American Men.

Signed the Bill.

DR. AMELIA M. KELLER.

EDGAR A. PERKINS AND FAMILY. All Members of Woman's Franchise League.

MRS. GRACE JULIAN CLARKE.

MRS. FELIX T. M'WHIRTER.

MRS. MEREDITH NICHOLSON.

MISS MARY HANNAH KROUT.

DR. ADAH M'MAHAN.

MISS HARRIET NOBLE.

MRS. G. M. HENDERSON.

INDIANAPOLIS NEWS/USA TODAY

After a dustup between woman suffrage organizations at a hearing at the Indiana Statehouse, Indianapolis suffragists launched a campaign to demonstrate their more sedate side with a full-page report about some of the suffragists and their families. The Perkins family decided to include all seven children in their photo.

board positions. It really did not matter. Surprisingly, the ESA backed the bill. Attorney Antionette Leach, the ESA member who had earlier argued that partial-suffrage bills such as this were unconstitutional, did not appear at the hearing. Graham had someone read a section of the Indiana Constitution that she claimed, "proved the bill constitutional." Central Labor Union member William Landgraf spoke in favor of the bill and said it would be a "wedge" to gain further suffrage. State ESA vice president Mrs. A. M. Noe warned the Democrats in charge that "the women of the state are going to stand by the party that stands by them." State Senator Charles Clarke, Grace Julian Clarke's husband, had charge of the hearing and allotted twenty minutes to each person for arguments. He, then, must take the blame for some of the chaos that erupted, as suffragists timed each other with watches to make sure

SUFFRAGISTS MARCH ON ASSEMBLY

—Photo by News Staff Photographer.

Members of the Woman's Franchise League of Indiana, the Equal Suffrage League and others who are interested in votes for women marched on the assembly yesterday to present a request for the amendment of the Constitution by eliminating the word "male" from the qualifications of electors. The picture was taken on the walk leading to the statehouse before the women entered the building. The first two women are Dr. Amelia Keller and Mrs. W. T. Barnes.

INDIANAPOLIS NEWS/USA TODAY

In a further attempt to demonstrate solidarity between suffrage organizations, the Woman's Franchise League and the Equal Suffrage Association staged a joint march to the Indiana Statehouse on the same day as the much larger woman suffrage parade in Washington, DC. Indiana suffragists proceeded quietly to the statehouse and pinned yellow suffrage sashes on accommodating state legislators.

each received her allotted time.[26]

The rivalry between the ESA and the WFL ruined the public hearing. After Graham gave her arguments in favor of the bill, she opened a can of worms with the statement, "I want to add just here that we are the only duly chartered organization of equal suffrage in the state of Indiana." The unnecessary comment only increased hostilities between the two suffrage groups and laid the split bare before the legislature and the public since newspapers eagerly covered the chaotic hearing. It helped no one. WFL speakers kept up a raucous pace and at one point, Mrs. Elizabeth Stanley from Liberty, Indiana, flung open a suitcase and "thousands of cards" signed by supporters of full suffrage spilled out in the chamber. Keller also spoke and unfortunately she and Graham had a "heated discussion" about the bill. A frustrated Senator Clarke closed the hearing by stating, "We thank you for this entertainment and leave Senator Stotsenburg to your mercy."[27]

The WFL quickly remembered the importance of positive publicity and moved to repair any damage to its reputation. Before the legislative session had even started and before this unfortunate display, they had invited members of the Indiana legislature to a dinner at the Claypool Hotel to argue for suffrage and they now used the dinner to try to mend fences. According to the *Woman's Journal*, "all the members of the Legislature who attended declared in favor of woman suffrage," although if local newspaper accounts are to be believed, only a few legislators dined with the women. Speakers at the meal included Keller, Charles and Grace Julian Clarke, and three other legislators in favor of suffrage. In addition to Clarke's husband, other spouses in attendance included Horace Stilwell, T. C. Day, Ernest Bross, Representative Carlin Myers, H. D Pierce, Edgar Perkins, W. T. Barnes, W. D. Pratt, Doctor Eugene Buehler (Keller's husband), John F. Barnhill, and W. W. Winslow. In early March the WFL followed up with a splashy article in the *Indianapolis News* complete with sedate photos and small blurbs about the family lives of some of the WFL officers. Mrs. Edgar A. Perkins posed with her husband, a labor organizer, and their seven children. The article juxtaposed WFL members who "are of high character, good homemakers and ideal mothers" and who worked "with a quiet persistency for the cause" while announcing their disapproval of militant suffrage tactics as seen in England (and by extension the behavior at the committee hearing including the spilling of the cards on the hearing room floor). Keller's biography stressed her husband (Buehler), her eight-year-old son, and explained her use of her birth name for her profession (that is the name she used when she began her medical practice). Eugenie Nicholson, the article stated, put her devotion to suffrage behind her devotion to her famous husband, her home, and their three children.[28]

The WFL wanted all legislators to see this more sedate suffrage support. They organized a peaceful march to the statehouse on March 3, which coincided with the date of the national suffrage parade in Washington, DC, that had been timed for the day before Wilson's inauguration to draw maximum attention to the suffrage movement. The parade drew about five thousand women to the nation's capital and it did not go as easily as the women had hoped. Some people in the crowd along the parade route assaulted and verbally abused the suffragists and any police who saw the disturbances did nothing to help the women. Nevertheless, the women persisted and finished the march. Harriet Noble and Mary (Mrs. Ovid Butler) Tarkington Jameson marched in the Washington parade to represent Hoosier women and carried the Indiana banner. In Indiana, suffragists planned to meet outside the state senate chamber to ask someone to present their petition to take the word "male" out of the proposed new state constitution. Graham of the ESA felt the need to make amends and asked the WFL for a meeting to devise a joint appearance at the Indianapolis march. Since the WFL had its plans in place, the group sent word to both Graham and to the press of those plans and invited both to join them. Graham apparently agreed, since she and presumably other ESA members joined the short walk to the statehouse.[29]

Channeling "The Charge of the Light Brigade," one reporter noted that the legislators found "women to the right of them and women to the left of them, women in the corridors and in the doorways, women everywhere, and on every woman a yellow streamer bearing in big black letters, 'Votes for Women.'" The statement is most likely true as an estimated five hundred women participated in the march. Even "Governor Ralston cheerily allowed Mrs. Felix T. [Luella] McWhirter to pin one of their streamers on his coat." Other politicians were not as cooperative, and Clarke's husband did not wear a streamer. Those legislators who donned suffrage streamers were known for their prosuffrage stances and Progressive Party senator Frank N. Gavit wore two. One sly House page neatly folded his streamer so that it read, "Votes for men." Keller and Graham apparently worked side by side and both declared the day a success. Graham noted that the two suffrage groups could not merge because men were a part of her group and not part of the WFL, but that both groups could always work together for events such as this one. In reality, while it was a success for the peaceful coexistence of the two suffrage groups, a proposed constitutional amendment that had been introduced while the women were in the statehouse and apparently did not even realize its existence due to the excitement, never made it out of committee.[30]

Convinced that its march to the statehouse had been a success, the WFL continued its "quiet persistency" of public meetings and garnering publicity. After a convention in May 1913 that found a "flushed" and "tardy" Keller arriving after, the newspapers were quick to note, having "just welcomed a new suffragist into the world," WFL members settled into a flurry of work. They planned ways to raise money, wrote letters to federal representatives about the Susan B. Anthony Amendment, and even received a letter of congratulations from NAWSA for the work they had accomplished over the previous year. Perhaps buoyed by that note, Clarke and Nicholson met with Ralston and asked him to place women on state advisory boards, especially on the Board of Education and the Centennial Committee, two very high-profile committees that

INDIANA CLUBWOMEN HAVE ORGANIZED TO
PROMOTE LEGISLATION OF INTEREST TO SEX

MRS FELIX T
M^c WHIRTER,
1ST VICE PRES.

MRS. S. C. STIMSON
2ND VICE PRES
TERRE HAUTE.

MRS GRACE JULIAN CLARKE,
PRESIDENT OF THE LEGISLATIVE
COUNCIL OF INDIANA WOMEN

MISS DORA
BOSART,
3RD VICE PRES.

MISS ALMA
SICKLER,
SECY.-TREAS

INDIANAPOLIS NEWS/USA TODAY

Grace Julian Clarke was instrumental in creating the Woman's Legislative Council. The Council, composed of several women's groups, became a powerful lobby and pushed for suffrage as well as other pieces of legislation.

garnered their causes, and any woman who served on those boards, a great deal of publicity. Clarke reported back to the WFL her impression that the governor "would do what the law requires and no more." Other activities included distributing suffrage literature at the state fair (a good way to reach women and men from rural parts of the state), holding an "open air meeting" on the working-class south side of Indianapolis, and celebrating the October 23, 1913, endorsement of suffrage by the Indiana Federation of Clubs. The WFL pushed the mayor of Indianapolis to appoint police women (he did not). The League created a "speakers' bureau." Speakers included Helen Benbridge, Sara (Mrs. Leon) Stern, and Mabel (Mrs. C. M.) Curry, all of Terre Haute; Reverend Daisy Douglas Barr of Muncie; Gerda Sebbelov of La Porte; Mrs. Alice Waugh of Tipton; and Keller, Clarke, Noble, O'Hair, Barnhill, Mrs. W. T. Barnes, Mrs. Ollah P. Toph, Mrs. Ida Gray Scott, Georgia Alexander, and Mrs. R. Harry Miller, all of Indianapolis. New WFL branches popped up across the state.[31]

In addition to devising its own state affairs, the WFL participated in events directed from NAWSA headquarters. The NAWSA declared May 2, 1914, to be women's Independence Day. At meetings in Hoosier cities and towns, women read a woman's Declaration of Independence and the proposed federal Anthony Amendment and crowds sang suffrage songs. The WFL organized the event in Indianapolis where at noon on May 2, a crowd of approximately three hundred gathered around parked cars decorated with the now familiar yellow suffrage banners on Market Street between Illinois Street and Monument Circle. Luella McWhirter read the woman's declaration of independence and the proposed federal amendment and Ida Gray Scott led the crowd in song. In a very overt demonstration of the WFL's willingness to now work with any politician who would help their cause, W. D. Headrick, a Bull Moose (Progressive) Party speaker, gave the main address. He called not only for women to receive the vote at the federal level, but also for a state constitutional convention to consider adding woman's suffrage, the referendum, and the recall—all Progressive Party initiatives—to it. His rousing speech proclaimed, "Woman is greatly interested in all social and moral reforms. She is called the queen of the home and should have the right to settle vital questions that so materially affect the home. She should not do this alone by praying on bended knee and in supplication, but she should do it fighting, and armed with the same weapon a man has, the ballot." The suffragists gave away suffrage material from the parked cars.[32]

The style of celebration varied at other May 2 gatherings across the state.

Evansville suffragists held a meeting inside the courthouse, where Stanley Coulter of Purdue University spoke to the crowd. The DePauw University suffrage group held its indoor luncheon at the women's gym. As at the Indianapolis meeting, suffrage songs and speeches highlighted the event with five speakers taking the dais that day. Richmond and Logansport branches held outdoor meetings. Richmond supporters met "on the steps of the North A street Friends church" and the Logansport group gathered at a local park. The Logansport meeting most likely lasted longer than the thirty-minute Richmond meeting. At Logansport, the crowd sang suffrage songs, including "The Battle Hymn of the Republic," which had long ago been adopted by the national suffragists as "their" song; two women gave speeches; and, as in Indianapolis, someone read the Declaration of Independence for women and the proposed federal amendment. Local Boy Scouts also participated in the meeting, although there is no record of precisely what they did. The Terre Haute franchise league hosted two hundred at a luncheon, where many women, and a local rabbi, spoke in favor of suffrage. Helen Gougar, who had died 1907, would most likely have been disappointed in the Lafayette program. The "conservative element" of the league there had apparently taken over the planning committee and held no outdoor meeting and no parade. In spite of a reported fifty women volunteering to participate in such a parade, the suffragists instead gathered at the Second Presbyterian Church to hear a discussion as to why the state constitution needed revision.[33]

Other cities across the nation held similar parades and outdoor meetings. New York City suffragists abandoned their annual parade in favor of open-air meetings in all parts of the city. As with the Indiana women, they used cars to gather attention and to be sure to cover all the territory in the city. An estimated sixty-five other towns across New York held parades and open-air meetings. In Geneva, New York, women placed suffrage literature in stores so that storekeepers could include it in packages that day. In Pittsburgh, a "monster parade" and an open-air meeting garnered a crowd estimated at two thousand and suffragists held meetings in sixty other locations in Pennsylvania, including Philadelphia. The large parade and open-air meeting there apparently drew "several thousand women and scores of men" who wore daffodils to signal their support. Anti-suffragists lined the route and wore red roses as a sign of where they stood on the issue.[34]

The same year as the big publicity splashes of street meetings across Indiana, members of the WFL also began to closely work with Indianapolis African

American suffragists. It seems that Branch Number 7 of the ESA disbanded as mention of it disappeared from newspapers. A variety of clubs that worked with both the WFL and the ESA replaced that original group. African American women in Indianapolis already belonged to a variety of women's clubs and hosted what was called an "echo meeting" of the National Association of Colored Women's Clubs convention in Indianapolis after the national meeting at Wilburforce University. Unlike the chilly reception African American women might receive at white women's clubs meetings at the national level, the WFL's Clarke and Laura Donnan and the ESA's Graham were welcomed to be among

INDIANAPOLIS NEWS/USA TODAY

Local newspapers noticed the uptick in suffrage publicity. This cartoon ran on the front page of the Indianapolis News *on May 2, 1913.*

the three hundred in attendance at the NACWC echo meeting. All three women had a history of working alongside African American women. Donnan is a prime example of the strong ties between Indianapolis schoolteachers, white and black, that bound the suffrage groups together. Donnan had taught for decades at Indianapolis/Shortridge High School and knew several African American women in Indianapolis because they were either fellow teachers (in this case at the elementary schools) or had been her pupils at the high school. In other words, Donnan found it easy to help start suffrage clubs because she already knew the women. A new suffrage group called the Women's Council, with Carrie Barnes again as the president, formed in 1914. Keller and Donnan spoke at several of their meetings. Two hundred women turned out for the Women's Council meeting at the Senate Avenue Young Men's Christian Association in October 1914. Donnan again spoke, as did both Elizabeth Mays of the old ESA Branch Number 7 and F. B. Ransom. One African American WCTU club distributed literature and Votes for Women streamers. The Woman's Council then disappeared from the newspapers and was replaced by the First Colored Woman's Suffrage Club in 1916. The Woman's Council's disappearance coincides with Barnes' departure from Indianapolis. In the summer of 1915, she had traveled to New York with Madame C. J. Walker, who considered Barnes to be like a daughter to her. While in New York, Barnes met Hubert W. Ross, an African American dentist who practiced in Boston. They married in Indianapolis in the summer of 1916 and then lived in Boston. African American churches entered the suffrage clamor by sponsoring debates with men from various churches offering prosuffrage and antisuffrage arguments. However, in spite of an active African American press and a sizable community, very little other information is known about suffrage activities among black women in Indianapolis. WFL members also worked with African American women in Terre Haute, but again, only the slightest information is available. In 1915 Sara Stern, Stella Stimson, and Helen Benbridge worked to help secure better facilities for a "day nursery" in Terre Haute, but there is no record of forming a WFL branch.[35]

The 1915 session of the Indiana General Assembly rapidly approached and the increasingly media savvy Hoosier suffragists were ready. They had accomplished a great deal since 1913 and had used innovative (for them) strategies such as automobile tours and street meetings to garner support for the cause. Their biggest obstacle remained the embarrassing problem that befell them in 1911 and 1913—how to cooperate with the ESA and other women's groups to present a united front to the legislature. They could get people's attention, but it had to be the right type of attention to accomplish their goals. The answer came in the form of a direct lobbying group, the Legislative Council, whose efforts focused on specific legislation supported by all member clubs. As *Indianapolis Star* columnist Belinda Brewster put it, "No more wrangling among themselves and no more this mistake of having one society ask for a measure and another society work against it." It was Clarke's idea. She first brought it up at the August 15, 1914, meeting of the WFL and met no objections. On September 3 delegates representing an estimated fifty thousand women who belonged to the Woman's Department Club (Indianapolis), the Local Council of Women (Indianapolis), the Consumers League, the WFL, the WCTU, and the Indiana Federation of Women's Clubs met to form the Woman's Legislative Council. That group invited the Council of Jewish Women, the ESA, the Association of Collegiate Alumnae, and the Mothers' Congress to join and they did. The Women's Press Club later also joined. Clarke had visited California in 1912 and learned that California women had formed a similar council prior to winning the vote there and then continued its use to work toward legislation they deemed important to women and children. Now Indiana women planned to do the same. Clarke had the idea to create the first efficient lobby that represented women of all stripes from the entire state.[36]

McWhirter, who had been very active in other women's clubs, including the WFL and the WCTU, seemed to find her niche with the WLC. Her leadership skills appeared from the first meeting when she insisted that the group write a constitution. It did and decided that each member association would have two representatives on the governing council unless that group had more than twenty-five branches, at which point the group could appoint one extra delegate for each additional twenty-five branches. Membership had to be continuous "to avoid having a society enter for one year and use the power of the WLC to support its pet issue before dropping out." They clearly delineated how the WLC chose what legislation to support in any given year: legislative proposals had to have a two-thirds vote of the committee for active lobbying to begin—a majority vote was not enough. If the WLC accepted an idea, the group that had made the proposal had to agree to contribute a lobbyist to the cause, who then worked under the guidance of a general lobbying committee. Excited and eager council directors introduced and accepted twelve proposals for their first year's work. Clarke strongly argued that they should work for no more than five measures, but the excited WLC members wanted to do more during the 1915 legislative session.[37]

Just as she achieved one of her greatest successes—the creation of a lobbying group that combined the forces of women across the state—Grace Julian Clarke became ill. The doctor diagnosed exhaustion. He and her friends insisted that Clarke go at once to Florida for the warmth and quiet and not think about suffrage or club work. After years of intensive labor on behalf of women, she just had to rest. She wrote to the only woman she thought could lead the new lobbying group in her place—McWhirter—to plead with her to take charge. Clarke was emphatic, "I have 'debated and decided' that YOU MUST BE PRESIDENT of the council. . . . There are very diverse elements to be amalgamated and controlled, and one with tact and at the same time a clear head is absolutely necessary." McWhirter accepted the post but signed her first circular to WLC members, "Acting President during the absence from the state of Mrs. Grace Julian Clarke." Unfortunately, in just a few weeks, McWhirter joined Clarke in Florida. McWhirter's husband had taken seriously ill and the couple went to Florida to see if the warmth, sunshine, and the slower pace of life would improve his health. Since Clarke's husband served

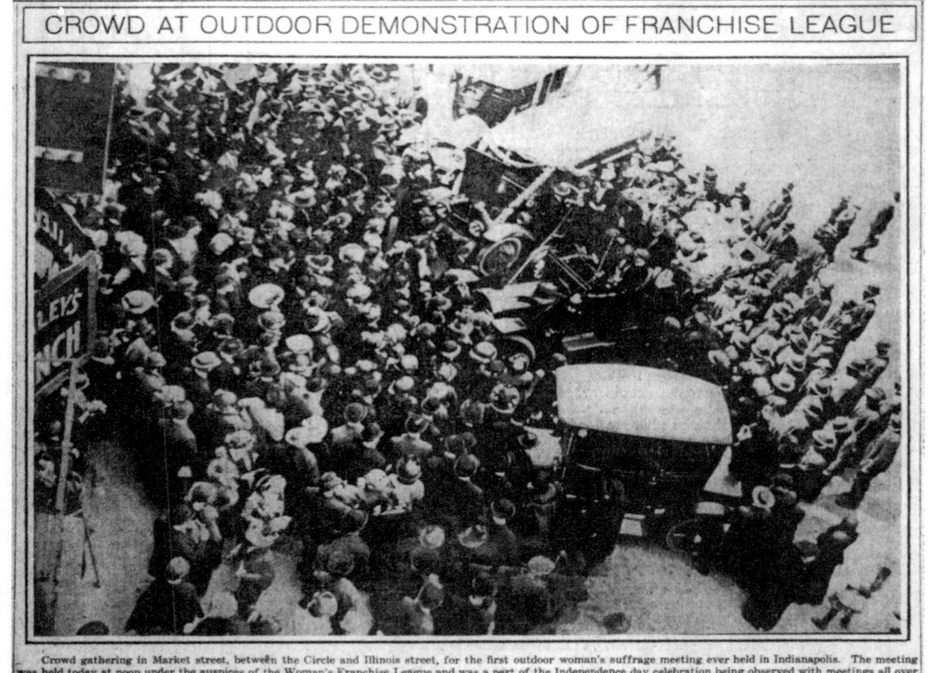
CROWD AT OUTDOOR DEMONSTRATION OF FRANCHISE LEAGUE

Crowd gathering in Market street, between the Circle and Illinois street, for the first outdoor woman's suffrage meeting ever held in Indianapolis. The meeting was held today at noon under the auspices of the Woman's Franchise League and was a part of the Independence day celebration being observed with meetings all over the country. The man standing in the auto is W. D. Headrick, who was one of the speakers.

INDIANAPOLIS NEWS/USA TODAY

Suffragists held a street meeting at the corner of Illinois and Market Streets in 1914 in a continuation of their emphasis of wider and more frequent publicity.

as a state senator, the two women kept in touch with statehouse events through him and with regular letters from WLC member Alma Sickler. Unlike the previous administration that did not give suffragists even a table in the Statehouse, Ralston gave them an office that Sickler staffed on a daily basis and Stella Stimson served as the chief lobbyist. They focused on the passage of a partial-suffrage bill similar to the one enacted in Illinois in 1913. They did not find sponsors for the bill until late February, when Senator Marion Maston and Representative Perry Rule agreed to help. Stimson and Culla Vayhinger of the WCTU telephoned 150 women to urge them to press their state legislators to vote for the bill (so much quicker and more efficient than the old letter-writing campaigns) and the women spoke directly to the governor. By that time, however, a statewide prohibition bill was also winding its way through the General Assembly and state legislators thought the two bills were related. The governor supported the suffrage bill and would not veto it should it pass, but he also did not publicly come out in favor of it. The bill sat in committee, where its chaimanr refused to bring it up for a vote. Women, once again, lost any chance at voting. On the positive side, Ralston had given them an office and as one historian noted, "a room of their own." Hoosier women found new, effective lobbying voices in Stimson, Sickler, and attorney Emma

Vice President Fairbanks loaned his car to publicize a mass meeting for the Republican Party in 1916 that suffragists attended.

White. Still, they had once again gone down to defeat because of a decades-old problem that dated back to at least 1881—the conflation of suffrage with prohibition.[38]

Hoosier suffragists had found common cause through the WLC and honed their expertise and seeming comfort at lobbying legislators. Just when things looked good for the future, things turned ugly later in 1915 when the Indiana Federation of Clubs had its own political battles—again because of suffrage and temperance. Clarke, back from Florida, rested and ready to resume suffrage and club work, found herself embroiled in the sort of conflict she did not relish—fights between friends and co-workers about private social habits. It is safe to say that the situation first hit Clarke's radar around July 7, 1915. A letter from Helen Benbridge, president of the Terre Haute Franchise League, warned Clarke of the impending fracas. The Indiana Federation of Women's Clubs held its officer elections each October and the campaigning for 1915 had already started. Clarke, as a longtime clubwoman and former president of the federation, had urged Lenore Cox of Terre Haute to stand for president of the federation. Stella Stimson, the outstanding lobbyist for the WLC during the latest general assembly session, also wanted to be president and started a campaign to besmirch Cox's reputation. Since both women lived in Terre Haute, most of the rumors and bile stemmed from local conditions. Benbridge warned Clarke to be prepared for "mud slinging, scandal mongering, innuendo, every sort of blackguarding." Even Sara Stern, treasurer of the Terre Haute WFL, got dragged into the mess. Stern and Stimson were evidently at odds about "several Jewish matters" in and around Terre Haute. Benbridge wanted Cox to win the election because Cox would put suffrage at the head of the federation's agenda and Stimson, an ardent prohibitionist, gave every indication that prohibition was more important for her ideas for the Federation's work than suffrage.[39]

The question in the minds of Benbridge and another Clarke correspondent, Helen Baumgartner, was whether Stimson would be loyal to the federation and its variety of club and reform activities, or whether she would use the federation to push the agenda of the WCTU in a manner that must have seemed similar to the Gougar years of the 1890s. When piecing together several letters to Clarke from a variety of women, it is clear that Stimson was spreading rumors about Cox's personal life and values. Baumgartner also hinted at some nefarious politicking by Stimson from several years earlier. They had good reason to be concerned. One of the rumors that Stimson apparently spread about

Cox was that she was the "liquor candidate." As Benbridge put it, "I doubt if the liquor element ever dreamed of having a candidate, knew there was such a thing as an election pending in the federation." The Terre Haute Brewery certainly did not like Cox and used her involvement with suffrage (not with the WCTU) as a reason to not donate to a charity that the Coxes supported. Stimson also made the ridiculous accusation that Cox favored prostitution and owned a home in Terre Haute's red-light district. Particularly offensive to suffragists was Stimson's insinuation that Cox would be fine as a president of a suffrage group, but for the presidency of the federation, one must have "high character," and be a "Christian woman." This would be news to the members of the Council of Jewish Women, who served as officers and members of the various women's clubs and suffrage groups across the state.

Stimson's attacks on Cox also included attacks on the suffrage organization in general, and according to Benbridge, Stimson spread lies across the state about suffrage officers and accused the treasurer of keeping money for herself. Housing reformer Albion Fellows Bacon tried to arrange a meeting with Clarke and Stimson in August at the Chautauqua House in Merom, stating, "there are some very important things that need to be discussed, and some things that we don't want to write." That same day Clarke had fired off a letter to McWhirter stating that Cox should be elected: "I am desirous of seeing her elected because of the utterly abominable warfare that is being made upon her, and because I feel that the most important thing to do in the present juncture is to rebuke such methods." McWhirter claimed no knowledge of the battle (even though she had been informed of the matter at about the same time as Clarke) that was raging and condemned it stating, "The DAR [Daughters of the American Revolution] is noted for its warlike proceedings, the suffragists for their lack of harmonious relations toward one another, but the clubwomen have been so busy with the very important things about them and concerning their interest in the home and children that they have loved and admired one another." Clarke also discovered rumors that Cox "smokes, drinks, serves strong drink to family and friend in her home, openly opposed to prohibition, and does not believe in a God" and she apparently played golf on Sundays.[40]

After gathering as much information as possible and even receiving a letter from Stimson herself, Clarke sent a stinging rebuke to Stimson challenging the gossip she had spread and criticizing her for spreading any rumors at all about a fellow clubwoman. She also sent a letter to Virginia Meredith repeating some of Stimson's rumors and the ones that were true—Cox's husband did own a

Fairbanks Automobile Makes Trips in Behalf of Suffrage

MISS CARINA EAGLESFIELD (LEFT) AND MRS. JOHN WESLEY TIMMONS.

INDIANAPOLIS STAR/USA TODAY

Novel publicity techniques such as this sign became more common in 1916.

building that housed a saloon. She ended her note, "I am not disposed to yield to such a woman [Stimson], for I consider it most dangerous to establish such precedents. No one would be safe if such methods are allowed to win. It is believed by some that she herself expects to be nominated and then expects the TEMPERANCE forces to rally and elect her. I am for temperance in all things, and particularly do I believe in curbing that unruly member, the tongue."[41]

What Clarke feared most was the adverse publicity any open fighting among the two women, both known to be strong suffragists in addition to being clubwomen, might have not just on the federation but also the WLC and the WFL. And she was right. Three extraordinary political cartoons about the federation chaos ran in the *Fort Wayne Daily News*. It was clear the cartoonist understood part of the nature of the fight, as drinking and smoking figured prominently in two of them. The papers also faithfully reported that neither Cox nor Stimson became president of the federation on October 29, but rather Fort Wayne clubwoman Caroline Fairbank, who admitted to having an occasional glass of beer, won. The unfortunate and even bizarre circumstances of

SUFFRAGE LEADERS WILL PLAN UNITED EFFORT

DR. AMELIA R. KELLER,
PRES., FRANCHISE LEAGUE OF INDIANA

MRS. CARRIE CHAPMAN CATT
PRES. NATIONAL AMERICAN WOMAN SUFFRAGE ASSOCIATION

MRS. WALTER McNABB MILLER,
DIRECTOR OF NATIONAL AMERICAN WOMAN SUFFRAGE ASSOCIATION

MRS. ANNA DUNN NOLAND
PRES. INDIANA EQUAL SUFFRAGE ASSOCIATION

Hallie W. Henderson; corresponding secretary, Mrs. Mary C. Luther; treasurer, Mrs. Emma C. Bogle; federation secretary, Miss Agnes McCrea; press correspondent, Mrs. Olive C. Shattuck; membership committee, Mrs. Zulemia A. Moore, Mrs. Hattie Halstead and Mrs. Nellie L. Weinland; program committee, Mrs. Clo B. Craig, Mrs. Helen G. Rouse and Mrs. Addie B. Cross; executive committee, Mrs. E. Stevenson, Mrs. H. Rouse, Mrs. Minnie Snyder, Mrs. C. B. Craig, Mrs. A. B. Cross and Mrs. Ella S. Falls; music committee, Mrs. Nancy McNutt and Mrs. Charlotte W. McCalip; civic improvement committee, Mrs. Lena T. Pollom and Mrs. Frances B. Robinson. The club has twenty-six corresponding

mony was performed in the presence of the immediate families and a few friends. Miss Bennett was given away by her guardian, William Burdell, of Columbus, O. Master William Staley, a cousin, acted as page. Walter W. Kuhn, of Indianapolis, was the best man, and August C. Bohlen, of Indianapolis; Lewis Wiggins and Edwin Kinnear, of New York, and Edwin Burdell, of Columbus, were ushers. Following the ceremony a wedding breakfast was served at the Hotel Manhattan. Mr. Stein, who is county clerk of Marion county, has taken his bride on an extended trip to California. On their return Mr. and Mrs. Stein will live at Wild Rose manor, their home, on Sherman drive, near Thirty-eighth street.

INDIANAPOLIS NEWS/USA TODAY

National American Woman Suffrage Association officers worked with Doctor Amelia Keller and Anna Dunn Noland to merge the two statewide suffrage groups but failed at the attempt.

the vote overshadowed the very real benefit that came from that federation meeting when members voted to recommend that the state purchase the land that became Turkey Run State Park and held a discussion about preserving the dunes of Lake Michigan (today a national park).[42]

In the end, Clarke and other members of the WFL board asked for Stimson's resignation from the same due to her actions not just toward Cox, but toward the board itself. The board charged her with "disloyalty and unfaithfulness to the trust placed in her as a member of the Board . . . in attempting to throw the representation of the State League out of the convention of the Indiana Federation of Clubs . . . equally unfair and unjust . . . is the flagrant charge made by Mrs. Stimson that 'the issue is one between the liquor interests and the non-church people.'" The sudden turn of events had so shocked the WFL that it could not conceive how they could continue to work with Stimson. Her work for the WLC had been extraordinary, as she held down the lobbying effort when Clarke and McWhirter were in Florida for health reasons. Now, she had turned on them because of her views on Prohibition and drinking as she gave away in her comment to the *Indianapolis News* when they asked about the conflict: "This is the same fight that is being waged before the American Federation of Labor at San Francisco and in Chicago. It is the fight of the nonchurch and liquor forces against the church and temperance forces. Everywhere, the nonchurch and liquor forces are trying to weed out the church and temperance forces. This is a fight of commercialism against principle and I shall not surrender one foot of ground." The year ended on an oddly discordant note for Hoosier suffragists. They had made great movement forward, but now seemed to be taking a step back.[43]

Chapter 6

"WE MUST BE FEARLESS"

For a few brief, wonderful months in 1917, Hoosier women registered to vote at county clerks' offices, studied civics through a special column in the *Indianapolis Star*, and prepared for the momentous task ahead of them—in November they could vote. Years of hard work paid off in the 1917 Indiana legislative session as not one, but two, suffrage bills were enacted. The partial-suffrage bill allowed for the vote right away in certain elections and the other bill needed to pass the legislature again in 1919 for full suffrage. The general assembly even passed a Constitutional Convention bill finally to rewrite the state's cumbersome document and hopefully include full woman suffrage in the state's organic law. Because of the enactment of the partial-suffrage bill, women could vote to send delegates sympathetic to woman suffrage to that convention. Doctor Amelia Keller, the Woman's Franchise League president, called the legislation "far-reaching and revolutionary."

It seemed that Indiana's women had secured all possible legislative ways to get the vote and would soon join women in many Western states and in Illinois at the polls. Rumors circulated, however, that some nefarious person or group might file a lawsuit to stop women from voting. And, within weeks, the rumors proved to be true. Two separate lawsuits challenged the laws and after many months of legal wrangling, the Indiana Supreme Court struck down the partial-suffrage law and the Constitutional Convention bill. Before then, however, women in Indiana, including perhaps the first—"the wife of Rev. J. E. McCloud"—voted for possibly the first time in state history on June 5 in Warren County in Washington Township on a local prohibition law that "helped oust four saloons." Women also voted in Porter County on July 10 to defeat the building of an expensive gravel road. Before the Court ruled that women in the state could not vote, the women of the town of Riverside in Delaware County voted for a town trustee and a town clerk in late September and became the last women in the state to vote. Discouraged but not defeated at the end of 1917 and armed with the information that when women voted no calamities befell the state, Hoosier suffragists resumed their work for the vote.[1]

It probably should come as no surprise that suffrage activity spiked in Indiana in 1916–17 because it happened across the United States. The National American Woman Suffrage Association, which had grown moribund under the leadership of Doctor Anna Howard Shaw, sprang back to life in in 1915 under the new leadership of Carrie Chapman Catt, who launched the organization into a highly active national suffrage campaign under her "Winning Plan." According to historians, Catt's success came in part because she chose to work with a board composed of "women with independent means who had ability as well as the willingness to devote themselves single mindedly to their new jobs" and if "a woman's health or family responsibilities precluded such full-time activity, neither sentiment nor gratitude for past achievement stood in the way of her replacement." A new national suffrage group, the Congressional Union, did the same. Of course, "it did not make for a socially representative leadership in either group; but it provided two brilliant leaders [Catt and Congressional Union chair Alice Paul] with trained and experienced staffs who measured up to any demands that were made upon them. . . . The day for the amateur reformer had given way to the professional organizer."[2]

Both Catt and Paul worked with what became three Indiana suffrage groups in 1916 and 1917, and while Catt urged the groups to work together and Paul urged the Indiana Congressional Union/Woman's Party to pursue its own course, both women can be credited for inspiring Hoosier suffragists to take a close look at their 1915 defeat at the statehouse, learn lessons from that defeat, and vigorously pursue suffrage once again.

In many ways it is amazing that two suffrage bills passed the legislature in 1917 because 1916 had been another contentious year for Hoosier suffrage organizations. With two separate, statewide suffrage organizations in place, the Woman's Franchise League and the Equal Suffrage Association, another suffrage group suddenly appeared in Indiana in 1916—an Indiana branch of the national suffrage group known as the Congressional Union. The CU grew from the controversial suffrage work of Paul and Lucy Burns, who had participated in raucous suffrage demonstrations in England. After their return to the states, they initially worked with the NAWSA. The association welcomed the energetic women into the suffrage fold and Paul took over the leadership of NAWSA's Congressional Committee. The CU, an outgrowth of that NAWSA committee and Paul's frustration with NAWSA rules and regulations about proper ways to agitate for the vote, was formed in 1913. The CU focused exclusively on gaining an amendment to the federal constitution and encouraged NAWSA to do the same. More important, the CU also held the political party in power culpable for the absence of federal suffrage legislation and believed in frequent street demonstrations and other tactics to draw attention to the suffrage fight. The NAWSA, on the other hand, had a long-standing policy of both pushing for the federal amendment and supporting states that worked to change suffrage laws only within their states. NAWSA leaders also felt that some of the bolder tactics used by the CU did more harm than good. While NAWSA saw the value of the CU's work, the two groups could not come to an agreement on tactics and goals and split in 1914.[3]

The CU got a foothold in Indiana in the same way it had taken hold across the country—mounting frustration with the lack of a suffrage amendment and a growing feeling that the movement's leaders were to blame for the lack of progress. In Indiana the WFL, the largest suffrage organization in the state, had been led by Doctor Amelia Keller for the past four years and she appeared to be on her way to a fifth term in office. In part because of concerns about the length of Keller's term of service and in part because of their sympathies with CU ideas, some of the estimated four hundred women from the five Indianapolis WFL branches—North Boulevard, North Indianapolis, Parkway, Brightwood, and Brookside—seceded from the organization and joined the CU. Eugenie Nicholson (who had testified for the WFL before the state legislature), a national CU board member, and Indianapolis lawyer Eleanor P. Barker apparently led the revolt. It seems that a new generation of suffragists were eager to join the more active demonstrations called for by the CU. The WFL and ESA had hosted street meetings and auto tours for years, but these women felt the need for more frequent events and to focus strictly on a federal suffrage amendment. According to Barker, "I think it worse than foolish to center all our time on state work. We probably all will be dead and buried before there is a new Indiana Constitution, and it is practically impossible to get an amendment that will grant us suffrage." Despite the unrest in its ranks, Keller won re-election to lead the WFL by a vote of 101 to 54 at a heated April 14 convention, where those who were about to form the CU still wanted to be able to vote for the WFL president. Other topics under debate at the meeting included whether to push for full suffrage in the state, with Grace Julian Clarke, Eleanor Barker, and Keller in favor and Emma White and Vanderburg County (Evansville) chair Rose Heilman favoring partial suffrage as better than nothing at all. Despite the mild acrimony, three hundred suffragists attended the annual banquet held at the end of the meeting. Two months later, on June 7, 1916, the WFL and the Indiana branch of the CU both marched through a driving rainstorm interlaced with snow as part of the suffrage parade held in Chicago during the National Republican Convention. The groups marched in their suffrage colors—yellow for the WFL (yellow capes and parasols) and yellow, white, and purple for the CU (white hat with yellow cord and purple rosettes across a white dress), but had additional accessories of overcoats, rainboots, and sturdy umbrellas. Betsy Edwards of Shelbyville held the banner at the front of the Indiana division—the same banner that Mary Tarkington Jameson and Harriet Noble had carried during the 1913 parade in Washington, DC, the day before President Woodrow Wilson's inauguration. Approximately seventy Indiana women walked in the parade and the Hoosier group tied Wisconsin for fielding the largest state delegation after host state Illinois.[4]

The lead up to Hoosier women's intense involvement in the 1917 legislative session really began at the joint meeting of the WFL and the ESA held just after the resounding success of the Chicago suffrage parade. Beginning in 1911, the WFL had made repeated overtures to the ESA for joint meetings and "amalgamation" or the merging of the two groups. Each time, the ESA offered no or only vague responses to WFL inquiries. Longtime state ESA president Anna Noland of Logansport did not, it appears, really want the two groups to merge. Indianapolis ESA leader, Hannah Graham, and WFL president Amelia Keller, usually did not work closely together, but had attempted to do so during the 1913 session when both groups marched to the statehouse to pin suffrage streamers on Indiana legislators. Despite this long history of only occasional cooperation, Catt of the NAWSA had arranged the joint June meeting to insure complete cooperation in state and national efforts to push the Susan B. Anthony Amendment through Congress. Catt firmly believed the two groups should coordinate their activities or simply merge (Catt's preference) to save time and money and help push through state and national victories. Catt had just come off a strenuous six-month stint of working in Iowa to get out the vote for the woman suffrage referendum in that state. It had failed on June 5 largely due to the votes of several Iowa counties that feared prohibition would be enacted if women could vote. She now had her sights set on helping Indiana.[5]

Women at the meeting spoke on topics, including "The Most Practical Plan for Suffrage Work in Indiana" and "Shall We Work for the Federal Amendment Only." Catt asked the women of Indiana "to mobilize a suffrage army and fight for the cause." In a show of solidarity and perhaps of Catt's persuasive skills, WFL and ESA leaders indicated that a merger would soon occur. The groups' differences, as should have already been plain from years of working for different pieces of legislation, had not pivoted on whether to work together, but rather what to work for. Many Hoosier leaders favored a singular focus on the Susan B. Anthony Amendment and others expressed impatience with a federal amendment that would take months, if not years, to ratify and wanted to pursue state laws. Suffrage, however, was still the ultimate goal. Catt warned against siding with either Democrats or Republicans during their suffrage campaigning. Men in favor of woman suffrage could be found in both parties and women should not choose one party and risk alienating the other. Everyone, it seemed, now realized that cooperation was the key to getting the vote.

LIBRARY OF CONGRESS

Luella McWhirter about 1915. McWhirter was active in the Woman's Christian Temperance Union and the Woman's Legislative Council. Her organizational skills proved to be invaluable to the suffrage movement.

Just as the convention came to a congenial end, Elsie Hill of the national CU put in a surprise appearance. Hill, from Connecticut, had been holding street meetings for the CU for almost two weeks in Indianapolis—noon meetings met at the corner of Senate Avenue and Washington Street with evening meetings at the corner of Market and Illinois Streets. The CU was about to meet with the Indianapolis WFL's five branches and some ESA women, as well as national CU leader Paul, to form a branch of the Union in Indianapolis. Just as approximately five hundred convention attendees applauded their hard work and fledging unity, Hill rose to comment on something Catt had said that Hill thought was "unfair" to the CU. A local newspaper played up the resulting kerfuffle by stating "harmony flies out the window" as Catt and Hill "stage a scene." Another newspaper declared that Catt "kicked up a row" that resulted not in the amalgamation of the state's two suffrage groups, but instead created a third. This was patently untrue, as plans for the creation of the CU in Indianapolis began before this meeting. Local newspapers played up a minor confrontation between Hill and Catt for their own purposes—perhaps to make a peaceful women's meeting more "newsworthy" and, given the response to the lack of harmony the previous year at the Indiana Federation of Clubs annual meeting, editors knew that a fight between women certainly sold papers. The CU formally organized in Indianapolis on June 24 with Barker as the state chair. In a show of unity and perhaps as a demonstration of lessons learned from prior dust-ups between suffrage groups, Keller attended the meeting and asked that all woman's suffrage groups in the state work together. A parade with an estimated fifty cars decorated with suffrage banners made its way through downtown streets after the meeting. Now, three suffrage organizations in the state had to work together, and it might not be an easy thing to do.[6]

Many women in Indianapolis pondered the differences between the CU and the WFL and wanted more information before deciding which to join. One suffrage group with that question was the First Colored Suffrage Club of Indianapolis. Carrie Whallon of Irvington and Lizzie Compton and Minnie Highbaugh, apparently the founding members of the club, had heard Catt speak at the joint meeting in Indianapolis. WFL member Harriet Johnson and Alma Sickler, manager of the WFL lobbying office at the statehouse, attended one of the group's first meetings. The new organization met regularly over the summer and held a tea in October to which men were also invited. The club remained intensely interested in the differences between the WFL and the CU throughout the fall. Sickler wrote a letter to explain the WFL to the editor of the *Indianapolis Recorder* and focused on the group's emphasis on securing both state and federal laws, as opposed to the CU's focus on a federal amendment. She also stressed the WFL's refusal to side with one specific political party. Without any evidence to the contrary, it seems the club worked with the WFL.[7]

By the end of the summer, the 1916 U.S. presidential campaign was well under way. True to their doctrine, the WFL and the ESA did not favor one party over the other, but rather pushed all political parties to come out in favor of suffrage. In spite of that nonpartisan pledge, when Republican presidential candidate Charles Evans Hughes, who had let it be known he favored the Anthony Amendment, came to Indianapolis in September, the combined forces of suffragists in Indianapolis created a large parade. Loud suffragists also filled the balcony, waved their banners and flags, and let their presence be known at the large Republican rally held that evening. Both major Indianapolis newspapers called attention to women "from all walks of life" who marched together in the suffrage demonstration. The CU may have supported Hughes due to their tenant of holding the party in power, in this case the Democrats, responsible for the lack of a federal suffrage amendment. For other Hoosier suffragists at the rally, support for Hughes most likely came from his support for the Anthony Amendment and from their support of and possible friendship with his running mate, former vice president Charles Fairbanks, a well-known supporter of woman suffrage.[8]

By October the WFL (no mention if the CU or ESA helped) had sent speakers to forty-five meetings across the state to lecture about suffrage at Chautauqua's, Farmers Institutes, political rallies, and street meetings; had given out 45,500 pieces of suffrage literature at the Indiana State Fair; and garnered endorsements for suffrage from thirty men's and women's groups across the state. A WFL-coordinated suffrage automobile tour covered all parts of the state from August 15 to September 1. Indiana was choosing a governor in 1916 and the nation a president, so women constantly worked to be sure someone with suffrage sympathies would find his way to both the statehouse and the White House. That November the country reelected Wilson (Democrat) and Indiana selected James P. Goodrich (Republican) as governor. Goodrich assured Indiana's suffragists that he would sign any suffrage bill the legislature enacted. The WFL and the ESA agreed by January to work together

Thousands Roar Approval of Hughes; Greatest Demonstration in City's History

Did Indianapolis Republicans Want to Hear Hughes? View This Portion of the Crowd That Packed Tomlinson Hall.

INDIANAPOLIS STAR/USA TODAY

At the rally for Republican presidential candidate Charles Evans Hughes at Tomlinson Hall in 1916, suffragists took over the balcony and unfurled a banner bearing the wording of the proposed Nineteenth Amendment to the U.S. Constitution.

(but not to a complete "amalgamation" as Catt had hoped), set up a table of suffrage literature (for educational purposes) staffed by suffragists in the hallway of the statehouse, and the 1917 legislative session began.[9]

While the ESA and WFL might have agreed on their plan, the Woman's Legislative Council had other ideas. The WLC, led by clubwoman and WCTU advocate Luella McWhirter, was essentially a powerful lobby that represented women's clubs from throughout the state. It had been formed under the leadership of Grace Julian Clarke (who was also a WFL member) a few years earlier. A vote of the representatives from the member clubs guided the lobbying efforts. When two-thirds of the representatives agreed with a proposed legislative objective, a lobbying committee at the statehouse attempted to guide that legislation through to successful passage. In 1916 the WLC had decided to work toward partial as well as full suffrage, the calling of a constitutional convention, prohibition, and protective labor legislation for women. The WFL and the ESA would have preferred to leave prohibition out of the mix that session. The WLC, however, lobbied for prohibition and for the passage of the other bills from a room in the statehouse—its headquarters for the legislative session granted to them by former governor Samuel Ralston and now continued by Goodrich. The council shared the office with a local newspaper and a reporter from the Associated Press and staffed it with savvy Hoosier women lobbyists who had graduated from Smith, Wellesley, and Vassar.[10]

There were, then, at least four groups pushing for some sort of suffrage for women at the 1917 legislative session—the WLC, the WFL, the ESA, and the CU. They all shared a sincere belief that women should vote. They only disagreed on the quickest path to success and whether to push any temperance legislation at the same time. Not all Indiana women agreed with these powerful women's organizations. A group of antisuffrage women from Indianapolis quickly petitioned the general assembly to stop any woman suffrage bill. They claimed that 90 percent of the women in the state did not want to vote and that a vocal minority of 10 percent pushing suffrage should not be allowed to impose voting on the majority. According to antisuffrage supporters, women performed their "civic duties" using their "tremendous influence through the press, through education, through our schools, through the training of citizens of the future, through the church, through organizations" without the fear of "a new party machine with the woman boss in control." The nineteen antisuffrage women who signed the petition were led by Mary Ella Lyon (Mrs. Lucius B.) Swift and most lived close together in an area just north of downtown Indianapolis. According to the *Indianapolis News*, members of an antisuffrage organization based on the East Coast had recently visited Indianapolis and stirred up support for their cause, leading to the petition. Suffragists quickly responded. In a letter to the *Indianapolis News* longtime suffragist Charity Dye cited a poll taken in Indianapolis's Eighth Ward in 1916 regarding suffrage. Of the 1,044 women polled, "in favor of suffrage, 628; opposed to suffrage 144; neutral, 272." She further noted that the 22,000 women members of the Indiana Federation of Clubs and the thousands of members of the Indiana State Teachers' Association (consisting mostly of women) had also endorsed suffrage and that in her travels for the state centennial (she was the only woman on the eight-member Indiana Historical Commission) "she met strong suffrage sentiment everywhere."[11]

Other women joined Dye in a swift response to the nineteen antisuffrage women. One woman told the *News* that the audacity of the women's claim to speak for 90 percent of Indiana woman had made her "a real dyed-in-the-wool suffragist." A group of nineteen stenographers and librarians sent a prosuffrage letter to the paper complete with their names, addresses, and sometimes their places of business. A group of Vassar College graduates claimed, "the cost of white paper is too high to publish the names of all the Vassar college women who are in favor of suffrage for women" and submitted nineteen names, including Harriet Noble and McWhirter's daughter. The final group of women to respond to the nineteen antisuffragists were nineteen prosuffrage women physicians.[12]

No one knows for sure why the antis rallied against woman suffrage. At the national level, many who worked against woman suffrage were well-to-do women who, in spite of having domestic workers to help them at home, complained about the extra duties women would have to endure if they could vote. Mrs. Arthur M. Dodge led the National Association Opposed to Woman Suffrage. Organizations such as hers received support from the liquor interests, mainly the national brewer's association, who still worried that suffrage would lead to prohibition. Other businesses, specifically manufacturers and railroads, also opposed woman suffrage. In this case, the worry was that women voters would vote in favor of labor legislation that banned child labor and decreased the number of hours that a woman could work in a given day. Antisuffrage groups such as these had led to the defeat of suffrage votes in Michigan in

1912 and in Iowa in late 1916. Would this small but vocal group of women, backed by unknown forces, do the same in Indiana?[13]

The answer was no. The Indiana General Assembly moved rapidly to enact suffrage legislation despite antisuffrage sentiment. Woman suffrage quickly found traction with Joint Resolution Number 2. The resolution, introduced in

CHARACTERS IN SUFFRAGE "MELLOW DRAMA"

INDIANAPOLIS NEWS/USA TODAY

While suffragists awaited the results of court cases that challenged the 1917 laws that gave Hoosier women the vote, Josephine (Mrs. Kin) Hubbard, Mrs. Walter Greenough, Lydia Parry Teasdale, Alma Sickler, and Sara Lauter composed a play about their dilemma. Pictured here are Sara Lauter as Sir Dark Knight and Mary Allerdice as Bill Suffrage.

the House of Representatives on January 26, asked for full woman suffrage. The WFL and the ESA sent a joint letter to every member of the state legislature asking for his vote in favor of this resolution. The letter stated,

> We think this an opportune time to ask for FULL suffrage because it is one of the foremost issues of the day, accepted and endorsed by every political party. In States where women vote it has been recognized as "a reform based upon justice, counseled by wisdom and justified by experience." The women of our state, for three generations have been asking for enfranchisement. Will not Indiana, NOW join in this great worldwide movement for democracy? We are depending upon you.

The WFL quickly followed up this notice to legislators with a letter to suffragists across the state asking them to write to their state representatives and senators to tell them to support the resolution.[14]

The enthusiasm for the resolution changed rather abruptly. Suffrage supporters withdrew it from consideration on February 1, when the legislature enacted a Constitutional Convention bill. A new Indiana Constitution could have full suffrage included in the document and eliminate the need to rely on a state law that could be overturned. The WFL debated whether to now expend its time and energy pushing for a full-suffrage plank in a new constitution and at the same time support the partial-suffrage measure that was winding its way through the legislative process. WLC members in Terre Haute did not hesitate and quickly rose to the occasion to support both the convention bill and the partial-suffrage bill by sending telegrams to the statehouse and by raising money to support lobbying efforts. The Executive Board of the Terre Haute Council of Jewish Women also quickly supported both measures.[15]

Perhaps seeing that their earlier antisuffrage letter had been in vain and their cause was almost lost, the Indianapolis antisuffrage group managed to have a legislative hearing called so that antisuffrage voices could be heard. Swift and one or two other antisuffrage activists spoke, but suffrage supporters from across the state descended on Indianapolis and packed the hearing room. The *News* waxed poetic about the evening and stated, "While Indiana looked on in proud pleasure, last night, woman suffrage staged in a legislative hall the most remarkable demonstration of its kind within the history of the state. Without an effort, Miss and Mrs. Indiana took charge of Mr. Indiana's sacred precincts, filled them with brilliant women and rode down the efforts of the Big Lobby until they shrank into insignificance. A public hearing demanded by the opponents of suffrage for women became, under the skillful guidance of those brilliant women, an unsuppressed riot of arguments for the passage of a part suffrage bill which the committee has under consideration." The *Star* noted that speeches "flashed humor, keen wit and an occasional bit of raillery or pungent sarcasm that brought laughter or stormy cheering."[16]

Suffragists and their supporters showed their strength again on February 16 when, according to the *News*, "suffragists from practically every town in the state came to Indianapolis today and overran the statehouse. Every train and every interurban car came loaded with men and women interested in the suffrage measure." The plan was to not "pester" the legislators, but rather to distribute information and show their support by wearing suffrage pins and yellow, the suffrage color. The paper relayed the rumor that the daughter of state Democratic Party chair Thomas Taggart was among those suffragists hard at work.[17]

Showing even more support for the prosuffrage groups, the *Indianapolis News* ran photos of suffragists who represented the various groups actively lobbying for the bills and stated, "The Woman's Franchise League of Indiana, as an organization, has devoted most of its efforts to the getting of a constitutional convention, although the individual members worked for the part suffrage bill. The Congressional Union worked for suffrage through federal amendment, and the Equal Suffrage Association always worked for suffrage both by state and federal amendment."[18]

Of these attempts at enacting prosuffrage legislation, the partial-suffrage bill that was the topic of the earlier hearing had bipartisan support and was early out of the gate. Marion Maston (Democrat), who had introduced the suffrage bill in 1915, and Arthur McKinley (Republican) introduced the partial-suffrage bill, Senate Bill Number 77, which gave "women the right to vote for presidential electors and certain other officers, and to vote in certain elections." It included an emergency clause so that women could vote in the March primaries. Those opposed to the bill suggested that instead of passing the measure, a special election should be held in September to ask voters if they wanted to enfranchise women, and that idea was rejected. To get the bill through, the committee removed the emergency clause and the bill was finally agreed to by both the House and Senate. The victory of Senate Bill 77 in the House by a vote of 67–24 had been unexpected. The House suspended its rules to take the vote. Many women, who would have enjoyed seeing this vote in person, had no time to get to the House chamber. The reasons representatives later gave for their votes varied widely. Chester Davis of Portland voted aye to stop the rumors he said were promoted by the "women's lobby" that he was antisuffrage. Another stated that he believed 750,000 women in the state did not want the vote, so he voted no. Another voted no because his amendment to give the vote only to white women had been defeated. Representative Alexander M. Scott of Indianapolis proudly voted aye, explaining, "I have been in six sessions of the Indiana Legislature, the first one nearly forty years ago. I well remember hearing Susan B. Anthony, one of the pioneer advocates of woman's rights make a speech here. Woman is God's first and best gift. To vote now to complete her civic power is one of the proudest moments of my life." A reporter for the *Star* praised the WLC for its work on pushing through the bill.[19]

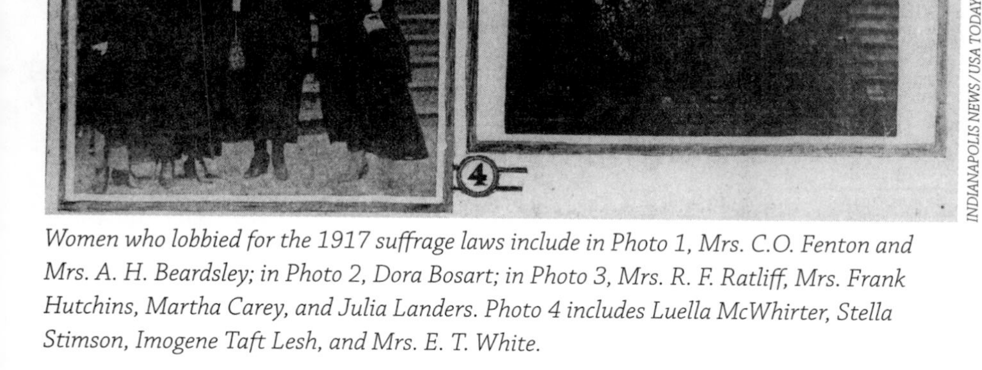

INDIANAPOLIS NEWS/USA TODAY

Women who lobbied for the 1917 suffrage laws include in Photo 1, Mrs. C.O. Fenton and Mrs. A. H. Beardsley; in Photo 2, Dora Bosart; in Photo 3, Mrs. R. F. Ratliff, Mrs. Frank Hutchins, Martha Carey, and Julia Landers. Photo 4 includes Luella McWhirter, Stella Stimson, Imogene Taft Lesh, and Mrs. E. T. White.

Suffragists celebrated with a banquet at the Claypool Hotel on February 27. Cora Goodrich, the governor's wife, presided over the meeting and offered remarks, as did the wife of the lieutenant governor. Goodrich reminded them, "we have been given the sacred power to help make a new constitution. We are not trained servants and it is most important that we study the need of the present constitution and that we make no mistake as to the attitude of the delegates toward prohibition and suffrage." The bill's sponsors, Maston and McKinley, gave a few brief remarks. On the council's behalf, McWhirter said, "Anything can be accomplished I believe by good women who seek it intelligently, if they have the press on their side and if the young women will lend their help." Culla Vayhinger of the Woman's Christian Temperance Union thanked the press for its reporting about the issue. The next morning Cora entered her husband's office and the governor signed the bill on February 28 with his wife as the only witness. The *Indianapolis News* covered his actions on

LEADERS IN THE SUCCESSFUL FIGHT FOR
PART WOMAN SUFFRAGE IN STATE OF INDIANA

MRS FELIX T. MCWHIRTER

MISS DORA BOSART
PHOTO BY BRETZMAN

MISS BLANCHE FOSTER
PHOTO BY BRETZMAN

MRS S.C. STIMSON

MISS VIDA NEWSOM

MRS CULLA J. VAYHINGER

MRS EDWARD FRANKLIN WHITE

endous advantage to the women to have
Room 75 on the assembly floor. The of-
ce is in charge of three young college
women, Miss Dora Bosart, a Smith grad-
ate; Miss Ethel Hutchinson, a Wellesley
ollege woman, and Miss La Steil Beck,
graduate of Vassar.
The idea of financing such a gigantic
work was an appalling one, and one
hat the women faced in trepidation.
Many a story of how a woman made a
acrifice to give to this fund has been
old, but with Mrs. Sara Messing Stern,
f Terre Haute, as chairman of the
inance committee, the necessary funds
ave been supplied. She asked the mem-
ership for 10 cents per capita. There
re no paid officers, the women giving
heir time without remuneration.

Work Divided.

The work was divided systematically.
Mrs. McWhirter perfected a plan for
uick action in case of emergency, and
or getting the members on short notice.
There never was a time when the women
f the bigger towns could not be notified
s quickly as telephone service would
ermit. The women at home did quite as
fficient work as those "at the front."
ine thousand letters were sent out and
any hundreds of telegrams and phone

INDIANAPOLIS NEWS/USA TODAY

The Indianapolis News *continued its publicity of suffragists from around the state following the 1917 legislative victories.*

the front page and implied that the governor wanted to avoid the very public ceremony planned by local suffrage groups. Regardless, the Woman's Suffrage Act of 1917, as it came to be known, meant that women who were twenty-one years old and older and a citizen (in Indiana men who were not citizens, but working toward citizenship could vote, but women in the same situation could not under this bill) could vote in Indiana as of June 1, 1917. They could vote for a myriad of local and state offices, including "attorney general, state geologist, reporter of the supreme court, judges of the various courts, members of the county council; county assessor; township trustee; for all elective officers of cities and towns; for all school officers in Indianapolis and Terre Haute and for all other elective offices not provided for in the constitution," for presidential electors, and perhaps, most importantly, for the delegates to a state constitutional convention, as well as for the new constitution that would come out of that convention. Oddly enough, women still would not be able to vote for higher state officers, such as governor or any federal representative or senator, and would have to use separate ballot boxes. Still, it was a significant victory.[20]

The other suffrage bill that passed the 1917 legislature was the Beardsley Full Suffrage Amendment. This bill amended the current state constitution to allow women to vote in all cases. A woman had to be twenty-one, a resident of the state for one year, and she had to have lived in her township for sixty days and in her precinct for thirty days and must be registered to vote. Because it amended the state constitution, the Beardsley Amendment had to pass the state legislature again in 1919 to become law. This must have reminded suffragists of the debacle of 1881/1883 when the 1881 woman-suffrage amendment was defeated in 1883 after intense work by the Democrats and those who feared that woman suffrage would equal prohibition. Still, it was worth it to try again. To round out the victories, a constitutional convention bill also passed.[21]

The other bill that the legislative enacted in this very busy and very short session was a prohibition bill. While suffragists struggled to work together toward the same goals, "all temperance organizations in the state except the Anti-Saloon league joined in the formation of the Indiana Dry Federation" in December 1916 to push for a prohibition law. (McWhirter was both a member of the Dry Federation and the president of the WLC.) The temperance forces were up against the "Big Lobby," which included liquor lobbyists and various other groups who opposed virtually everything suffragists and temperance advocates wanted to see enacted in 1917. It seems though that the Big Lobby had no chance to defeat a prohibition bill. Prohibition lobbyists and members of the Dry Federation overran the statehouse. They arrived in decorated automobiles, brought along bands, posed for photos on the statehouse lawn, paraded inside the building with banners, sang songs, and even got an assist from former presidential candidate William Jennings Bryan, who was that unique blend of a "dry" and a Democrat. The bill was approved in February 1917. The bill prohibited the sale, trade, making, or keeping of alcohol and banned liquids, malts, or wine containing more than one half of 1 percent of alcohol. Medical, scientific, and religious uses were exempt. It would go into effect in April 1918.[22]

At the end of the surprisingly productive legislative session, the WFL met to clearly delineate goals for the coming year. The group decided to focus on "electing the proper candidates to the Constitutional Convention, the nominating of friendly candidates for the 1919 Legislature," and "getting out the referendum vote on the Constitution." In other words, this was no time to rest, there was more work to be done. The ESA also stepped up its efforts. Plans formulated at its Fifth District meeting in Greencastle included the creation of civics courses with arrangements to be made so that women who worked outside the home could attend. In a rousing speech to the convention, suffragist, club member, and good friend to Eugene and Kate Debs, Mabel Curry of Terre Haute, spurred on the crowd with a call for unity: "It will take the pooled efforts of all the women to enlighten and crystalize the suffrage sentiment in the state. We must consider it in the light of a prolonged Lenten period in which we give up our personal convenience and interests for the common good. We must be fearless."[23]

The WFL also made one last attempt to merge with the ESA. Mary Garret Hay, now of New York but a native Hoosier and a well-known suffrage leader at the national level, returned for the April WFL state meeting to negotiate the merger after receiving assurances from Anna Noland, state ESA president, that she would attend to consider the plan. In a speech that was meant to arouse their fervor but also sounded exasperated, Hay tried to rally WFL members: "You must get together on a big, strong ground in the fall. Forget personalities and individuals. Elect as your leaders those best qualified to lead you, irrespective of your friends or your foes. Unite—and unite for harmony and success in Indiana." The merger never came. The WFL did gain a new president that year, Marie Edwards of Peru. As newspapers noted, she was "one of the younger suffrage leaders of the state," but also "untiring" and "enthusiastic."[24]

The final major suffrage group in the state, the CU, changed its name to the Woman's Party at the end of March 1918 at the direction of the CU/Woman's Party national officers. Barker still led the Indiana organization and declared that all three groups must work together and emphasized what still needed to be done to secure a new state constitution. By this time, the WP had begun picketing the White House to draw attention to woman suffrage. The WP had branch leagues in cities throughout Indiana and in Indianapolis. Barker stayed with the group only until August, when she abruptly resigned. Without directly mentioning picketing, which had become very controversial once the United States had entered World War I in April 1917, Barker told the *News*, "I am no longer connected with the Woman's Party because I am no longer in sympathy with its policy. . . . I followed the Woman's Party as long as I could, but I can stand by it no longer." She became the chair of the women's division of the Indiana Republican Party. Perhaps her beliefs about securing the vote had become more in line with those of Clarke of the WFL. Clarke had visited the WP's headquarters in Washington, DC, in July. She spoke with a member, Florence Bayard Hilles, who, like Clarke, had a father who had served in Congress. While she and Clarke disagreed about picketing the White House, Clarke thought Hilles "a type that exists in connection with every reform. They are the extremists . . . William Lloyd Garrison and his nonvoting anti-slavery apostles were of

FIRST WOMEN to REGISTER

MRS. MINDWELL C. WILSON
MISS LORETTA BERNSTEIN, GARY
MISS BEATRICE CROW
MISS MARIE BARNETT
MISS MARY RINGWALT
MISS SYLVIA LOWREY, WINAMAC
MRS. GEORGIA BERRY CONLEY, GOSHEN
MISS FLOY ETTER
MISS SADIE A. McGROARTY
MRS. JOSIE ESTHER RINKER
MRS. HARRIET WILMA WALKER, LEBANON
MISS ETHA MASSENA, LOGANSPORT
MRS. HARRY W. MOORE, GREENCASTLE
MRS. MARGARET REICHART, NEW CASTLE
MRS. RALPH S. TODD
MRS. CASPER BUTLER, KOKOMO
MRS. LULA C. CURRY, MARION
MRS. NANCY MULVIHILL, GREENFIELD
MRS. MARY C. KENNEDY, LAFAYETTE
MISS LORNA DRESSER, PERU
MISS MARGARET IRVIN, CANNELTON
MRS. JULIA P. PERDUE, TERRE HAUTE
MISS ANNA FAGEL, SHELBYVILLE
MRS. MARY E. SMELSER, WAYNE COUNTY
MISS ANNA TOOKER, WINCHESTER
MRS. ERMA GALUSHA LEMON, MADISON
MRS. DAVE GILES, SULLIVAN
MRS. OMAR I. DEMAREE, FRANKLIN
MISS ROSAMOND AGNIEL, PRINCETON
MRS. JACOB F. DAVIS, HUNTINGTON

name," she said. "Is there any way it can be arranged so I can vote, even if I can't read or write?"
"Surely," said Mrs. Reed, who then filled out the registration blank for the woman, held her shaking hand while she made the cross in place of her name, and then administered the oath to her. That done, the woman walked slowly away, without saying another word. It was learned later that the woman's husband had died of intemperance and that she wished to save her son from the same fate by having prohibition written into the Constitution.
"Most of the women of forty-five or

county clerk, went the honor of being the first woman to register in Putnam county. She is an ardent suffragist. The Putnam County Woman's Franchise League was active in getting out the registration of all women and Mrs. N. C. O'Hair, county chairman of the league, pushed the organization of branches. Many townships now have leagues, and they are discussing constitution making and other questions vital to the new women voters.
Elkhart county women took a keen interest in qualifying to vote, especially in Goshen and Elkhart city. In one

est woman to register was Mrs. Nancy Riggle, age eighty-six, who lives near Sullivan. Mrs. Dave Giles, wife of the county clerk, was the first woman to qualify.
The first person to register in Dearborn county was Mrs. Tillie C. Cole, age twenty-six, wife of George C. Cole, county superintendent of public schools. Following her were Miss Lessie Stauss, Miss Emily J. Sauers, Miss Margaret E. Ritzman, Miss Elizabeth M. Stark and Mrs. Margaret E. Collier.
Mrs. Josie Esther Rinker, wife of Lewis D. Rinker, living at Brooklyn, was the first woman to register in Mor-

the clerk's office she made arrangements with the registration board to distribute blanks among the young women that they might fill them out at home and later file them with the county clerk. In this way many women were registered. She also took advantage of a party held in the afternoon to present each woman with a registration blank and explained to them the simplicity of the action. It was proposed to make an auto tour of the farming communities, each party being accompanied by a notary public, and save the women the trouble of a trip to the city.
The women of Boone county have kept

INDIANAPOLIS NEWS/USA TODAY

The Indianapolis News *gave extensive coverage to the first women to register in June 1917 and in some cases included their photos in the report.*

this type. So were the British militants [likely referring to suffragettes in England]. Their ways are not our ways. They embarrass the great mass of orderly, respectable, law-abiding, sometimes impatient, but on the whole long-suffering suffragists. But . . . their place will be among the real helpers. . . . It will be said that it was well they did thus, but also that it was fortunate that they were a small minority. For in the long run it is the slow-moving, law-abiding, patient forces that keep the world in order and propel it onward."[25]

Amid Hoosier suffragists celebrating their great victories and planning their strategy to be sure that women registered to vote, the United States entered the war raging in Europe, which had begun in 1914 and had been a constant shadow hovering over the suffrage movement. While suffragists deplored the war and many suffragists strongly advocated for peace, they also hoped that their participation in the war effort—conserving food, working in factories, nursing, Red Cross work, and knitting socks and sweaters for soldiers—would demonstrate to everyone women's dedication to the country and their strong belief in civic duty. War work just might lead to the passage of a federal suffrage amendment. True, this line of reasoning had proven false after the Civil War, but this was a different time and women's war work was more easily seen and reported in the press. President Wilson had named one of the most popular suffragists in the nation, Doctor Anna Howard Shaw, to chair the Women's Division of the National Council of Defense, the government agency that coordinated women's war work across the nation. The NAWSA pledged that its members would throw themselves into war work and they did. The overwhelming publicity about women's work and the federal government's sanction of a specific branch of the defense council dedicated to their assistance might motivate the remaining antisuffrage holdouts to recognize women's right to the ballot. This must have been a heady time for Hoosier suffragists, with three laws enacted that would surely lead to the vote. For some members, the passage of the prohibition law was another success. And, by throwing themselves into war work, women's value as citizens would surely no longer be questioned by anyone.[26]

Lurking in the background for many suffragists, however, was the knowledge that an argument had been made for the envisioned new Indiana Constitution to not include woman suffrage in the main body of the new document, but rather to make it an amendment. There was also the sure belief that both suffrage laws would be tested in the courts. As to the first matter, Clarke neatly summed up the arguments for and against including woman suffrage in the new constitution or adding it as an amendment in an article written for the *Indiana Forum*. The idea, according to some, was that a new constitution would go down to defeat if woman suffrage was included in the main body of the document. Women, therefore, should trust that a future amendment would give women full suffrage. Clarke had none of that argument. She reminded her readers that at the passage of the Fourteenth and Fifteenth Amendments, "women were told that if they would just withdraw their opposition to that enactment their turn would come next. They need only wait a little longer, and then their wants would be attended to. They have waited more than forty-seven years for that federal amendment, and it is still in the indefinite future." She also argued that many Hoosiers would not want to amend a "new" constitution right away; that they would want to test it out first, leading to another indefinite wait for woman suffrage. The answer was, she thought, fully obvious that woman suffrage should be a part of the body of the constitution, not as an amendment. The other concern for suffragists that spring, the threat of lawsuits, followed by actual lawsuits, led to an intense correspondence between new WFL president, Marie Edwards, of Peru, and her brother, Lafayette attorney Allison Stuart, who was unsure as to the constitutionality of the partial-suffrage bill and told his sister the same. He declared himself willing to work with her on any case that might challenge partial suffrage and recommended other attorneys to represent the suffragists.[27]

The first legal challenge to suffrage arrived in May 1917 and took on both concerns—the constitution and the partial-suffrage law. The plaintiff, Henry W. Bennett, "president of the State Life Insurance Company" and "an active member of the Republican party," challenged the constitutionality of the Constitutional Convention law and of partial suffrage for women. Bennett apparently filed the suit because, in part, he thought a constitutional convention was an unnecessary government expense. Bennett estimated that the convention would cost $500,000 and that since voters (all male of course) in 1914 had voted down the call for such a convention (for the proposed Marshall constitution that included the word "male" under voter qualifications), there was no reason to believe that a mere three years later public sentiment had changed. His suit went to the Marion County Superior Court. Judge William Thornton ruled the constitutional convention law valid, but said that partial suffrage violated Article II, Section Two, of the current state constitution which defined voters as male. Still, Thornton knew that if women could not register to vote while the WFL appealed the case, they might not be able to participate in the upcoming constitutional convention vote should a higher court overturn his ruling, so he allowed women to register to vote for the election of constitutional convention delegates. As Thornton later explained to Marie Edwards, he supported woman suffrage. His wife worked for the suffrage cause. He believed, however, that he had to rule on the merits of the case. Edwards, who had sat in the courtroom during the arguments, empathized with Thornton and thanked him for his work.[28]

Hoosier women who kept up with national news would not have been surprised by this turn of events. As Ida Husted Harper pointed out in late June, partial suffrage had been granted to women in North Dakota, Nebraska, Arkansas, Michigan, Indiana, Ohio, Rhode Island, and Vermont in 1917 and in each case, except Rhode Island, antisuffragists had sued to have the law declared unconstitutional. Harper claimed that in many states "ballot boxes have been stuffed against them and voters have been intimidated" into repealing the laws. Her answer was a federal amendment. Certainly, Harper's evidence of the futility of partial suffrage did not give Hoosier women much hope.[29]

While waiting for the courts to process the suffragists' appeal in the Bennett case, women in Indiana, hopeful for a positive outcome, began civics lessons. A column on government and citizenship titled "The Star's Home Study Class for Women Voters" ran every Tuesday, Thursday, Saturday, and Sunday in the *Star*. Suffrage organizations ran similar civics classes in many places across the state. Keller and Cora Goodrich spoke at a meeting for African American women at the Second Christian Church in Indianapolis on women and citizenship at the invitation of Mrs. Nellie Gilliam who supervised the domestic science classes at a local school. Other women created several more clubs "to make a study of the duties of citizenship" in addition to or possibly to replace the First Colored Suffrage Club, which seems to have disappeared. A well-known teacher in local African American public elementary schools and later a literary and book review columnist for the *News*, Frances Berry Coston noted that the war with its consequent increased presence of women in the workplace and other civic affairs meant that all women should confront their new-found suffrage from a solid base of knowledge. Coston listed current suffrage organizations, including "the Fourth Ward League of North Indianapolis, the Women's Advance Franchise League, the Colored Women's Republican Club, the Women's Suffrage League of the Second Baptist Church, and the Women's Suffrage Club of Irvington." Some organizations evidently let men join their groups and others did not. Coston urged club members to study the issues and opt for the best course for their group. She noted that "with the nation at war, with a new state Constitution almost in the making, with thousands of women soon to cast their first ballot, with the cost of living steadily increasing, thus forcing greater numbers of mothers into the wage earning channel, it is only soberness and common sense to place good municipal government among the most vital issues" and women should study those issues. They especially needed to reach out to those who were so busy with their daily lives that they did not even realize they could vote. She disagreed with some white suffragists, however, on the role of political parties. While some suffrage groups warned women away from partisanship, Coston implied that women needed political parties because "whatever hardships the people of this city are going to be called on to suffer, because of the unequal advantages in industrial opportunities and economic status, the negro is going to suffer most" and thought that they needed affiliation. She expressed concern about an influx of African Americans from the South flooding the northern labor market and that party politics might control employment options during the war. Coston's article emphasized that women in African American suffrage clubs needed to do more than meet and discuss, they needed to quickly reach out to the community and discuss pressing issues with the new voters.[30]

In addition to civics lessons and closely monitoring the progress of the Bennett suit, suffrage groups and the press focused on voter registration of women for the election for delegates to the constitutional convention. A group consisting of the state attorney general and two other men approved by Goodrich and the state Republican and Democratic chairmen, designated June 22 through August 20 as the time for both men and women to register for that election. (Registration for other elections in various towns had begun in May.) The WFL mobilized quickly as women's participation in this special election could secure the inclusion of woman suffrage in the constitution. The group's registration drive almost had been dealt a death blow when Thornton ruled against woman suffrage in the Bennett case. Before Thornton decided to allow registration to continue, women had flooded registration sites in case they could not register later. Local officials had difficulty processing so many forms. The *News* ran a special report on the women's registration drive. It stated that women in rural areas were more "apathetic" to voting than women in cities, but that suffragists conducted a "house-to-house canvass" to spur interest, even taking notaries with them, or becoming certified notaries themselves, to certify the registrations. Supposedly more women than men registered for this special constitutional convention delegates election.[31]

The *News* sent its reporters throughout the state to witness eager and excited women registering to vote at local clerk's offices. The paper printed women's names, the names of their towns, and in many cases even the photos of the first woman to register. The personal stories they found varied as much as the women themselves. One woman in Muncie could not read or write so the clerk helped her make an X by her name on the registration form. Some women in Anderson did not want to state, "their husbands full name and nativity, since men are not asked whether they are married." Women in several counties arrived before registration headquarters opened so they could be the first in line to register. In Tippecanoe County, women comprised 75 percent of the registrations that first day. More women than men registered the first day in other places as well and the *News* thought that perhaps men had purposely delayed their registrations in a show of chivalry to allow the excited women to go first.[32]

In Bartholomew County, Fanny Davis and Elizabeth Hubbard, both African Americans the newspaper noted, registered first. Octogenarians registered first in several counties as did many professional women, wives of professional men, and members of the WFL and/or the WLC. The first woman to register in Parke County "had been a consistent opponent of woman suffrage." The second was reportedly an ardent suffragist. In Clinton County Addie Cohee, aged ninety-two, filled out her own registration form and stated, "I can't see why some women are so foolish that they don't want to vote." For some reason, the *News* repeatedly reported that only a few women scattered here and there throughout the state were reluctant to give their ages to complete the registration form. Perhaps this had been a concern on the part of some women prior to the registration drive, but no mention of it can be found in any suffrage group's papers.[33]

Early in June, suffragist Mabel Curry traveled throughout Marshall County and other northern counties to campaign for suffrage. She started in Plymouth with a cadre of "twenty-five automobiles filled with enthusiasts." Over the course of the next week she spoke at Culver, Argos, Tippecanoe, Bourbon, Bremen, Millersburg, Goshen, Mishawaka, and Nappanee. At Tippecanoe she stood on a chair in a drizzle to speak to a crowd of two hundred. Curry rallied the women in attendance by reminding them that, "The ills of democracy may be many but the only cure for them is more democracy." Miami County suffragists, led by Marie Edwards, sent a "Flying Squadron," otherwise known as an auto tour, throughout Miami County for a two-day registration drive during what the government had termed "patriotic week" as part of the effort to encourage men and women to engage in war work. Auto tours like the Miami County tour took place in other parts of the state as well. Patriotic week had begun with a Woman's Citizen Day on Sunday and the WFL asked members to speak with local clergy in hopes that they would support woman suffrage from the pulpit. Lafayette organized a community religious service for the event as did other towns in the state.[34]

The Indiana Supreme Court finally ruled on an unlucky Friday, July 13, in the Bennett case. The outcome surprised everyone. Unlike the lower court, the Supreme Court ruled that the constitutional convention bill was unconstitutional and did not rule on the partial-suffrage bill. This left suffragists with the Beardsley full-suffrage amendment in place (but uncertain that it would help since it might not pass out of the 1919 legislative session), the partial-suffrage bill in limbo, and no chance to participate in electing men to participate in or serving as delegates themselves to a constitutional convention. Catt returned to Indianapolis the following month to plot the suffragists next move. As might be expected, different suffrage groups wanted to respond in different ways. Following Catt's lead, the WFL decided to focus its efforts on getting the 1919 legislators to enact both the Beardsley Amendment and the federal Susan B. Anthony Amendment. The WLC urged Goodrich to quickly call for "a special election" so that voters could decide whether to have a constitutional convention. The governor refused and the WFL concurred. WFL leaders feared that the cost of a special election would appear frivolous in wartime and still held onto the belief that women's war work would convince everyone who doubted that women should vote.[35]

With the question of partial suffrage still on the table after the court's odd ruling, it came as no surprise that another legal challenge to the partial-suffrage law quickly followed. On August 9, 1917, William W. Knight sued to have the measure declared invalid. Bennett's arguments against the constitutional convention resurfaced in Knight's suit—woman suffrage added costs and it violated Article II Section 2 of the state constitution. Unlike the well-known and influential Bennett, Knight was a relatively unknown and probably not wealthy man from Indianapolis. Suffragists could not fathom why he brought the suit or how he could pay the costs of pursuing it. They suspected he was a front for someone else. A Republican, he hired a Democrat as one of his lawyers. The rumor spread that many women had registered as socialists and that apparently the two major parties (as evidenced by a Republican and Democrat working together) wanted to be sure they could not vote. Hoosier suffragists picked up on something that the chair of the U.S. Food Administration during World War I (and future president) Herbert Hoover had stated to argue their point in favor of the bill. Hoover thought that women would help win the war effort by conserving food and saving money for other war expenditures. The editors of *The Hoosier Suffragist* drew on his remarks and stated, "Mr. Hoover says he expects the women of this country to save enough to pay for the war. Mr. Knight says that ballot boxes and 'fixings' for women to vote will cost at least six thousand dollars. If we pay for the war can't the men scrape up the money for those ballot boxes?"[36]

Edwards and her brother again consulted on the matter and the WFL put together an impressive team of lawyers, including Indiana attorney general Ele Stansbury, Abram Simmons, U. G. Lesh, Emma Eaton White, W. W. Spencer, and Catharine McCulloch, who had helped Illinois women gain partial suffrage in 1913. Catt returned to Indianapolis to offer advice and support. Republican Party state chair Will Hays offered to assist the suffragists, and it appears he suggested another lawyer, William H. Thompson, to help with the case. A petition drive led by women from both the WFL and the local branch of the Woman's Party tried to rally public and legislative support by citing women's war work. "Whereas," they stated, "The women of the United States by their readiness to work and sacrifice, are abundantly demonstrating not only their patriotism but their intelligent grasp of the meaning of the great world crisis; and whereas, it is generally admitted that the successful termination of the present war can only be brought about with the help of women," they deserved the vote. The Marion County Superior Court heard the case. Part of the argument revolved around Helen Gougar's failed attempt to vote in 1894. The state had ruled against her then, and it seemed that there was no reason, according to Knight's lawyers, to view the partial-suffrage bill as anything different.[37]

Despite an impressive closing argument by Stansbury that reminded the court "this law is a milestone in the history of Indiana and a milestone in the pathway of civilization," on September 17 the court issued a forty-three-page ruling from the majority against the partial-suffrage bill. The suffragists immediately appealed and, as with the Bennett case earlier that summer, the court allowed women to continue to register to vote, this time for the November elections. The ruling had applied only to Marion County so, perhaps, women outside the county could still vote and if the Indiana Supreme Court overturned the ruling, so could women in Marion County.[38]

The court's ruling clearly upset Luella McWhirter, who blamed the "combined forces of the liquor elements and the corporate interests" for the decision. At no other time except during the current war, women, she noted, "have been called upon for service as they are now, and no time when they have given service more willingly." Somewhat amazingly, Marie Edwards called upon one of the political parties to come to the aid of suffragists. "If either party," she stated, "were shrewd enough to come out openly for suffrage, to help financially and to push suffrage as a party measure, it would line up the biggest floating vote the state has ever known, because women are at this time sorting their friends and enemies and keeping a record for future use." After years of nonpartisanship, the president of the WFL now declared that whichever party gave women help in achieving suffrage, women would reward them with their votes.[39]

Just as the lower court declared the suffrage law invalid and the WFL appealed to the higher court, "suffrage season" opened in Indianapolis. Every year local suffrage groups held a tea to kick off fall and winter events. In 1917 a group of suffragists presented a unique play, which they termed a "mellow drama." In the play November 6 (election day) is the day that Lindy Anna (a clever nod to Indiana) and Bill Suffrage are to marry. Lindy's aunt, Anti Suff, tells Lindy that Cally Fornia (California), Carrie Zona (Arizona), and other girls who have married into the Suffrage family regret their marriages and fears that Lindy will as well. At Anti Suff's insistence Lindy's father, P. Pull, forbids the nuptials. The villain in the play, Sir Dark (who happens to be a knight), has strong feelings against the marriage although he never really states the reasons for them. He dresses as a clergy man and just happens to run into Bill Suffrage who is looking for someone to quickly marry he and Lindy. Sir Dark, still dressed as a minister, persuades physicians to test Bill's "constitution." Bill endures a physical exam that includes "pounding him and reciting passages from the state constitution." Poor Bill yells that "Milly Noise (Illinois) did it; why not Lindy Anna?" During this turmoil, P. Pull, who has had a change of heart, enters with a real pastor and exposes Sir Dark as a fraud. Lindy Anna and Bill Suffrage wed and Sir Dark admits that all along he had only been worried about "the taxes."[40]

With this optimistic view of a successful decision in mind, on October 9 more than fifty women attended the Indiana Supreme Court to hear the arguments for and against Knight. They brought along their knitting, most likely as part of their knitting for soldiers campaign to support the war effort, and sat through four hours of arguments. The Court ruled on October 26, 1917, that the partial-suffrage law was unconstitutional. The *News* ran a front-page banner, "SUPREME COURT HOLDS INDIANA WOMEN CANNOT VOTE." The *Star* immediately reported the decision and the WFL's official response, "The decision was not unlooked for, although this organization has hoped for a favorable return from the Supreme Court. We feel that the women of Indiana are being very unjustly treated at the hands of the men voters. The women of this state are being called on for all kinds of war service and we are giving up every other interest in order to answer to the calls. Our men are so short-sighted and so lacking in patriotism that they are still willing to see us work under this growing disadvantage. This we resent." The reporter also interviewed suffragists and antisuffragists from around the state for their reactions. While some suffragists expressed dismay and surprise at the negative decision, most had expected the outcome and readily admitted that a federal amendment was their only chance to receive the vote. Clarke, for example, deemed the federal amendment "a safe and sane enterprise with all things in its favor." Eldena Lauter, who with her sister had long participated in the suffrage movement, tied suffrage to war work, "The country is asking us to devote our energies to war work and we are doing everything we can for the safety of the nation. Now we are denied the right of suffrage. The decision means women will have more work to do. We must and we will do the war work, but we will have to work harder now because we will work for suffrage, too." Swift, one of the now infamous nineteen women who stated that women did not want suffrage, declared, "I believe the decision removes an element of danger to the state, and that it is for the benefit of a very large majority of the women of the state. The leaders of suffrage are a menace to good government so long as they continue their present policy of blacklisting every public man who can not subscribe to suffrage." Another antisuffrage sentiment focused on the war. Mrs. E. C. Atkins noted that, "I believe the members of the Supreme Court have a collection of very sensible wives. . . . it is a very good thing just now that the suffrage question should be squelched. The war, the work we have to do, and the state of the nation are such that we should put forth our very best efforts and I do not believe we should settle this question now." The former leader of the Indiana Woman's Party and now a Republican, Eleanor Barker, stated that it was what she expected since she thought that partial suffrage was unconstitutional. She explained, "I have never been opposed to it, but I have never believed that the Supreme Court would give a favorable decision on it. The women of Indiana, I believe, have learned the value of party affiliation.

We have in the past worked along non-partisan lines and have not accomplished a great deal. I believe that the women's political organizations are here to stay, and we now unquestionably will center our efforts on obtaining the Federal amendment."[41]

The WFL wanted to appeal and when no other lawyer would pursue it, Edward's brother, Stuart, did so as a favor to his sister, but the court denied their petition. In the opinion of WFL attorney Abram Simmons only three avenues remained open for women in Indiana to obtain the vote: amending the federal constitution, amending the state constitution, or through a state constitutional convention that included a provision for woman suffrage. WFL secretary Dora Bosart noted, "the women have refuted the argument that they are indifferent to suffrage and duties of citizenship in this state. They have demonstrated that not only will they vote eagerly when the privilege is extended to them, but also will vote with full understanding and information as to what the state and their immediate communities need. . . . This awakening to civic life has been a large factor in the ready response the women have given to the government's call for war work. Through suffrage they had begun to feel that the Government was as much theirs as the men's, and consequently were learning to take active interest in its welfare."[42]

The Wabash Valley Conference, a regional WFL meeting, gathered in November in Terre Haute four days after what would have been the day for the first votes. The Indianapolis "mellow drama" resurfaced at the meeting, this time, of course, with a tragic ending. In this version, Bill Suffrage's physical exam resulted in his death by poisoning. Sir Dark supplied three of the four attending physicians (representing the Supreme Court justices) with poison—the fourth refused to kill Bill. Bill does not realize he has been poisoned until he is about to marry Lindy at which point he keels over at the point of death. He tells Lindy "that he cannot die, that he will return again, if she will only love him and wait." Sir Dark rewards the suppliers of the poison as the fourth doctor turns away in disgust.[43]

Defeated in Indiana, at least one suffragist, fifty-six-year-old Nellie (Mrs. Charles W.) Barnes, took the fight to Washington, DC. Barnes served on the Woman's Party state board and went to Washington to serve as an Indiana representative on the picket line at the White House under the direction of the Women's Party, as other suffragists had been doing for months. There is a good chance that Barnes heard Margaret Whittemore, one of the early picketers who had been arrested, speak at the Woman's Party meeting in Indianapolis in August. Woman's Party members stood as "silent sentinels" outside the White House, holding banners critical of Wilson and Congress for not enacting the Anthony Amendment. Many had been arrested and sent to the Occoquan federal workhouse, where they were held in terrible conditions and sometimes manacled to the cell bars, beaten, or force fed. The police arrested Barnes along with Doctor Harvey Wiley's wife, Anna, (Wiley was a Hoosier native, former Purdue University chemist, and chief chemist of the U.S. Department of Agriculture who championed the Pure Food and Drug Act) and forty other women. At her court appearance, after "laying aside her knitting," Barnes stated her reason for picketing to the court, "I came to picket for the disfranchised women of Indiana because we were granted political liberty only to have it taken away from us before we could use it." The court sent Barnes to Occoquan. How Barnes later felt about her experience varied according to who interviewed her and where. In an interview in Washington with a reporter from the *Star*, Barnes reported that she had been arrested twice, but would not have picketed for the second time had it not been for the Woman's Party's officers who, Barnes stated "absolutely dominated the rest of us." Barnes said they made her feel like a "slacker" if she chose not to return to the picket line and to jail for the second time. She wanted to return to Indianapolis to let Woman's Party members there know "we simply have been misled by our national leaders." However, in an interview with the *News* at her home in Indianapolis a couple of days later, Barnes, surrounded by a national organizer for the Woman's Party (it is not known who this was, but both Mabel Vernon and Margaret Whittemore of the party had been in town six days prior to the interview) and several Indianapolis members of the group, stated that she learned a lot from her experience, had no intention of leaving the Woman's Party, and favored "picketing the White House with suffrage banners because it makes so much publicity." The *Star* quickly picked up on her change of heart and used it as an example that women's politics would not be "purer" since the reporter felt Barnes had been pressured to recant her previous statement. Both of Barnes's interviews must be carefully considered. One given while she was ill and just after she had been released from jail, and the other given while she was still ill and surrounded by those who wanted her to put a positive spin on the experience. We do not really know how she felt about the experience, but it is apparent she participated to protest the suffrage defeat in the Indiana courts.[44]

WFL president Edwards's next monthly circular to league members began, "Dear Near Voters," but otherwise did not dwell on the suffrage proposals defeat. Instead, the WFL turned its attention to the probable introduction to Congress, in December 1917, of the Susan B. Anthony Amendment to the federal Constitution. Petitions had to be sent to Indiana's Senators and Representatives in Washington, DC, and money raised to fund promotion of the ratification of the amendment once Congress passed it. Edwards reminded members "to emphasize the relations between suffrage and patriotism. Real patriotism demands that we serve the Government no matter how out of patience we get with state authorities. . . . Suffrage is not lost."[45]

Chapter 7

"WORKING TOGETHER . . . THERE IS NOTHING WE CANNOT ACCOMPLISH"

After the defeat of the suffrage bills, new Woman's Legislative Council president Emma White penned a bitter editorial for the *Indianapolis News*. "The state," she explained, "which is giving millions to make the world safe for democracy, should be willing to spend a few hundreds or even thousands to establish democracy within its own borders. . . . There was once a very plausible objection to giving women the vote, because they could not go to war. No one in Indiana dares make that objection now, for women do go to war, do support the war in every way except to carry a gun, and thousands of aliens carry a vote who do not carry a gun, and who can not be drafted in the war because they are not citizens." These two themes, women's war work and an Indiana law that let male immigrants vote after filing "first papers" of their intent to become naturalized citizens, dominated suffragists' arguments after the 1917 defeats in the state courts. They stressed the first argument, but frustration with the naturalization law led to disparaging comments about male immigrant voters. More important, suffragists did not drop their pursuit of the vote to focus on war work as they had during the Civil War. Then, women had dropped suffrage campaigning in exchange for tackling war work and believed, erroneously it turned out, that war work would win them suffrage. That disappointment festered, and this time they did not make the same mistake.[1]

In 1917 women in Indiana had fought for laws that could give them suffrage under the shadow of World War I. After years of isolationism, several events, including the sinking of the RMS *Lusitania*, the Zimmerman telegram, and the overthrow of a fledgling government in Russia led President Woodrow Wilson to declare that the United States must enter the war to make the world "safe for democracy." Since many suffragists had advocated for peace and viewed the war as immoral, there was no guarantee how suffragists across the country, or in Indiana, would react to the president's announcement. In Wisconsin, for example, the statewide suffrage organization split in two as its president and other suffragists advocated that war work proved their deep sense of civic duty and should secure them the vote. Other Wisconsin suffragists believed women could achieve suffrage without betraying their pacifist beliefs. In 1914 in Indiana, the Woman's Franchise League dedicated a meeting to world peace and offered resolutions that included asking women to "begin immediately to shape sentiment in favor of peace and the arbitration of disputes." Grace Julian Clarke spoke about the loss of possible future authors, philosophers, and scientists to the guns of war. Charity Dye more bluntly stated that "war is wrong because the final decision is with might and not necessarily with right, because it breeds hate instead of love, because it destroys the best of young manhood, and because there is a better way to settle disputes."[2]

Like the WFL, the Indiana Federation of Clubs advocated for peace in 1914–15 (many suffragists belonged to both organizations). Eventually, both groups changed their positions and enthusiastically supported women's war work. Most suffragists probably did so from a sense of both patriotism and pragmatism. They hoped that embracing war work proved the depth of their civic duty and finally would lead to a national woman suffrage amendment. Still, it seemed a good idea to rouse Hoosier women to the task at hand. Indianapolis journalist Betty Blythe, who had reported many years earlier on the suffrage automobile campaign to Boone County, alerted Hoosier women that much work needed to be done to win the war. "Business must continue," she declared, "and government contracts must be filled on time and thousands upon thousands of women must take the places of those boys who have marched away." She urged what she called "the great Hoosier army of women" to register for war work with the Indiana State Council of Defense and exclaimed, "THE WAR CANNOT BE WON WITHOUT OUR HELP."[3]

While the war certainly increased the attention paid to women's civic participation, other factors also pushed suffrage legislation over the top in Congress and in Indiana. Woman suffrage had been a topic of national conversation since 1848 and in Indiana women had agitated for the vote almost continuously since 1851. Since the emergence of women's clubs in the 1880s and 1890s, suffragists could be found in literary clubs, social-service clubs, religious-based groups, groups defined by ethnicity, college alumna groups—they were everywhere. During the 1917 voter registration drives, Hoosier suffragists had reached the remotest areas of the state and registered tens of thousands of women to vote. Even before the push to enter war service, politically active women across the state lobbied for the vote. What the war managed to do was to finally focus the energies of all these suffragists and clubwomen, so they acted in concert for one goal—win the war and in the process win suffrage for themselves. Disagreements among suffragists about the means to reach the vote faded away with the path in front of them so clearly defined.

LIBRARY OF CONGRESS

Lawyer Eleanor Barker was the first president of the Congressional Union/Woman's Party in Indiana. Barker later left the Woman's Party to join the Republican Party.

When the war began in Europe, even though the United States had declared its neutrality, the federal government created the Council of National Defense to coordinate any government and civilian activities related to the European war. Despite urgings from the National American Woman Suffrage Association for the government to do so, the government did not create a federal woman's committee as part of the council. Not content to wait on the government to act, women took the matter into their own hands and created the National League for Women's Service to coordinate women's war work. After the United States officially entered the war in April 1917, instead of working with the league and its existing programs, the federal government decided to formally add a woman's committee to the Council of National Defense. Former NAWSA president Doctor Anna Howard Shaw chaired that committee (sometimes referred to as the Woman's Section) and coordinated the mobilization of women across the country. Each state also created a state Council of Defense and following the model of the federal agency, created a state woman's committee. In Indiana, Governor James Goodrich organized the Indiana State Council of Defense in May 1917, which in turn created county councils, each with its own woman's committee. The governor appointed Indiana Republican Party chair Will Hays to lead the effort and Caroline Fairbank, president of the Indiana Federation of Clubs, to chair the Indiana Woman's Committee. Although Fairbank tried to serve, poor health delayed her efforts. Fortunately, Julia E. Landers already had formed the Indiana League for Woman's Service after hearing about the national group at the convention of the Daughters of the American Revolution. Helen Boyd and Marie Edwards, representing the WFL, served on Landers's committee. Reporter Blythe (her real name was Marie Chomel) provided publicity. Until October 1, 1917, the ILWS coordinated its work with the Indiana State Council of Defense, creating the unusual situation of an official state Council of Defense working with an unofficial state women's group. The

ILWS's first task was to help the quartermaster at Jeffersonville find enough women to make two million shirts for the army. They found approximately ten thousand women from southern Indiana who agreed to make shirts in their homes. In response to the federal government's statement that women would be needed to fill men's places in factories, Landers's group also did an early registration of women for war work with fifty thousand registrations submitted. Although that was an impressive number, persuading women to register had not been easy. Landers reported on "the opposition of men, the selfishness and ignorance of women who did not want to help with the war or who feared conscription of women." After Fairbank resigned due to her failing health from the inactive yet official state woman's committee, Hays asked Landers to take her place. Landers refused, since the job required her to use her own money to travel to Washington for periodic meetings. She agreed, however, to continue the registration of women for war work.[4]

Anne Studebaker Carlisle of South Bend took over for Fairbank. Therefore, the Woman's Committee of the Indiana State Council of Defense did not really commence work until November 1917, not long after two of the woman suffrage bills went down to defeat in Indiana's courts. Despite suffragists' profound disappointment at the loss of the suffrage legislation, they enthusiastically took on war work. Suffrage organizations or organizations known to be sympathetic to suffrage—the Collegiate Alumnae Association of Indiana, the Indiana Federation of Clubs, Indiana Equal Suffrage Association, Indiana State Teachers' Association, National Association of Colored Women, State Federation of Colored Women's Clubs, WFL, and the Woman's Press Club—all worked with the state Woman's Committee. The editors of the WFL's small newspaper, *The Hoosier Suffragist*, embraced the work and filled its pages with reports of war work and advertisements for Liberty Loan drives, War Savings Stamps drives, and other items that depicted suffragists enthusiastically tackling war work.[5]

Each county council of defense answered to the state council. These county councils named one woman to its council and her task was to create a county woman's committee. Often using existing women's and suffrage clubs as its base, the county woman's committee then organized women at the township, precinct, and even block level so that, hopefully, it reached every woman in the state and persuaded her to take on some type of work. Doctor Amelia Keller, for years the master organizer of suffrage groups, perfected this organization of state and county committees. Several committees already created by the national women's committee began their work immediately and Indiana added Socks for Soldiers, Fourteen-Minute Women, Americanization, Motor Corps, Entertainment, and Liberty Loan committees with suffragists chairing these state-level groups.[6]

For example, Eleanor Barker, the woman who had organized the state's Congressional Union/Woman's Party (the CU/WP did not promote war work, unlike the NAWSA), toured Indiana and several other states advocating for food conservation for the war effort and then took over the Women in Industry committee in December 1918 after original committee chair, Mabel Many, president of the Garment Workers' Union, stepped down. Suffrage supporter Jennie Ralston, wife of former governor Samuel Ralston (a Democrat), and Cora Goodrich, wife of the current governor (a Republican) and a staunch suffragist, also worked with the women in industry committee. With so many more women working in factories during the war (in 1919 Governor Goodrich estimated 175,000 women workers as compared to 30,000 in 1910 and 70,000 in 1917), the long-standing fight for improved industrial working conditions for women and for children became a war measure. Governor Goodrich stated that "no objection can be offered to the employment of women in industry if such employment is not used as a means to lower wages, if the principle of equal pay for equal services is firmly fixed and such employment is properly safeguarded by laws limiting hours of service and working conditions." The governor appointed a woman to lead the division of Women and Children of the Indiana Industrial Board and named Mrs. Arthur T. Cox as the inspector of women and children's labor. Keller had pushed the governor to use his wartime contingency fund to create Cox's job. The Women in Industry committee's final report optimistically stated that "the value of the work done by this committee lies in the fact that enough interest has been aroused to keep the problems alive in the public mind."[7]

Leading another state committee, Julia Henderson, the WFL's longtime and recently retired secretary, "conceived the idea and began the organization of a group of speakers known as the 'Fourteen-Minute' Women of Indiana" after she accepted the post of deputy food administrator for Marion County. Fourteen Minute Women took a proactive approach to its work. If an organization in her district did not request a speaker, Henderson contacted the group and asked to send a speaker to its next meeting with the result "that in two weeks more than 100 addresses had been made." The Marion County Fourteen Minute Women drew the attention of Carlisle and she asked Henderson to expand her group of speakers, to lead them in a statewide effort, and to expand the content of the speeches to include every aspect of war work. Henderson agreed. Some of the best-known suffragists in the state became Fourteen Minute Women, including Keller, Clarke, Barker, Mary Tarkington Jameson, and Belle O'Hair from Indianapolis and Sara Messing Stern and Helen Benbridge from Terre Haute. By the end of the war, Fourteen Minute Women had given thousands of speeches on every conceivable war-related topic at every conceivable venue. Henderson and her speakers provided the work without charge, a point they emphasized to encourage the scheduling of more speaking engagements. They spoke about whatever the state council wanted to emphasize that week—food, Liberty Loans, child welfare, or any other concern. Henderson's office supplied materials to other women and groups as well for their local work. One woman from a difficult to reach rural area in the southern part of the state traveled by train to get information to carry back to her township. Towns and county councils across the state thanked the Fourteen Minute Women for its work and declared that, in at least one case, the speech helped "in arousing in our county the greatest spirit it has had since the war began." By May 1918 a total of 750 Fourteen Minute Women had traversed the state. Some local groups of speakers had astonishing speaking schedules as seen in Wayne County, where enthusiastic Fourteen Minute Women gave eighty speeches between March 1 and May 14, 1918. That summer, Fourteen Minute Women spoke at various lakeside vacation communities in the northern part of the state and at other scattered vacation spots. The final report showed that Henderson's speakers spoke in seventy-four of Indiana's ninety-two counties and received accolades from the Council of National Defense.[8]

Columbus suffragist and Indiana Federation of Clubs past president Vida Newsom chaired the Committee on Maintenance of Existing Social Service Agencies. Her group worked with county charities, children's guardian homes, and other social-service offices to make sure they were staffed with clerical workers (women had other, higher-paying job options during the war) and had adequate funding to continue offering their crucial community services. If an agency needed workers, Newsom made referrals with the help of war work registration cards so they could hire women from their communities. The committee also worked with the Board of State Charities to maintain staffing and funding at prewar levels.[9]

Somewhat reluctant suffrage supporter Albion Fellows Bacon, known across the state for her work in housing reform and friend to many ardent suffragists, led the Child Welfare Committee. This active woman and her active committee organized the Children's Year with its emphasis on providing free physical examinations for every child in the state and encouraging everyone to register their children—in other words, to secure birth certificates for them. By the end of the war, at least 94,814 children had been examined and from one-third to one-half of those children had been diagnosed with any one of several maladies, including "diseased tonsils, adenoids, undernourishment, bad teeth, circumcision needed, hernia, tuberculosis, defective eyes, heart trouble, defective hearing." The committee provided follow-up operations and other corrective measures. At the end of the war the committee did not disband but planned a legislative agenda that covered a wide range of child-welfare issues.[10]

INDIANAPOLIS NEWS/USA TODAY

Frances Berry Coston taught in the Indianapolis Public Schools, worked for suffrage, and served as a literary critic for the Indianapolis News.

Even when suffragists did not lead a committee, they participated in its activities. Suffragists completed their war work registration cards along with everyone else. Specific reasons given to register included "to give every woman an opportunity to offer to her country such service as she is best fitted to render," "to have in every community lists of women carefully classified who are willing to be called upon for trained or untrained service to the state or nation," "to furnish accurate information to the government of the capacities in which women are now serving, whether in their own homes or in paid pursuits, trades, or professions," to discover which women were available to work outside the home, to find women who wanted to train for war work, to help women find "salaried positions whether in government service or not," to help women find volunteer work, and to have a handy list of women should the need for them arise. As one historian pointed out and suffragists noted, registration served the purpose of raising "the importance of the volunteer worker" and hence the importance of women. Each county maintained the completed cards. A total of 626,292 Hoosier women registered for war work, making Indiana "second only to Michigan in the percentage of women registered." Lake County estimated that it registered the largest number of women at 20,000 to 21,741, with Henry County following at reportedly 7,000 to 10,500. Registration chair Landers emphasized that no woman would be forced to work but deemed women "the moral force of the country, and it is the greatest encouragement to the heads of our government to know that the women are standing back of them." No one asked a woman to work without a wage if she needed the wage. A case in point was the need

The day after Congress approved the Nineteenth Amendment, the Indianapolis News *welcomed women voters on its front page.*

for stenographers. The government, it was reported, was willing to pay "from $100 to $250 more per year for beginners than ever before. . . . Uncle Sam will pay these women well, he needs them."[11]

The woman's committee created an Americanization Committee in May 1918 and named Mrs. Arthur S. Hurrell as the chair. Its purpose was "to unify our nation in language, ideals and allegiance." Hurrell created six units: education, social service, industry, health standards, naturalization, and war information. The education group focused on teaching English around the state and to soldiers, who were not native English speakers, training at Fort Benjamin Harrison. The social-services section attempted to improve neighborhoods with playgrounds and Mother's Clubs. The section also intended to use the state Motor Corps, staffed also by women, to take a "kitchen on wheels" into predominantly immigrant neighborhoods to discuss food conservation and canning methods, as it did elsewhere in the state as part of the federal food conservation project. The industrial section looked at factories to investigate working conditions of immigrant women. The health-standards committee worked with public-health nurses, anti-tuberculosis groups, and the Indiana University child-welfare group. The WFL led the committee's naturalization efforts with a focus on explaining to women why they and their husbands should complete the naturalization process after filing first papers. The war-information group worked in neighborhoods heavily populated by immigrants. Hurrell moved out of the state in August and Mrs. Arthur Charles of Richmond, Indiana, took over her work just before belligerents signed the armistice and "other agencies" (unnamed then and now) took over her work.[12]

In the Woman's Committee official report, only two of Indiana's ninety-two counties reported on their Americanization efforts. In Saint Joseph County, the home of the industrial city of South Bend, most Americanization activities took place at existing community centers and playgrounds. Women focused on teaching English to children and their families and sponsored school activities. They also used July 4 to recognize newly naturalized citizens. The only other county to report activity, Wayne County, the home of Mrs. Charles, reported Americanization work accomplished through "four afternoons a week given to cooking and sewing in the foreign districts." As has been pointed out in a recent work on women and World War I, Americanization was not the same thing as nativism or what others confusingly referred to as "100 percent Americanism." While nativism could degenerate into violence against and hatred of specific groups, Americanization as practiced by the Woman's Committee echoed social-reform work characteristic of the Progressive era that many suffragists and clubwomen had done before the war. Suffragists stressed that immigrants should feel part of the United States and essential to the war effort. While acknowledging that Americanization was "laden with ethnocentrism and condescension," at least one historian suggested, "these women's approaches to Americanization nonetheless suggest that many women reformers who supported the war consciously countered the illiberal nativism of the war era by portraying immigrants in a positive light and did so from a distinctly female point of view."[13]

The spike in nativism across the country contrasted with the overall goal of adapting immigrants to their new communities. Anger toward "hyphenated Americans" led to violence, and sometimes death, across the nation. Suffragists in other states were not immune to this frightening idea. Not surprisingly, they aimed much of the vitriol at German Americans who suffragists, and others, had blamed not just for the war but also for decades of working against suffrage legislation. Brewers of German heritage rightly feared that woman suffrage meant the enactment of prohibition legislation and thus the end of their economic and social ways of life. Recent studies of suffrage in Wisconsin, Minnesota, South Dakota, and Iowa note the connection between defeated suffrage legislation and fear of prohibition, especially in the case of the Great Plains where suffragists wantonly used nativist rhetoric to attempt to gain suffrage. In addition to blocking suffrage legislation, the laws of many states, including Indiana, had in common the infuriating, to most suffragists, law of allowing foreign-born men to vote after filing first papers of their intent to become citizens, while women born in the United States and already citizens had their attempts to gain the vote blocked. While other historians clearly document the anti-immigrant rhetoric used elsewhere in the country, in Indiana, most suffragists moderated any nativist rhetoric, especially in the capital city.[14]

The reason for the modulation most likely lies in the state's history and in the heritage of suffragist leaders. Indiana had strong German communities in Indianapolis, Fort Wayne, Jasper, Evansville, Terre Haute, Hammond, and a few other pockets scattered across the state. One historian called Indiana's German population the "largest and most influential minority racial group" in the state. While Indiana, as a whole, had a foreign-born population of only 159,663 (16.9 percent) in 1910, Germans constituted 62,170 of those. Of the 509,873 Hoosiers who had at least one parent born abroad or were themselves born there, 264,198 listed the German states as the country of origin. While this German population was smaller than found in other states, such as Ohio and Wisconsin, their widespread influence on Indiana's cultural, economic, and government institutions made them a powerful presence.[15]

The Indianapolis German community had always had a strong influence on the city. In 1850 a total of 1,045 people or 12.9 percent of the total Indianapolis population were German. By 1890, depending on who one counts as having German heritage, anywhere from 18 percent to 25 percent of Indianapolis's population claimed German heritage. Over the years, persons of German descent led or owned many Indianapolis cultural institutions—art societies, the press, social, and musical groups—and many large businesses. Among Indianapolis suffragists, women of immigrant parentage held leadership positions. For example, Keller's parents left Baden due to the political unrest

WOMAN, AGE 79, WHO WILL NOT SCRATCH TICKET, LEARNS HOW TO OPERATE VOTING MACHINE

MRS. CATHERINE CURRY PAYNE. MRS. MARGARET CURRY. MISS NELL M. TAYLOR.

INDIANAPOLIS NEWS/USA TODAY

Nell M. Taylor demonstrates a voting machine to new voters Catherine Curry Payne and Margaret Curry.

AN ADDRESS

to the

CONGRESS OF THE UNITED STATES

by

Carrie Chapman Catt

President of the National American Woman Suffrage Association

From The Woman Citizen

National Woman Suffrage Publishing Company, Inc.

171 Madison Avenue New York, N. Y.

Hoosier suffragists supported the government's efforts in World War I. This speech by NAWSA president Carrie Chapman Catt resonated with their dedication to the war effort.

of 1848. Once they reached the United States, her father edited German-language newspapers in Cleveland, Evansville, and Indianapolis including, the *Die Union*, *Frei Presse*, the *Telegraph*, and the *Spottvogel*. Sara and Eldena Lauter's father, the son of a philosophy professor and rabbi from Berlin, came to the United States around the time of the Civil War and sometime later opened a large furniture factory in Indianapolis. He helped develop the manual-training program at Manual High School. When he died in 1907, his biographer noted that "while of foreign birth he was intensely American, a believer in the institutions of his adopted country and admired especially the freedom of worship and of personal action according to the dictates of the individual conscience."[16]

Governor Goodrich did not pursue nativist policies during the war. The Republican Party in Indiana wooed the German American vote in 1916, as did the Democratic Party. Consequently, politicians used little nativist rhetoric and the Republicans did all they could to keep former President Theodore Roosevelt out of the state because of his strong, overt, anti-German feelings. Goodrich later stated that he initially supported Germany in the war, but then decided that entering the conflict against Germany was the right thing to do. As governor, he issued a proclamation that forbade anyone in Indiana from hurting someone because of their ancestry. To drive home his point, Goodrich appointed he and his wife's friend, the father of Indiana's conservation movement and of the state park system, Richard Lieber, as his military secretary at the rank of colonel for the duration of the war. The German-born Lieber had three brothers serving in the German army, but both Goodrich and Hays admired Lieber a great deal and his assignment met with little opposition. Keller, Lieber, and suffragist Lucy Riesenberg's husband, Henry C., all worked with the nationally organized Friends of German Democracy group and held pro-American rallies throughout the state. Riesenberg, born in Prussia, moved to east Texas at the age of twelve, and then moved to Indianapolis as an adult. He gave lectures for the Council of National Defense and the Committee on Public Information (the government's propaganda committee to promote the war) at meetings across the country. So, while Indiana suffragists in some cities echoed nativist rhetoric found in other states, in general their views were less extreme. One historian has stated that "nativism sparked by World War I shattered the tolerance of ethnic diversity in the Midwest," and certainly there were some problems in Indiana. In Indianapolis, Das Deutsche Haus, the home of a theater, gymnastics club, and a biergarten decided to change its name to one less German, Athenaeum. The final German-language newspaper in the city closed its doors as reading anything in German could constitute suspicious activity. German had long been the proud second language of Indianapolis and of Indiana, but the state legislature enacted a law, after the end of the war, that forbid the teaching of German in Indiana's public schools. The bill even had the support of some college professors. German remained off the secondary school curriculum for about ten years before being restored. Still, except for a few local leaders, such as Fort Wayne's Alice Foster McCullough, who blamed the "German element" and the power of local brewers for the loss of a suffrage bill, for the most part, leading Hoosier suffragists, while making disparaging comments about "alien suffrage," did not focus on nativist rhetoric as has been reported for other midwestern areas and was carried out by some NAWSA leaders.[17]

In addition to individual suffragists working with the state Council of Defense, the WFL separately had answered the call to war work in August 1917 while the state Woman's Committee struggled to organize and while the WFL waged its legal battle in the state courts. The group placed "the services of the Woman's Franchise League of Indiana with ten thousand members and a closely-knit state organization . . . at the disposal of state and nation to help make the world safe for democracy. There is no relaxation in suffrage propaganda, which is regarded as an essential plank in a democracy platform; but there are additional problems to be met and additional tasks to be performed." True to its statement, the WFL boldly set out to secure the vote while pursing war work. In December 1917 the WFL urged the Indiana State Council of National Defense to officially support the Susan B. Anthony Amendment, now referred to as the Nineteenth Amendment because of the hopes of its swift passage. The chair of the council's policy committee happened to be former vice president Charles Fairbanks. His committee readily endorsed the amendment "as a matter of sheer right and common justice," according to Hays.[18]

The WFL set up five war committees of its own: agriculture, thrift, Red Cross, war census, and war industrial, and, once the national council began the campaign, Liberty Loan. Of these committees, the Red Cross and the Liberty Loan campaigns filled most of the WFL's time. The Indianapolis branch of the WFL put in a great deal of effort at a Red Cross workroom located in the W. H. Block Department Store. The women from the WFL knitted socks for soldiers alongside members of local churches and charitable organizations. They also used leather from car seats to make hospital slippers for soldiers recuperating from trench foot and made hospital comfort kits. Their work eventually expanded to include clothing for French and Belgian children. On the anniversary of Abraham Lincoln's birthday, author and suffrage supporter Meredith Nicholson visited the workroom and presented a "patriotic program" while the

ARE YOU WITH US?

Are you awake

to the fact that 14,000,000 women throughout the world have been enfranchised in war time?

Are you aware

that the women of nineteen states can vote for the President of the United States?

Are you alive

to the enormous demand of the women of this state who in large numbers are petitioning for the vote?

Are you ready

to fight in this great war for democracy?

SIGN THE PETITION

Support the Federal Suffrage Amendment.

NATIONAL AMERICAN WOMAN SUFFRAGE ASSOCIATION

171 Madison Avenue 154 New York City

Printed July 1918

INDIANA HISTORICAL SOCIETY

Hoosier Ida Husted Harper led the publicity bureau of the NAWSA during the war and kept suffrage and the war effort on everyone's mind.

AS A WAR MEASURE

The Country is Asking of Women Service

AS

FARMERS
MECHANICS
NURSES and DOCTORS
MUNITION WORKERS
MINE WORKERS
YEOMEN
GAS MAKERS
BELL BOYS
MESSENGERS
CONDUCTORS
MOTORMEN
ARMY COOKS
TELEGRAPHERS
AMBULANCE DRIVERS
ADVISORS TO THE
COUNCIL OF
NATIONAL DEFENSE

AND

The Country is Getting It !

Women Are Asking of The Country

ENFRANCHISEMENT

Are the Women Going to Get It?

National Woman Suffrage Publishing Company, Inc.  171 Madison Ave., New York City

Women worked hard to support the war effort and only asked for one thing in return.

women worked. At the Red Cross parade in Indianapolis on May 19, a plethora of suffragists walked with other Red Cross workers.[19]

Mrs. Walter Greenough led the WFL Liberty Loan committee for the state's third Liberty Loan drive. She devised a plan to encourage every WFL member and every WFL branch league to purchase a bond to both support the war effort and to have funds for future suffrage work. She worked closely with the state Council of Defense Liberty Loan chairperson, McCulloch, who also led the Fort Wayne WFL, and they achieved impressive results. By May a total of $1,527,150 in bonds had been sold by branch leagues, with the largest total ($200,000) coming from Terre Haute's joint committee of suffragists and county women's committee members.[20]

Indiana suffragists also enthusiastically worked with NAWSA to create field hospitals in France. These hospitals treated wounded soldiers and one specifically treated soldiers who suffered from the effects of the newest deadly weapon, poisonous gas. NAWSA staffed the hospitals with suffragists from across the country. A hospital cost about $125,000 each year to run and Indiana pledged $2,000 to the cause, $1,000 more than NAWSA requested.[21]

The most concise report of local war work is found in the *Report of the Woman's Section of the Indiana State Council of Defense*. County chairs submitted final reports complete with names of local women who participated in the council, statistics of the work accomplished, and sometimes brief descriptions of the work. Activities across the state varied, in part, due to geography. For example, Brown County's report noted, "We must not fail to take into consideration the fact that Brown County has no railroads, and has many hills, which makes it extremely difficult to go from place to place. To overcome this difficulty Mrs. Shulz organized what she called her 'messengers.' These messengers were girls and boys who rode horseback and who were ready at all times to carry her messages, etc. to the members of her food clubs and other committees. The largest town in this county has less than three hundred inhabitants."[22]

Carroll County adopted twenty-two French orphans. Cass County sent 2,435 books to soldiers and sailors. Fayette County's public-health nurse, Miss Stoops, worked with the Child Welfare Committee to examine, they claimed, all children under age seven and found children who were underweight, supplied eyeglasses, dental work, tonsil and adenoid operations, and help for two children with back problems. Not to be outdone, Lake County claimed to have examined 12,931 babies and waged an extensive campaign to bring in clean milk resulting in a "negligible, almost non-existent" infant death rate in Gary over the usually sickly summer season.[23]

While some African American women's clubs including the Daughters (Household is the official name of the organization) of Ruth (the African American women's auxiliary of the African American men's Odd Fellows), the Colanthe Court of the K. of P. Women (Knights of Pythias African American women's group), the National Association of Colored Women, and the State Federation of Colored Women's Clubs sponsored the state Woman's Committee along with other women's groups, comparatively little is known about African American women's activities as coordinated by the state-level committee. Other states reportedly created "parallel organizations" for African American women except for Illinois, North Carolina, and Massachusetts, which created councils with no barriers between white and African American council members. In Indiana Vanderburgh County reported six hundred gardens and two food clubs organized in Wayne County. Marion County, on the other hand, had an extremely active group of African American women to take on the task. Mrs. William L. Elder of the Marion County Council of Defense Woman's Committee appointed one African American woman volunteer to serve on each of the county's women's committees. The women also met separately as their own African American woman's committee with Emma Duvalle as the chair. The new committee named Mrs. Minnie Whitaker as the Liberty Loan chair; Mrs. Celia Maxey led registration; Mrs. Mary E. Cable and Mrs. Sallie Phillips oversaw food production; Mrs. Rhoda Hanley worked with home economics; Mrs. Duvalle took on child welfare; socialworker for the Woman's Improvement Club, Mrs. Daisy Brabham (her husband, Rev. Brabham, had given a talk supporting woman suffrage at his church), chaired home and foreign relief; Mrs. M. A. Clarke led the effort to work with social agencies; Ella Clay worked with the education committee; Mrs. Daneva W. Donnell coordinated public speaking; Mrs. Mollie Saunders led the women in industry group; and journalist and suffragist Frances Berry Coston directed publicity efforts. They also formed three other committees not found in the larger Marion County Council—Training of Boys led by Mrs. Hattie Porter, Training of Girls under the auspices of Miss Pearl Jones, and a Unit Work committee led by Mrs. Laura Profit.[24]

Mrs. Samuel Perkins ran Marion County's registration for the women's war service drive. She named one vice chair for each township, except for Center Township, which had four. Within Center Township, four African

American women served as vice chairs to register women in Indianapolis's African American neighborhoods. The chair of the Marion County Education Propaganda Committee, Mrs. Angeline Carey, a teacher at Shortridge High

FEDERAL SUFFRAGE AMENDMENT

DO YOU KNOW?

DO YOU KNOW that the women of one-fourth of the States of the Union voted for President in 1916 and that these States are: Illinois, Montana, Wyoming, Kansas, Colorado, Idaho, Utah, Washington, California, Oregon, Nevada and Arizona?

DO YOU KNOW that it is nothing less than a national scandal that the women of the East and South remain unenfranchised while the women of the Equal Suffrage States in the West have the right to vote?

DO YOU KNOW that there are two ways in which women may get the vote? One is by asking consent of all the men of the United States, rich or poor, native born or naturalized, good or bad, intelligent or ignorant; the other is by a Federal Amendment.

DO YOU KNOW that the descendants of early land holders in the thirteen original colonies got their vote by Colonial Constitutions?

DO YOU KNOW that the foundations of Male Suffrage were laid in twenty-four States before the Civil War and in five States since then by **legislatures and constitutional conventions whose constitutions were not submitted to the people's vote?**

DO YOU KNOW that the easy road to self-government which was thus opened to men is in every State but Delaware, now closed to women?

DO YOU KNOW that no disfranchised class of men in the United States has been compelled to appeal to a vast body of voters for their enfranchisement?

DO YOU KNOW that three-fourths of the present voters got their vote through naturalization or the naturalization of their ancestors?

DO YOU KNOW that foreigners who become citizens of the United States are naturalized by the FEDERAL GOVERNMENT? Indians are enfranchised by the FEDERAL GOVERNMENT? Negroes were enfranchised by the FEDERAL GOVERNMENT?

Why should a government which gives the vote to all men deny the easiest process for women to work for theirs?

NATIONAL WOMAN SUFFRAGE PUBLISHING COMPANY, INC.
171 Madison Avenue **New York City**
Printed Feb., 1917

INDIANA HISTORICAL SOCIETY

Suffragists emphasized that a federal amendment was the surest way to secure the vote.

School, worked with Clay to spread war information through Indianapolis, just as the Fourteen Minute Women did in other parts of the state. Under Clay's direction, twelve women delivered talks at neighborhood meetings, club

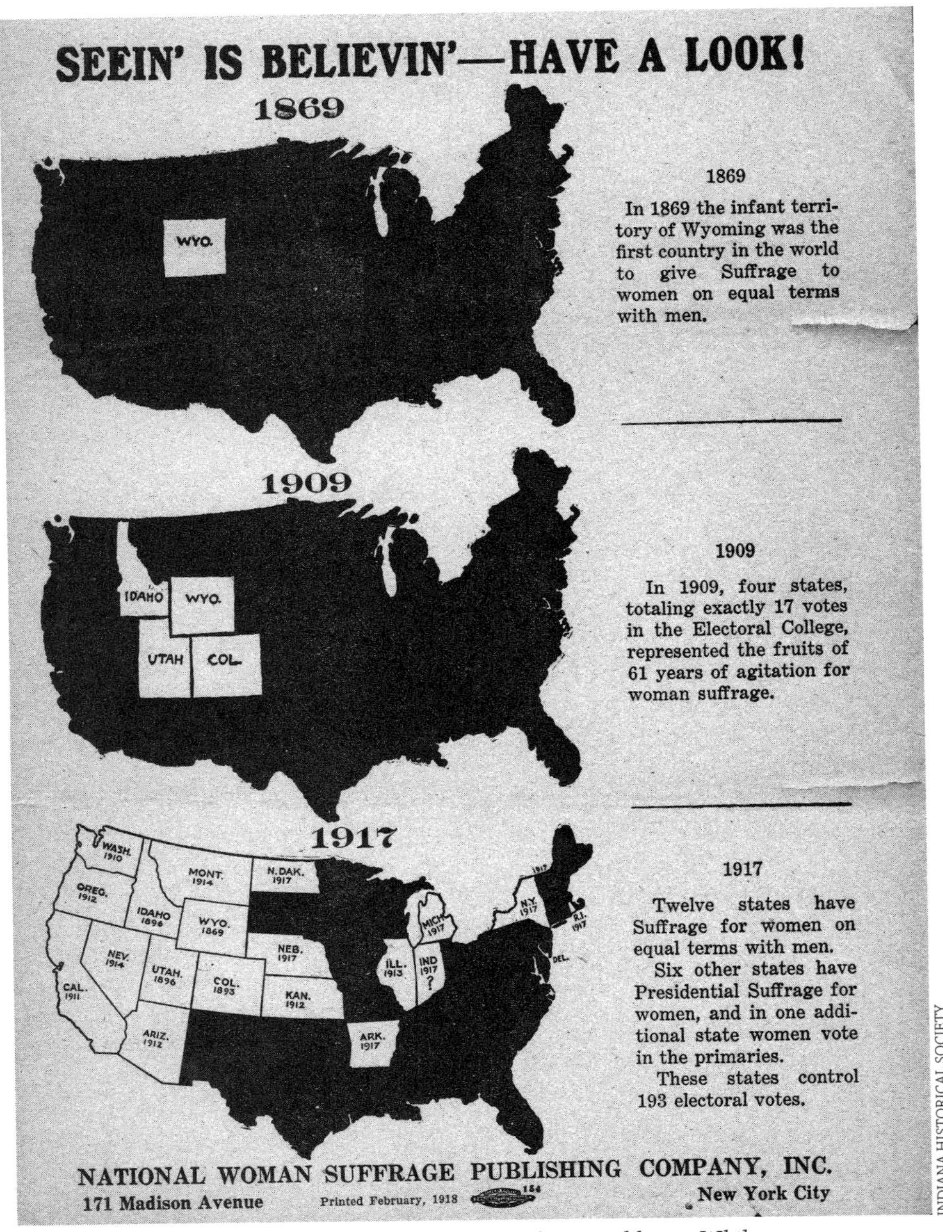

The flyer was premature in stating that women in Indiana could vote. While women won the vote in 1917 in the Hoosier State, the Indiana Supreme Court declared the suffrage laws unconstitutional so women could not vote until the federal amendment was enacted in 1920.

meetings, church meetings, and any other gathering. The women spoke on the same topics as the other Fourteen Minute Women: registration of men for the draft; registration of women for war work; registration of children (birth certificates); public utilities; drives for Liberty Loans and Thrift Stamps; use of substitutes for meat, wheat, and sugar, and coal conservation; prohibition; labor; "the farming army;" and the "duty of reporting disloyal words and acts, and of refraining from idle talk and censure." "Mrs. Charles Baughman, Mrs. W. H. Armstead, Mrs. Thomas Simms, Mrs. Henry Milliken, Mrs. Walter Price, Miss Donnell, Mrs. Alfred DuValle, Frances Berry Coston, Mrs. Weir Stuart, and Mrs. Hummons "all became speakers in the city's African American neighborhoods. Clay encouraged the women to "forget every question of race and racial grievances ... to preach the gospel of unqualified loyalty and do its part for the success of the war measures."[25]

The active role in war work by these committees can be seen through numerous short newspaper items and the *Indiana War Records Colored Section* report. Eighty-six women registered for first-aid training at Flanner House and another 125 women attended nurse-training classes and were called to service during the flu epidemic. Flanner House also had its own Red Cross unit, which made "pajamas, men's white underwear, bath robes, shirts, underskirts, and gowns for children, surgical bags, and house wife kits for soldiers." "White and colored friends" loaned twelve sewing machines for the work. Another unit was formed in Haughville, located just west of downtown Indianapolis. The Household of Ruth focused on relief for African American soldiers. Emma Duvalle worked with F. B. Ransom to form food clubs, which appear to have been organized mostly by churches. In recognition of its contributions to the war effort, a women's division led by Clay marched in the August 20, 1918, parade of African American soldiers through downtown Indianapolis. The 1,258 recently drafted men were on their way to Fort Dodge, Kansas, for training. The women then joined the crowd at Tomlinson Hall to hear speeches from Indianapolis mayor Samuel L. Shank and Governor Goodrich.[26]

There is no question that Hoosier women, both suffragists and nonsuffragists, proudly took on war work. There is also no question that much of the war work was organized and directed by suffragists, who had been mobilizing large numbers of women for years. Their competence was readily recognized and used by the Indiana State Council of Defense just as the Council of National Defense had called on NAWSA presidents Shaw and Carrie Chapman Catt to mobilize the nation's women. These well-organized national and Indiana suffrage groups came together when a special session of NAWSA's executive council met in Indianapolis in April 1918 at the same time as the state WFL convention. The timing was purposeful. The NAWSA's executive council usually met during its annual national convention, but it needed a special session to coordinate the group's war work. Indianapolis seemed the logical place to convene given its central geographic location, but also because the NAWSA thought that Indiana and its surrounding states seemed poised to pass suffrage legislation. NAWSA president Catt spoke at a dinner on April 17 and urged Hoosier women to not give up the fight for suffrage during the war, forcefully reminding the women that, "it was because the American ideal of democracy—the democracy that means equal votes—was threatened that this great country went into war, and if the question of woman suffrage is set aside now it would mean that our country is living a lie." She emphasized that women should be able to vote instead of the "ignorant foreigner." (NAWSA officials consistently used this rhetoric in their messages although Shaw was much more vociferous than Catt along these lines.) How Indiana suffragists, many of them the daughters or granddaughters or wives or friends of immigrants felt about this is not known, but the local group did approve a resolution against teaching German in local elementary schools. Looking to the future both in suffrage work and war work, NAWSA executives planned fund-raising drives to support ratification of the Nineteenth Amendment since Congress seemed almost certain to approve it that year. The group wanted to pool contributions from all state suffrage societies to aid ratification efforts in every state and asked all women's organizations to contribute. At that same dinner, WFL president Marie Edwards announced the upcoming membership drive that included, for the first time, an emphasis on enrolling men as new members stating, "an organization of 10,000 [this is a misprint in the *Indianapolis Star*, the goal was actually 100,000 as stated in the *News*] men and women in Indiana will be a factor which the Legislature can not afford to ignore." Shaw, the chair of the Woman's Committee of the Council of National Defense, happened to be in Indiana on council business at the same time as the NAWSA meeting. Speaking on behalf of the federal Woman's Committee, she noted that the war could not be won without women's war work. The *News* commented that many women attending the NAWSA/WFL meeting also played important roles in the state Council of Defense, which was exactly the point suffragists had hoped the paper would make. Woman's Committee chair Carlisle hosted three hundred suffragists who did war work at a luncheon where both Shaw and

Catt spoke about the importance of women's war service. Cora Goodrich, Jennie Ralston, and the wife of Indianapolis mayor Charles W. Jewett attended the meeting, surely a sign of both personal and political support for women's war work from the highest levels of Indiana government.[27]

The WFL also prepared for the 1919 Indiana legislative session. The only piece of suffrage legislation from the 1917 session that the Indiana Supreme Court did not strike down, the Beardsley Amendment (that would change Article II, Section 2 of the state Constitution so that women could vote), would be taken up again in 1919 since an amendment had to pass two legislative sessions before it became part of the constitution. Edwards, still president of the WFL, offered her annual report at the joint NAWSA/WFL meeting and encouraged Hoosier women to begin lobbying for the vote by noting that in 1917

> Overnight we became of interest to both political parties. I believe we all thoroughly enjoyed our sudden popularity and were amused at the way we were courted. That taste of power has been fatal. Many women hitherto not interested in suffrage, now demand to know why they may not

USA TODAY

This group of Miami County women fanned out through the county in July 1917 as part of the Woman's Franchise League voter registration drive. Judges allowed women to register to vote while suffrage court cases were pending. In the end, Indiana women lost the vote.

> vote. The withdrawal of the voting privilege has enormously increased the number of women interested in suffrage. To the general public, political or otherwise, we can never again be the negligible quantity we were before. The fact remains that for a while we were voters, and all the effect of that is not lost.

She noted that "no [WFL] league can work by itself—irrespective of the state plan and independent of the state organization—and get anywhere . . . what each league does or does not do affects vitally the other leagues in the state and the consequent state campaign. So, we must each feel a part of a whole—closely related—and interdependent."[28]

Edward's comments built on those from earlier, local WFL meetings that summer, but without the derogatory comments about immigrant men that had recently been voiced at the Fifth District meeting at Terre Haute. The theme there had been "Suffrage Patriotism" and included jabs at men who voted on first papers. Keynote speakers stressed the need for women voters when it came time to negotiate peace stating, "there has never been a settlement of any way in which the women took part. . . . Men will be more concerned about boundaries than human life. The only way we can insure that element being

Indiana suffragists attended the Democratic National Convention in 1916 to push for the inclusion of a suffrage plank in the Democratic platform.

as much as considered is of having women at the peace table. . . . This war will last five years more perhaps. In that five years, a large percentage of the voters will be disloyal, ignorant, alien enemy." Another speaker, Lenore Cox from the Indiana Federation of Clubs election a few years earlier, stressed that maternal point of view and noted, "I have a son who will go to France in a few months. I have a daughter already over there. Whether or not they get the things they should have depends upon the legislature of this state. We must get a legislature that will allow women to vote. I want my vote to count in getting for my son and daughter the things to which they are entitled just as much as the vote of the alien enemy." Benbridge wrapped up the day's speeches with a rousing call to action: "Are we suffragists going to stand for certain men of the administration getting up and saying that we should not have the ballot because we haven't brains enough and then turn right around and ask these same women who haven't brains, to sell Liberty bonds, Thrift stamps and do a thousand and one other things? Are we going to let them get by with it? . . . We don't need to neglect suffrage to do war work. . . . This is our time to make a great gift to the next generation. Let's make it!"[29]

In July Edwards announced the start of the WFL membership drive, claiming that the "psychological moment for all good suffragists" had arrived. The upcoming August campaign coincided with a "lull" in war work when "the War Savings Stamp drive is over, the next Liberty loan not due till October, and the Red Cross demands not so heavy right now for Indiana." The WFL wanted to scour the state in a house-to-house canvas for new members and signatures on a petition supporting the Nineteenth Amendment. The group hoped to have 100,000 members by the end of the membership drive and to get 700,000 signatures on the petition to Congress (as requested by NAWSA headquarters). The WFL created a new league officer, the county organizer, to lead at the local level and to blitz counties with the now familiar suffrage tactics of auto tours, literature, speeches, newspaper articles, and anything else that would help enroll new members. The group created training schools to prepare its speakers. Edwards stressed that, "every suffragist knows, that the cause of suffrage is closely linked with every hope of real democracy, with every idea of real progress. We all believe that enfranchisement of women on equal terms with men is an actual war measure." Clarke promoted the registration drive in her column in the *Star* and continued Edwards's theme, noting that women needed to show "that we are truly patriotic, not only by knitting and doing the conventional kinds of war work, but by the utmost exertions to secure for the women of our country their rightful place as equal partners in the tremendously important enterprise of government. . . . Women of all religious denominations, club women, women who work whether in the home or in the many fields outside; young women and old, colored women and white, all women with sufficient wit to discern right from wrong, daylight from night, should enlist in the present suffrage drive."[30]

Membership drive workers received detailed training and written materials to study before the canvass. One "Instructions of Precinct Workers" reminded canvassers to "be pleasant but not apologetic. You are doing your country a patriotic service." Detailed responses to a list of possible objections women might encounter hopefully made the canvassers feel more comfortable at the task. For example, if someone mentioned women picketing the White House, the WFL suggested canvassers point out that the WFL was part of NAWSA with more than two million members and the picketers were part of a much smaller group, the Woman's Party, with only a few thousand members. If someone countered that they had too much to do to worry about woman suffrage, they were reminded that "President Wilson has declared suffrage a war measure" and that "our allied nations, with the guns of the Germans at their very hearts, have paused long enough to enfranchise their women or to make definite plans for it as a war necessity," implying that women in Indiana could not be more busy than those who lived in the midst of war in Europe. Anyone who declared that pushing for suffrage was unpatriotic in a time of war met two arguments in response. First, the WFL stated that "the United States is the only English-speaking nation in the world which has not enfranchised its women." Second, a canvasser could point out that "Indiana allows her alien enemies to vote if they have taken out their first papers. Why not offset that with the vote of patriotic American women who ARE citizens of the U.S. The enfranchisement of women by the Federal Amendment, means giving the country a patriotic vote of defense. We must fight for democracy in the trenches of France and at the polls at home." Once the new member had signed up and paid her dues, the canvasser issued a receipt and asked her to sign a petition in favor of the Nineteenth Amendment.[31]

WFL speeches similarly stressed the two major arguments for women to have the vote—men who voted on first papers and war work. One again emphasized that "the alien is permitted to vote on his first papers, after he has been in the state only six months. He can claim exemption under the draft law because he isn't a citizen, and so cannot be made to fight for his country, but he can vote and help govern it." Another, much longer, sample followed along the same lines, but much more extensively focused on women's war work as a reason for women to gain suffrage: "President Wilson calls suffrage 'an act of right and justice.' It is more than that. It is an act of sound common sense. Women can help win the war at the polls quite as well as by conserving food and doing government work." Women, the WFL noted, "share in all the war work, they share in all the deprivations and anxieties . . . whether they work in munition factories or at the Red Cross Shop." Women should be able to vote to help make laws because "most important of all, some of these laws have to do with arrangements for the soldiers in America and across the seas, their comfort and protection, their clothing, and military equipment, their very guns and shells." And again, speakers needed to remind Hoosiers that, "men who are citizens of those countries with which we are at war, men whose countries are fighting our men in France today can vote, can make laws in Indiana, can be and are mayors of Indiana cities."[32]

Suffragists also criticized both the state legislature and the U.S. Senate. Speakers stressed "that practically the only way Indiana women can get the vote is through an amendment to the constitution of the United States . . . we learned last year that no matter how much the Indiana men wish to give it to us, it cannot be done that way." The U.S. Senate also seemed out of control because "this suffrage amendment . . . passed the House of Representatives January 10th, but has been held up in the Senate ever since. . . . Our Senate in holding up this measure is in line with the parliaments of Germany and Austria both of which defeated suffrage bills this year. It is not in line with England and Canada, both of which have enfranchised their women since January 1st." An unnamed senator took direct fire, "here, in America, a senator who is opposed to suffrage gets up on the floor of the Senate and makes fun of woman's efforts of woman's work in the world, worst of all—of woman's services in the war!" The canvass paid off. By October the WFL had 283 branch leagues in place across the state.[33]

The war ended November 11, 1918. That night a massive celebration took place on Monument Circle in Indianapolis. The expansive English Hotel on the northwest quadrant of the circle displayed the flags of all allied nations. The hotel also hosted bands that played allied country's national anthems from its balconies. Schools and businesses closed that day and some the next. On November 12 a group of revelers celebrated inside the statehouse. According to the *Star*, "delegations headed by bands and with the flags of the allied nations

Marie Edwards of Peru, Indiana, led the Woman's Franchise League through the crucial years 1917 to 1919. She increased membership in the organization and kept the pressure on state legislators.

marched riotously through the corridors." Goodrich joined the celebrations as best he could. In August after leaving a dinner at Keller's home that honored some medical personnel who were about to enter the war, his car collided with a streetcar and by November he was still recuperating from several broken bones, including a broken hip (Keller was one of the doctors who attended to his injuries). With assistance, the governor made it into the crowd to deliver a short speech. He chastised the Kaiser and noted that "a nation founded on brute force can not rule the world." Goodrich could not join the "street demonstration" later that afternoon, but his wife, Cora, represented him (Keller was there as well). The *News* reported (in the colloquial) that a man watching the festivities noted, "see them women celebratin.' They can't vote yit, but it's coming' to em' and they orto have it. I didn't use to be for it, but I'm fur 'em now."[34]

The WFL assumed the lead in getting suffrage enacted after the war. The effective and powerful Indiana women's lobby, the Woman's Legislative Council, changed its leadership in 1918 after Luella McWhirter stepped down as its chair. While a friend hinted that perhaps she resigned due to conflicts within the organization, McWhirter had also taken on representing Indiana at the General Federation of Women's Clubs and mostly devoted her time to a new federation war work committee. Emma Eaton White, the woman who had offered the council solid legal advice, replaced her. One historian has stated that the change in leadership was an unfortunate turn of events. White, a lawyer, brought to the job her legal skills, but also her belief, unusual for an Indiana suffragist, that lobbying did not get legislation enacted. Therefore, the WLC, instead of acting like the strong woman's lobby it had been, simply let each organization do its own lobbying at the 1919 Indiana General Assembly and did not coordinate the work or even offer a clear list of legislative measures to pursue.[35]

So, the WFL went to work. The membership drive's stunning success had demonstrated the strength of suffrage sentiment in the state and lifted suffragists' spirits. However, the WFL probably already had support for the vote without the extensive membership campaign. Both the Democratic and Republican Parties of Indiana came out in favor of woman suffrage and Goodrich agreed, too. At the state Republican convention in May 1918, he announced that suffrage was "an act of tardy justice." There did not seem to be anything that could go wrong in 1919, but state WFL leaders left nothing to chance. They set up a "bureau of reference" in its statehouse office to answer questions about suffrage legislation and to closely monitor the progress of bills. The group asked WFL members to stay near the telephone and check for telegrams in case they needed to quickly act on a piece of legislation. The group asked branch leaders who visited Indianapolis during the legislative session to report to the its office and assist with any work that needed to be done. The WFL tried to get errant branches to send in any leftover signed petitions from the summer membership drive so the group could put them on display at the statehouse. The victories and subsequent defeats in 1917 weighed heavily on the WFL and this time the group wanted no surprises.[36]

On the opening day of the 1919 legislative session, "immediately after Governor Goodrich finished reading his message," State Senator John S. Alldredge of Anderson introduced a resolution to encourage the U.S. Senate to pass the Nineteenth Amendment (the U.S. House of Representatives had already approved the amendment; the holdup was in the Senate), "Whereas, The women of our country in the past world's war again demonstrated their unfailing patriotism and eminent ability in every way deserving of the ballot. . . . Be it resolved that we . . . urge upon the United States Senate and the immediate passage of said measure in the end that this session may ratify the same." The body approved the resolution by a voice vote in front of Keller and Cora Goodrich. This gave women hope, but they still assumed nothing.[37]

Fortunately, they did not have to wait long for success. A new partial-suffrage bill that gave Indiana women the right to vote for presidential electors passed the House 90–3 in late January and in the Senate 44–3 in early February. Although a partial-suffrage bill had been declared unconstitutional in Indiana in 1917, WFL attorneys assured suffragists this new legislation passed muster and NAWSA offered to help with expenses if someone challenged the bill. Legislators who spoke in favor of the measure gave women's war work, which to them signified women's loyalty, as the reason to support the partial-suffrage bill. As Alldredge noted, "The work of the women has spoken eloquently in their behalf. The war could not have been won without the sacrifices and toil of the women of this land." Senator Oliver Kline, Republican from Huntington and Whitley Counties; Senator John Erskine, Democrat from Vanderburgh County; and Senator Charles Hagerty, Democrat from Saint Joseph and Marshall Counties, all voted against the measure. Kline spoke at length and argued that his constituents did not want women to vote, that something nefarious must be going on in concert with the Indiana Supreme Court to get the bill through, and that women were not ready for the ballot as evidenced by their support of President Wilson's promise to keep the United States out of war. He praised women for their war work, but insisted that it proved that keeping women out of politics had made them better than men for such work. He ended his diatribe on a note of concern about "race suicide," noting, "There are women in this state who should be reproducing their kind, but they are not doing so. The greatest scandal of the state of Indiana is that strong, healthy couples, paired in the bonds of wedlock, are reproducing but one child, or none at all." Finally, he declared, "If the secret minds of the members of the Senate could be pictured on a screen by the pressing of a button, there would be few reproductions that would be in accord with the verbal votes of those men." When the governor signed the bill the next day, he gave the pen to the WFL which supposedly stored it with its gavel made with wood from the Indiana constitutional elm in Corydon and "other trophies owned by the organization."[38]

Legislators then withdrew the Beardsley Constitutional Amendment Bill that was up for its second vote. Goodrich wanted to modify the 1917 Beardsley bill, but if he did and it passed the legislature again, it could not be voted on the second time until 1921. So, it seemed prudent to withdraw the Beardsley bill and introduce a new one that covered some issues the original bill did not. The new bill modified Article II Section 2 of the state constitution so that women could vote in all elections and a new provision allowed only native-born citizens and fully naturalized citizens to vote and not, as currently happened, those who had filed to become, but were not yet, citizens. This bill passed without dissent.[39]

The U.S. Senate did not have the votes to pass the Nineteenth Amendment out of that chamber while the Indiana legislature was still in session, but in June the Senate finally acted and the amendment was sent to the states for ratification. Women across the country would be able to vote in all elections once thirty-six states ratified the amendment. New WFL president Helen Benbridge met with Goodrich to urge him to immediately call a special session to ratify the amendment. For such a strong supporter of suffrage, the governor did not want to do so until other states had ratified. Emma White and Sara Lauter, current president of the Indianapolis WFL, publicly called on Goodrich to order the legislature into session. The *News* calculated the special session might save the state the extra costs of the partial-suffrage law, estimated to be $100,000. The *Star* thought the governor should wait until it was clear that the amendment would be ratified before he called a special session. The governor at first hinted at a late August/early September date, but then changed his mind. When Lauter personally asked him about the date of the session, he said that he had decided to "postpone" the session, but assured her that "Indiana will be by no means the last state to act."[40]

Indiana suffragists did not like that answer but had to wait. In the meantime, they celebrated the Senate vote. Suffragists in Anderson organized a parade and carried banners that read "It Took Forty Years," "At Last, At Last," "Thanks, Gentlemen," "Over the Country at Last," and "You're All Right, Gentlemen." In Marion "several hundred persons, both men and women, gathered on the courthouse lawn Thursday night and celebrated" with Edwards as their speaker. In Edwards's hometown, Peru, the local WFL used the celebration to pin yellow tags on supporters and ask for their donations to push through ratification. The Richmond celebration included a talk by William Dudley Foulke who had presided over the AWSA in the late 1880s. The Indianapolis branch of the WFL organized a "suffrage week" to celebrate. In addition to a week-long series of traditional suffrage teas that were open to all women and held across the city, they honored "pioneer suffragists" of Indianapolis at a public reception held at the home of Zerelda Wallace's (early suffragist and temperance lecturer) granddaughter, Mrs. Arthur B. Grover. The pioneer suffragists included Charity Dye; Mrs. John T. Dye; Mrs. Charles E. Kregelo; Mrs. Henry D. Pierce; Mrs. John M. Judah; Mrs. John C. New; the sisters Martha McKay, Elizabeth Nicholson, and Mary Nicholson; and Laura Donnan—all reportedly members of the 1872 Indianapolis Suffrage Society started by the McKays and Donnan. Judah (granddaughter of Ovid Butler, founder of Butler University and a suffrage supporter) and Pierce (a friend of Elizabeth Cady Stanton's daughters), highlighted the educational backgrounds of many suffragists (both had attended Vassar College). Kregelo had not only been an officer in local suffrage organizations, but she also served as a reminder of Indianapolis's ties to national suffragists who she often hosted in her home. Rather than celebrate, other suffragists wanted to jump directly into the political fray. However, at a WFL district meeting in Elkhart, district chair Mrs. A. H. Beardsley, wife of the author of the Beardsley amendment, urged suffragists to not "be tied up in political entanglements rather assume an attitude based on intelligent comprehension of the opportunities and obligations now come to women." The WFL Indianapolis branch channeled its energy into a Citizenship School scheduled for late September and assumed that thirty-six states, including Indiana, would indeed ratify the amendment. "The universities and colleges of the state" sent instructors to Indianapolis for the weeklong school. The WFL charged a fee, but the Indianapolis branch felt sure that members would "find it a necessary and beneficial course of instruction." The school warned women not to form strong ties to any political party just yet.[41]

By December Goodrich had still failed to call a special session devoted to ratifying the amendment. Goodrich most likely feared that some of his "pet" pieces of legislation from the last legislative session might come under siege at the special session and he wanted to protect his legislative accomplishments. Exasperated with the delay, Benbridge and several other suffragists presented petitions to Lieutenant Governor Edgar D. Bush signed by a reported 86,000 Hoosiers asking for a special session. Benbridge also directly wrote to the governor for an explanation. He stated that he did "not want to delay the ratification of the Suffrage Amendment and desired to give the women the benefit of early action on the part of our State." On the other hand, he knew that he would need to call another special session "to enact certain additional legislation to take care of the big increase in the number of voters" he expected after ratification. However, he told Benbridge, "that if assurance can be received from the members of the General Assembly that they will upon call meet for the purpose only of acting upon the Suffrage Amendment, I will upon the receipt of such assurance, immediately call the General Assembly for that purpose." In another communication to Benbridge, the governor put the number at two-thirds of the legislators. She immediately went to work to secure those assurances.

On January 3, 1920, the WFL sent letters to state legislators asking them to send a response by January 15 if they agreed to attend a special session for the sole purpose to vote on the Nineteenth Amendment. The WFL sent a separate letter to its local officers asking them to contact their local legislators and reiterated the importance of a positive answer. Most legislators' answers came back very quickly. Those who did not respond with dispatch might have received a visit from a suffragist. Benbridge at one point asked Mrs. J. G. McNutt to travel to Madison, Indiana, at the WFL's expense, to nudge Representative Joseph Cravens along with his answer. When legislators did respond, they usually stated a reason on whether to agree. James M. Knapp of Wayne County specifically cited the war for his affirmative reply noting, "During the last four years, the women of the United States have not only earned their right to the ballot, but they have proven their fitness for suffrage in every way." In less than two weeks, two-thirds of the general assembly responded in the affirmative. Goodrich called for the special session three days later. As word went out, women in the state rejoiced. Dora E. Clark of West Lebanon sent a letter to Benbridge to congratulate "your women workers for splendid success . . . I have longed these many years for Indiana women the right to vote. It now seems a certain thing." On January 16, 1920, as Clark hoped, at a special session, the legislature voted to allow Indiana to become the twenty-sixth state to ratify the Nineteenth Amendment.[42]

At the onset of the special session, Goodrich announced its purpose was "to recognize the political equality of the women of the nation but also . . . to pay tribute to them for their valiant services and ceaseless devotion in the great crisis through which we have just passed." WFL members Edwards, Benbridge, McCulloch, and Elizabeth Cooper had the honor of sitting at the speaker's platform in the House and with the lieutenant governor in the Senate as each body voted. The Senate vote was 43–3. One Democratic senator, Hagerty of South Bend, who had voted no on the Indiana bill in the previous session, and two Republicans, Kline of Huntington, who had also voted in the negative on the Indiana bill, and McCray of Indianapolis, voted no. Erskine, who had also voted no on the Indiana bill was not present. An estimated three hundred women wearing the yellow flower of Indiana suffragists applauded the enactment. Senator John H. Furnas, a suffrage supporter, then, by prearrangement, moved to reconsider the vote, and Senator Harry Negley moved to lay that motion on the table. This was done so that the "resolution could not be reopened." The scene in the statehouse grew raucous after the bill went to the House and all ninety-three members unanimously voted for it. Three hours had passed. Indiana had ratified the Nineteenth Amendment. The band that someone had the forethought to invite to the statehouse for the day struck up "Glory, Glory Hallelujah." Women sang and according to the *News*, "scenes of the wildest joy and confusion prevailed." Cora Goodrich and Mary Tarkington Jameson waltzed to

"Until We Meet Again." The *News* banner headline read, "STATE LEGISLATURE PASSES SUFFRAGE RESOLUTION." The *Star* more succinctly noted, "INDIANA JOINS SUFFRAGE LIST" and placed a photograph of Goodrich signing the bill under the headline. When Goodrich had signed the Maston-McKinley bill in 1917, only his wife had been present. Now he signed the bill with several pens and distributed them to the fourteen suffragists in attendance.[43]

If anyone thought that Hoosier suffragists would now disband their organizations and relax, then they had never really understood the depth of their commitment to suffrage. They forged ahead with their work while waiting for the final ratification of the Nineteenth Amendment by the other states. The WFL citizenship booklet, "An Aid to the Citizen in Indiana," had sold 8,500 copies since the previous September. An estimated ninety towns and approximately fifty-three clubs held suffrage schools like the one Lauter had organized in Indianapolis the previous September and used the course in their programs. Colleges and public schools also adopted the WFL citizenship program. Women across the state, it seemed, wanted more information on the workings of government and current state and national issues. The ground in Indiana was fertile for the creation of a new woman's organization. In her role as president of the WFL's Indianapolis branch, Lauter invited presidents of other women's groups to attend a March 19 meeting in Indianapolis to discuss the creation of an Indiana branch of the national League of Women Voters. Edwards, who had already accepted the position of treasurer for the national league, ran the meeting to organize the new Indiana group, formed to be nonpartisan in its work. League members studied legislation and issues and offered their members a forum to discuss those topics without promoting a political party. The NAWSA rolled its memberships into the league, but some members chose instead to join the National Woman's Party, which became a one-issue party and focused on advocating for the Equal Rights Amendment. The movement of women into the league has been criticized because it might have "short circuited the political strength of the most gifted suffragist women" by making them seem less interested in the hurly-burly political world than in reform and thus made male politicians more likely to ignore them. On the other hand, NAWSA president Catt publicly stated that the league, "is not encouraging women to leave their parties for it is through the political parties that we must work" and encouraged women to work against "lynching, compelling kissing of the flag and deportation" and "to set their shoulders against intolerance which will cause the crumbling of any foundation."[44]

Tennessee became the thirty-sixth state to ratify the Nineteenth Amendment on August 18, 1920. Republican and Democratic women embraced the news. Landers, now with the national Democratic Committee, and Mrs. Joseph B. Kealing with the state Republican Party, emphasized the importance of women for the coming November elections. Mrs. Wilmer Christian of the Indianapolis LWV hoped that women voters could push through legislation on issues such as child labor. Lauter asserted that the league was the vehicle for woman's work since she did "not see what either political party has given them [women]." McWhirter had worked for both temperance and suffrage and mentioned that the vote would keep things "dry" and that women would rally behind laws that reduced deaths among mothers and infants. State officials claimed to be ready for the additional voters, although without extra machines, paper ballots might be needed. With the 750,000 to 800,000 women voters expected to register in the state, the total number of voters in Indiana could reach an estimated 1.6 million for the November election. The only women ineligible to vote would be those under twenty-one and those who were not citizens. Additionally, women citizens married to men who were not naturalized could not vote since citizenship traveled with the husband—the new suffrage legislation had not fixed that oddity of Hoosier voting. Senator James E. Watson of Indiana, chair of the Senate committee on suffrage and credited with its skillful maneuvering through that body, hoped that enfranchised women would fight socialism. Republican National Committee chair Hays almost burst with praise for the amendment. He stated, "the effects of the approaching presidential election will influence our national life for weal or for woe, for at least fifty years. . . . We want these women in play. We want them in play this year more than ever before. Ratification of the amendment clears the political atmosphere, and makes possible the functioning of a very great element for good in our political life and is a final triumph of supreme justice for American women." Catt released a statement saying she hoped women would not follow the model of "kid-gloved men slackers whom I have heard proudly boast that they would not touch politics with a ten-foot pole." Rather she hoped that women might "swell America's army of voters who put conscience and thought into the scales with party politics and party candidates."[45]

Word came on August 26, 1920, that the final papers to complete the ratification process had been signed in Congress (this is the day women celebrate as Women's Equality Day). Women across the land had the vote. At noon,

INDIANAPOLIS NEWS/USA TODAY

Hoosier women voted in large numbers on November 2, 1920. The top photo shows women voting in the Third Precinct, Eleventh Ward, at 631 South Alabama Street, Indianapolis. The women in the bottom photo are voting at the Second Precinct, Fifth Ward, at 904 Indiana Avenue.

church bells rang for five minutes and the chimes at Monument Circle's Christ Church rang out with a musical number. Factory whistles blew as the NAWSA asked suffragists across the country to arrange for that particular celebration. Other cities in the state held similar celebrations with factory whistles blown in Anderson and Fort Wayne. The Fort Wayne League of Women voters also managed to have an airplane drop leaflets on the city. In Indianapolis, a celebration, or what the papers termed a "jollification," took place on Saturday, August 28. The Claypool Hotel, the site of many suffrage meetings over the previous decades, hosted the celebration. The day included a unique tableau performance of the events in Tennessee and several well-known Hoosier suffragists dressed as some of the movements most recognizable national suffrage pioneers: Charity Dye appeared as Susan B. Anthony, Luella McWhirter as Dr. Anna Howard Shaw, and Keller as Carrie Chapman Catt. Grace Julian Clarke spoke about her father's work for suffrage in the U.S. House of Representatives. The festivities rippled out across the state and the Shelbyville branch of the WFL, now a branch of the LWV, waited until September for a celebration.[46]

Now that they had the vote, and there was a national election in November, Hoosier women dove into the political process. Joining the LWV did not, it turned out, stop them from also working for a political party. Many women, including Landers, McCulloch, Hortense Tapp Moore, Olive Beldon Lewis, Jennie Ralston, Mrs. Samuel Perkins, Eugenie Nicholson, Dr. Hannah Graham, Mrs. Kin Hubbard, and Clarke joined the Democratic Party. Other suffragists joined the Republican Party including Keller, Eleanor Barker, Emma White, McWhirter, and Julia Henderson.[47]

Most women left no record of their reasons for following a particular party but looking at their speeches on behalf of their respective parties the League of Nations jumps out as an important issue. Barker, as a Republican, stated that the League of Nations might lead to more wars and that "Wilson fooled some of the women of the United States four years ago on a war issue, but they won't bite twice at the same bait." Clarke, on the other hand, supported the League of Nations. Clarke had taken a less public role for the suffrage cause just before the special session because she had been speaking around the state on behalf of the League of Nations. She garnered both praise and criticism for her stand including one letter with the simple, one-line message, "Madam, <u>You are a damned fool</u>!" She explained to a group in South Bend that she supported the League of Nations and worked for the Democrats even though she really considered herself to be an independent voter. The League of Nations as a body, she stated, promoted better working conditions for all and cited a treaty that called for an eight-hour day and "humane provision" for women and children wage earners. She worked staunchly against the candidacy of Warren G. Harding in 1920 for president and told Edwards, "I have little interest in anything Senator Harding may say at any-time on any subject." She particularly excoriated him for his stand on the League of Nations and what she called "his cowardly attitude on woman suffrage during the pendency of that question in congress." Clarke already penned a regular column for the *Indianapolis Star* and after winning the vote she also contributed to the "Women in Politics" column as the Democrat, while Mrs. Joseph B. Kealing represented the Republicans.[48]

Women, children, and a "riot of colors" enlivened an otherwise drab, dreary election day on November 2, 1920. Indiana had to choose a president, governor, senator, and other officials. It was the first election after the war and national political debates added to the excitement and the largest voter turnout in the state's history. Women turned out in large numbers, sometimes with their children in tow, who they either took into the voting booth with them or handed off to another voter for a moment. Women also worked at the polls, most often, it appears, as the registrar or as a poll watcher who stood outside, bundled against the cold. Some reports indicated that voters arrived in three waves in Indianapolis that day. Men voted as they went to work. The *News* tried to add some fun to its report by noting that "by 8 o'clock, with breakfast over, the dishes washed, and the house straightened up a bit, Mrs. Voter was on the way to vote." While we do not know what women's activities were before they went to the polls, it is apparent that women voted from a little later in the morning until noon, the time period when, by most reports (including from around the state), more women than men voted. The third wave included more men as some factories let workers leave at noon to be sure they could vote. Other scattered reports had women waiting in line for the polls to open to be sure to be the first to vote. Everyone agreed that by noon most Hoosier women had finished making their way to the polls. In Indianapolis men seemed to vote a straight ticket (as evidenced by their short time in the voting booth) with a distinct possibility that women voted for the candidate, not the party. High voter turnout of men and women in precincts populated by African Americans and German Americans were reported. The day did not pass without incident. The voting machine proved to be an obstacle for at least one shorter woman, who could not reach the levers. Mrs. F. T. Reed suffered injuries in a car accident as she drove to the polls. After a brief visit to the hospital and a quick rest at home, someone took her to vote in the afternoon. It was estimated that "less than 5000 of 76,000 women" in Marion County did not vote although how that number was determined is not clear.[49]

Elsewhere in the state, women arrived early at the polls and in Greenfield all eleven precincts reported women as the first voters. In New Albany women had been encouraged to vote early and many appeared at the polls wearing "I Will Vote by 10" pins. One of the oldest voters, 103-year-old Sarah Cannon of Washington, Indiana, arrived in a wheelchair and had to have someone mark her ballot for her due to poor eyesight. Raised as a Republican, she proudly voted for the Democratic ticket because of her support for the League of Nations. South Bend reported that almost all the 38,477 women registered to vote actually voted. In North Manchester "five sisters, all past 74 years" voted. In Lafayette the nuns from Saint Elizabeth Hospital "marched in solemn procession to the polls." In Richmond women voted early in the day and the overall voter turnout was high with three-fifths of the total registered voters at the polls by 1:00 p.m. It appeared that most women in Richmond favored Republicans.[50]

Like the Richmond voters, Indiana and the nation chose the Republicans that day. Warren G. Harding easily swept into the presidency with his "return to normalcy" campaign that promised to leave war and reform behind. Hoosier women appeared on the ballot in a few places. In Lake County Margaret McClure Turner and Myrtle Meara both ran for the legislature but did not win. Also, in Lake County, Mrs. Fred Carter sought to become a county commissioner. Julia D. Nelson became the first woman elected to the Indiana legislature. As chair of the Republican women of Delaware County, she replaced Clark D. McKinley on the ballot after he died the Saturday before the election. Nelson thought that "we don't want women politicians—we want political women, that is women who are interested in the affairs of the city in which they live, in the state and in the country." Another important first was the selection, by incoming Governor Warren T. McCray, of Adah Bush as his private secretary, the first time in the state's history that post had been filled by a woman. Bush had served McCray as his secretary for twenty years at his place of business and was his wife's cousin. A leading suffragist, while not serving in an elected capacity, had her place next to the highest official in the state.[51]

While women celebrated, joined political parties, and voted, national antisuffragists did not give up their crusade. NAWSA president Catt foresaw this possibility and hired 1916 Republican presidential candidate and suffrage supporter Charles Evans Hughes to defend the amendment in court. In February 1922 the final legal challenge to the federal amendment went down to defeat.[52]

Ida Husted Harper had spent the last years of the suffrage movement managing the NAWSA's publicity. She composed pamphlets, articles, flyers, letters to the editor, and anything else that could inspire someone to believe that women should vote. Her national vision let her offer a few final words on the results of the suffrage movement. She quoted the *New York Tribune* on the conduct of the election, "The most striking fact of all is that this great change in our political structure has come almost unnoticed—it is today as if women had always voted. The predicted disturbances of cherished institutions has not shown a trace. . . . The miracle has happened and the world has not tipped." Harper herself commented that "older suffragists are happy over the election, whether their favorite candidates were elected or not, for it was the fulfillment of the dream of three generations." Women could now "vote on equal terms with men at a national election . . . 'elected by the people' would not mean 'elected by half of the people.'" The president-elect had remarked that he would consult both men and women on important questions of the day. "When," Harper asked, "before now have women been seriously considered for members of the President's cabinet?" Suffragists were also relieved. They no longer had to approach each session of Congress with anxiety over women gaining, or not, the vote. They were no longer, Harper thought, "bored" or "resentful" or panicked at the idea of an antisuffragist congressman.[53]

Decades earlier Zerelda Wallace had become a suffragist when one Indiana state senator compared ten thousand women's signatures on a prohibition petition to the signatures of ten thousand mice. Things had changed. Harper reminded her readers, "For the first time in all history, the members of the United States congress in their deliberations on all questions will have to take into account the opinions of women, and when their minds revert to their cherished constituents they will have a vision of women sharing the seats of the mighty."[54]

Notes

Introduction

1. Information about Way is found at http://www.in.gov/history/markers/4117.htm/ as well as in Eric L. Hamilton, "The Role of Quakerism in the Indiana Women's Suffrage Movement, 1851–1885" (master's thesis, Indiana University–Purdue University at Indianapolis, 2013). Dane Starbuck, *The Goodriches: An American Family* (Indianapolis: Liberty Fund, 2001), 13, for Goodrich's birthplace.

2. *Richmond Palladium*, October 11, 1910.

3. A recent issue of the *Indiana Magazine of History* discusses that point: *Indiana Magazine of History* 112 (December 2016). For Read, Louise R. Noun, *Strong-Minded Women: The Emergence of the Woman-Suffrage Movement in Iowa* (Ames: Iowa State University Press, 1969), 24–25, 272. *The United States Biographical Dictionary and Portrait Gallery of Eminent and Self Made Men: Iowa Volume* (Chicago and New York: American Biographical Publishing Company, 1878), 494–96, includes details about Read at the end of a biographical article about her husband. Noun, *Strong-Minded Women*, 270–71 has information about Harbert. Steven M. Buechler, *The Transformation of the Woman Suffrage Movement: The Case of Illinois, 1850–1920* (New Brunswick, NJ: Rutgers University Press, 1986), refers to Harbert in many places in his work. The merger of the two national suffrage groups is found in Susan B. Anthony and Ida Husted Harper, eds., *History of Woman Suffrage*, vol. 4 (1883–1900; repr., Salem, NH: Ayer Company Publishers, 1985), 164. Three Hoosiers technically served in the NWSA group since Elizabeth Boynton Harbert was born and raised in Crawfordsville, Indiana. Harper is described in Nancy Baker Jones, "A Forgotten Feminist: The Early Writings of Ida Husted Harper, 1878–1894," *Indiana Magazine of History* 73 (June 1977): 79–101 and mentioned in Genevieve G. McBride, *On Wisconsin Women: Working for Their Rights from Settlement to Suffrage* (Madison: University of Wisconsin Press, 1993), 283. More on Hay is found in: Charity Dye, *Some Torch Bearers in Indiana* (Indianapolis: Hollenbeck Press, 1917), 216–22; Edward T. James, Janet Wilson James, and Paul S. Boyer, eds., *Notable American Women, 1607–1950: A Biographical Dictionary*, 3 vols. (Cambridge, MA: Belknap Press of Harvard University, 1971), 2:163–65; and Melanie Gustafson, Kristie Miller, and Elisabeth Israels Perry, eds., *We Have Come to Stay: American Women and Political Parties, 1880–1960* (Albuquerque: University of New Mexico Press, 1999), 97–107. The best biography of Sewall is Ray E. Boomhower, *"But I Do Clamor": May Wright Sewall, A Life 1844–1920* (Zionsville, IN: Guild Press of Indiana, 2001). For Clarke, Linda C. Gugin and James E. St. Clair, eds., *Indiana's 200: The People Who Shaped the Hoosier State* (Indianapolis: Indiana Historical Society Press, 2015), 62–64.

4. Anthony and Husted Harper, eds., *History of Woman Suffrage*, 614 and Ida Husted Harper, ed., *History of Woman Suffrage*, vol. 6 (1900–1920; rept., Salem, NH: Ayer Company Publishers, 1985), 166.

5. Sara Egge, *Woman Suffrage and Citizenship in the Midwest, 1870–1920* (Iowa City: University Press of Iowa, 2018), 1–20. Xenia E. Cord, "Black Rural Settlements in Indiana before 1860," in Wilma L. Gibbs, ed., *Indiana's African American Heritage* (Indianapolis: Indiana Historical Society, 1993), 99–110. Robert M. Taylor Jr., and Connie B. McBirney, eds., *Peopling Indiana: The Ethnic Experience* (Indianapolis: Indiana Historical Society, 1996), 12–21 covers the history of African Americans in Indiana for the time period of this study. French inhabitants of what became the Indiana Territory owned slaves and were allowed to keep them following statehood. Some

white settlers who came to Indiana tried to introduce slavery into the state, even though it was prohibited. Differing views by Hoosiers about slavery and the status of free blacks living in early Indiana can be found in Donald F. Carmony, *Indiana 1816–1850: The Pioneer Era* (Indianapolis: Indiana Historical Bureau and Indiana Historical Society, 1998), 562–67 and for attempts to keep free blacks from entering Indiana and to possibly expel those already in Indiana see Carmony's explanation of the convention to draft Indiana's 1851 Constitution, 442–51.

6. *Indianapolis Daily State Sentinel*, June 10, 1869; *Indianapolis News*, May 19, 20, 1882, for more reporting on the meeting.

7. Taylor and McBirney, eds., *Peopling Indiana*, 12–15. Information about Ralston and Lively is found in B. R. Sulgrove, *History of Indianapolis and Marion County, Indiana* (Philadelphia: L. H. Everts and Company, 1884), 25, 26, 29 and David J. Bodenhamer and Robert G. Barrows, eds., *The Encyclopedia of Indianapolis* (Bloomington and Indianapolis: Indiana University Press, 1994), 1164. Statistics are found in Bodenhamer and Barrows, eds., *Encyclopedia of Indianapolis*, 55. Emma Lou Thornbrough, *Indiana in the Civil War Era* (Indianapolis: Indiana Historical Society, 1995), 541–43, contains pre-twentieth century population statistics. Richard B. Pierce, *Polite Protest: The Political Economy of Race in Indianapolis, 1920–1970* (Bloomington: Indiana University Press, 2005), 3, on the growth of the city. Information on Indianapolis's schools, Taylor and McBirney, eds., *Peopling Indiana*, 16; Bodenhamer and Barrows, eds., *Encyclopedia of Indianapolis*, 7–8; Pierce, *Polite Protest*, 26–55; and Emma Lou Thornbrough, "The History of Black Women in Indiana," in Gibbs, ed., *Indiana's African American Heritage*, 72–74. Thornbrough notes that Gertrude Mahorney, class of 1887, was the first African American to graduate from Butler University. She then taught school in Indianapolis and evidently was "the only black teacher in the system who taught German." More on Clarke is found in Bodenhamer and Barrows, eds., *Encyclopedia of Indianapolis*, 445–46 and Gugin and St. Clair, eds., *Indiana's 200*, 62–64.

8. Taylor and McBirney, eds., *Peopling Indiana*, introduction, for an overall look at immigration and Indiana. Bodenhamer and Barrows, eds., *Encyclopedia of Indianapolis*, 51–60 for immigration and Indianapolis. Emma Lou Thornbrough, *Indiana in the Civil War Era*, 543–55 gives detailed information about German and Irish immigrants. George Theodore Probst, *The Germans in Indianapolis, 1840–1918* (Indianapolis: German-American Center and Indiana German Heritage Society, 989) for a detailed look at Indianapolis's German heritage and culture. Thornbrough, *Indiana in the Civil War Era*, 39–40 for immigrant men becoming eligible to vote in the state after living in Indiana for only six months. Egge, *Woman Suffrage and Citizenship in the Midwest*, 1–10 for more information on "alien suffrage."

9. Sylvia D. Hoffert, *When Hens Crow: The Woman's Rights Movement in Antebellum America* (Bloomington: Indiana University Press, 1995) and Wendy Hamand Venet, *A Strong-Minded Woman: The Life of Mary A. Livermore* (Amherst: University of Massachusetts Press, 2005) address the various ways women were critiqued including using the term strong-minded and referring to women as crowing hens.

10. Clifton J. Phillips, *Indiana in Transition: The Emergence of an Industrial Commonwealth, 1880–1920* (Indiana Historical Bureau and Indiana Historical Society, 1968), 289–90; Probst, *Germans in Indianapolis*, 33–35, 86; Taylor and McBirney, eds., *Peopling Indiana*, 166; Bodenhamer and Barrows, eds., *Encyclopedia of Indianapolis*, 349–50.

11. Will H. Hays, *The Memoirs of Will H. Hays* (New York: Doubleday and Company, 1955), 130. *Indianapolis Star*, June 2, 1918, and *Indianapolis News*, May 29, 1918. See, Woman's Franchise League 1914–1919 Collection, SC 1761, box 1, folder 2, Indiana Historical Society William Henry Smith Memorial Library, Indianapolis, model speech for the membership drive.

Chapter 1

1. Elizabeth Cady Stanton, Susan B. Anthony, and Matilda Joslyn Gage, *History of Woman Suffrage*, vol. 1 (New York: Fowler and Wells, 1881), 306. Eric L. Hamilton, "The Role of Quakerism in the Indiana Woman's Suffrage Movement, 1851–1885: Towards a More Perfect Freedom for All" (master's thesis, Indiana University, 2013), has a good discussion of the relationships/kinship between those who called for the meeting. Many of the earliest advocates for woman's rights, both in the nation and in Indiana were Quakers. In Indiana two of the most prominent leaders, Amanda Way and Dr. Mary Thomas, later joined the Methodist Episcopal Church because they felt their Quaker congregations did not do enough to fight slavery.

2. Emma Lou Thornbrough, *Indiana in the Civil War Era, 1850–1880* (Indianapolis: Indiana Historical Society, 1995), 19–25; Peggy Brase Seigel, "Moral Champions and Public Pathfinders: Antebellum Quaker Women in Eastcentral Indiana," *Quaker History* 81, no. 2 (1992): 87–106. Ties to abolition and temperance on the part of the women at the Seneca Falls, New York, woman's rights convention are explained in Sally G. McMillen, *Seneca Falls and the Origins of the Women's Rights Movement* (New York: Oxford University Press, 2008) and Lisa Tetrault, *The Myth of Seneca Falls: Memory and the Women's Suffrage Movement, 1848–1898* (Chapel Hill: University of North Carolina Press, 2014).

3. Thornbrough, *Indiana in the Civil War*, 28–32.

4. This discussion of women and the law in Indiana is drawn from: Virginia Dill McCarty, "From Petticoat Slavery to Equality: Women's Rights in Indiana Law," in David J. Bodenhamer and Randall T. Shepard, eds, *History of Indiana Law* (Athens: Ohio University Press, 2006), 177–92.

5. McCarty, "From Petticoat Slavery to Equality," 179–80; Thornbrough, *Indiana in the Civil War*, 34–35. The comments about the importance of securing the law within the state constitution and about the silver pitcher are found in, Sarah T. Bolton to William Wesley Woollen, September 16, 1882, Sarah Tittle Barrett Bolton Papers 1832–1893, SC108, Indiana Historical Society William Henry Smith Memorial Library, Indianapolis. The silver pitcher is now housed at the Indiana State Archives. The New Harmony experiment is explained in Donald F. Carmony and Josephine M. Elliott, "New Harmony, Indiana: Robert Owen's Seedbed for Utopia," *Indiana Magazine of History* 76 (September 1980).

6. McCarty, "From Petticoat Slavery to Equality," 180.

7. An excellent discussion about how the men and women who were involved in the formation of the IWRA gained procedural experience from their roles in the Society of Friends (Quakers) is found in Hamilton, "Role of Quakerism in the Indiana Woman's Suffrage Movement." Indiana women were not unique in the path they followed in the 1850s. Many other woman's rights associations pursued the same goals. A good explanation of the overall woman's rights movement at this time is found in Eleanor Flexnor and Ellen Fitzpatrick, *Century of Struggle: The Woman's Rights Movement in the United States* (Cambridge, MA: Belknap/Harvard University Press, 1996), Chapters 5 and 6.

8. Minutes for October 1851, Indiana Woman's Suffrage Association Record Book, 1851–1886, Collection SC 1792/BV 2577, Indiana Historical Society (hereafter IWSA Minutes); Stanton, Anthony, and Gage, *History of Woman Suffrage*, 306.

9. IWSA Minutes October 1851; Stanton, Anthony, and Gage, *History of Woman Suffrage*, 306.

10. IWSA Minutes, October 1851

11. Flexnor and Fitzpatrick, *Century of Struggle*, 66–72; Lori D. Ginzberg, *Elizabeth Cady Stanton* (New York: Hill and Wang, 2009), 52–76.

12. Ibid., 52–76.
13. Ibid., 77–79; Flexnor and Fitzpatrick, *Century of Struggle*, 79–80.
14. IWSA Minutes, 1852
15. Ibid.,1853
16. Ibid.,1853–59
17. Ibid.; Stanton, Anthony, and Gage, *History of Woman Suffrage*, 311–14.
18. IWSA Minutes, 1854, emphasis in the original, 1855 and 1857 for other remarks. Frances Dana Gage was an active organizer of woman's rights meetings in Ohio and also spoke at national conventions. Ernestine Rose was born in Poland, but left there after she refused to marry the man her father chose for her. She eventually arrived in England where she met Robert Dale Owen, married a jeweler, and immigrated to the United States in 1835. She traveled the country in support of woman's suffrage and improved married women's property laws, especially in New York. Some have called her the "first Jewish feminist." See Jewish Women's Archive, https://jwa.org/encyclopedia/article/rose-ernestine. Lucretia Mott worked with Elizabeth Cady Stanton and others on the Seneca Falls convention in 1848. Mott and her husband, James, were active abolitionists. For more on Mott and Bloomer, see Flexnor and Fitzpatrick, *Century of Struggle*, 66–71, 77–79.
19. *The Lily*, Richmond, Indiana, February 1859 issue, photocopy in author's possession. In a small article entitled "The Committee," the editor noted, "But half of the committee appointed by the Woman's Rights Association to have a hearing before the legislature and present the petitions, met at Indianapolis on the 19th, and they were those who had no expectancy of being placed on active duty."
20. *Indianapolis Daily Journal*, January 20, 1859, for comment on the "cornstalks." Thomas's remarks are mentioned in *The Lily*, February 1859. They are also found in the *Indianapolis Daily State Sentinel*, January 21, 1859, and at http://www.mrlinfo.org/history/biography/petition.htm through the Morrison-Reeves Library in Richmond, Indiana. Birdsall's comments were not printed in the press and no copy of them has been found. A brief summary of the event is found in IWSA, "Presentation of Petition to the Legislature in 1859," written by Thomas. The standard scholarly article on this event is Pat Creech Scholten, "A Public 'Jollification': The 1859 Women's Rights Petition before the Indiana Legislature," *Indiana Magazine of History* 72 (December 1976): 347–59.
21. *The Lily*, February 1859. *Indianapolis Daily Journal*, January 20, 1859; *Indianapolis Daily State Sentinel*, January 20, 1859. Admittedly, *The Lily* reported on the historic event from the eyes of the women. If one looks at the events from other views, the report is less straightforward. *Brevier's Legislative Reports*, 1859 Regular Session, vol. 2, pp, 55–56, relates the overall excitement and agitation present in the House chambers that day including the taunting of the unmarried representatives. *Journal of the House of Representatives 1859*, Indiana State Library Digital Collections, gives perfunctory comments on the session (157–58), records that the next day at 2:00 p.m. the House met to consider the women's petition and it was referred to the "committee on the rights and inhabitants of this State" (182). On February 10 that committee reported that "it would be inexpedient to legislate on the subject" (472).
22. *Indianapolis Daily Journal*, January 20, 1859, for problems with hearing Thomas's remarks and the mention of Mrs. Ferguson. Ibid., January 22, 1859, for the other remarks.
23. *Indianapolis Daily Journal*, January 22, 1859.
24. Edward T. James, Janet Wilson James, and Paul S. Boyer eds. *Notable American Women, 1607–1950*, vol. 3 (Cambridge: Belknap Press of Harvard University Press, 1917), 552–53; Stan-

ton, Anthony, and Gage, *History of Woman Suffrage*, 311–12; B. F. Austin, ed., *The Temperance Leaders of America*, Part 1 (Saint Thomas, Ontario: Alma College 1896), 20; "Obituary Amanda M. Way," *Pacific Friend* 21 (1914): 14–15. Some of the best work on Amanda Way is found in Hamilton, "Role of Quakerism in the Indiana Woman's Suffrage Movement." Many thanks also to the Indiana Historical Bureau for sharing their historical marker file on Amanda Way.

25. "Mother of Women," *The Woman's Journal* (September 29, 1888); Hamilton, "Role of Quakerism in the Indiana Woman's Suffrage Movement," 40.

26. Hamilton, "The Role of Quakerism in the Indiana Woman's Suffrage Movement," 40–43.

27. Ibid.," includes much information about Thomas throughout the thesis. "Mother of Women"; Pauline T. Heald, "Mary F. Thomas, M.D. Richmond, IND," *Michigan History Magazine* 6 (1922): 369–73 (Heald was Thomas's daughter and this article is taken from a paper she read to the Michigan League of Women Voters in 1920). "Dr. Mary F. Thomas Obituary," *Richmond Evening Item*, August 20, 1888; James and Boyer, eds., *Notable American Women*, 450–51.

28. *History of Wayne County Indiana*, vol. 1 (Chicago: Inter-State Publishing Company, 1884), 606–8.

29. IWSA Minutes (no date), "Some further history of the work of the Indiana Woman Suffrage Association," in Thomas's handwriting.

Chapter 2

1. Recent books about women's war work and the Sanitary Commission include: Jeanie Attie, *Patriotic Toil: Northern Women and the American Civil War* (Ithaca, NY: Cornell University Press, 1998); Judith Ann Giesberg, *Civil War Sisterhood: The U.S. Sanitary Commission and Women's Politics in Transition* (Boston: Northeastern University Press, 2000); Judith Giesberg, *Army at Home: Women and the Civil War on the Northern Home Front* (Chapel Hill: University of North Caroline Press, 2012); and Wendy Hamand Venet, *A Strong-Minded Woman: The Life of Mary A. Livermore* (Amherst: University of Massachusetts Press, 2005).

2. Eleanor Flexnor and Ellen Fitzpatrick, *Century of Struggle: The Woman's Rights Movement in the United States* (Cambridge, MA: Belknap/Harvard University Press, 1996), 99–107. Chapter 7 is concise synopsis of the woman's rights movement during the war.

3. "Some further history of the work of the Indiana Woman Suffrage Association," in Thomas's handwriting, Minutes (no date), Indiana Woman's Suffrage Association Record Book, 1851–1886, Collection SC 1792/BV 2577, Indiana Historical Society William Henry Smith Memorial Library, Indianapolis (hereafter cited as IWSA Minutes).

4. Emma Lou Thornbrough, *Indiana in the Civil War Era, 1850–1880* (Indianapolis: Indiana Historical Society, 1995), 170–76. The state and national sanitary commissions did not always work together. Indiana had a strong, reliable sanitary commission and did not want the guidance of the national organization. W. H. H. Terrell, *Report of the Adjutant General of the State of Indiana*, vol. 1 (Indianapolis: State Printer, 1869), 314–59, for all types of relief work completed in the state.

5. *Indianapolis Daily Journal*, November 18–21, 1863, for the large fair held in Indianapolis. Thornbrough, *Indiana in the Civil War Era*, 170 for fairs in general. Joan Marshall, "Aid for Union Soldiers' Families: A Comfortable Entitlement or a Pauper's Pittance? Indiana, 1861–1865," *Social Service Review* 78 (June 2004): 207–42.

6. Thornbrough, *Indiana in the Civil War Era*, 142, gives the number of Indiana men who served in the Civil War as 196,363. Thornbrough mentions that Indiana's adjutant general, W. H. H. Terrell, gives the number as 208,367 in his final report on the war. The Allegheny arsenal

explosion is found in Giesberg, *Army at Home*, 68–72. For more on Indiana women in the war, see Anita Morgan, "'The Responsibilities of a Community at War': County and State Government Aid to Soldiers' Families during the Civil War," *Indiana Magazine of History* 113 (March 2017): 48–77.

7. Eric L. Hamilton, "The Role of Quakerism in the Indiana Woman's Suffrage Movement, 1851–1885: Towards a More Perfect Freedom for All," master's thesis, Indiana University, 2013, 58–59. Peggy Brase Seigel, "She Went to War: Indiana Women Nurses in the Civil War," *Indiana Magazine of History* 86 (March 1990): 8, 26. "An Act Granting a Pension to Amanda M. Way, as Army Nurse," *Statutes at Large of the United States of America from December 1895 to March 1897*, vol. 29, 1897. "Amanda M. Way," *Civil War Pension Index: General Index to Pension Files, 1861–1934*.

8. "Mother of Women," *Woman's Journal* (September 29, 1888): 307–8.

9. Edward T. James, Janet Wilson James, and Paul S. Boyer eds. *Notable American Women, 1607–1950*, vol. 3 (Cambridge: Belknap Press of Harvard University Press, 1971), 450; "Dr. Mary F. Thomas," *Woman's Journal* (September 1, 1888): 278; Thornbrough, *Indiana in the Civil War Era*, 172–73. For information on Stones River and the large number of women sent to Nashville, see Seigel, "She Went to War," 24.

10."Mother of Women," 307–8; Janet M. Cramer, "For Women and the War: A Cultural Analysis of the *Mayflower*, 1861–1864" in David B. Sachsman, S. Kittrell Rushong, and Debra Reddin van Tuyll, eds., *The Civil War and the Press* (New Brunswick, NJ: Transaction Publishers, 2000), 209–26; and "Samuel G.A. Read, A.M., M.D.," in *The United States Biographical Dictionary and Portrait Gallery of Eminent and Self Made Men: Iowa Volume* (Chicago and New York: American Biographical Publishing Company, 1878), 494–96. Issues of the *Mayflower* are housed at the Schlesinger Library, Radcliffe Institute, Harvard University.

11. *Mayflower*, March 1, 1861; *The United States Biographical Dictionary and Portrait Gallery of Eminent and Self Made Men*, 494–96. More about Read after she moved to Iowa and how the extant issues of the *Mayflower* were discovered is found in Louise R. Noun, *Strong-Minded Women: The Emergence of the Woman-Suffrage Movement in Iowa* (Ames: Iowa State University Press, 1969), 272.

12. Cramer, "For Women and the War," 209–26. The first eight issues of the newspaper have not been found.

13. Thomas's first extant article is found in the *Mayflower*, July 1, 1861. The article on Richmond is found in the July 15, 1861, issue.

14. *Mayflower*, August 15, September 1, October 15, 1861.

15. Ibid., March 1, June 15, 1862.

16. Ibid., November 1, December 1, 1861.

17. Ibid., September 1, June 15, 1862, May 1, 1863.

18. Ibid., August 1, 1861, for Indianapolis, September 1, 1862, for the deaths.

19. Ibid., June 15 and July 1, 1862.

20. Ibid., February [no day] 1864. Noun, *Strong-Minded Women*, 120.

21. *Mayflower*, September 1, 1862.

22. Ibid., December 15, 1861.

23. Thornbrough, *Indiana in the Civil War Era*, 259; *Journal of the House of Representatives of the State of Indiana, 1865 Special Session* (Indianapolis: W. R. Holloway, 1865), 316–17; Flexnor and Fitzpatrick, *Century of Struggle*, 139.

24. Flexnor and Fitzpatrick, *Century of Struggle*, 136–48, and Lori D. Ginzberg, *Elizabeth Cady Stanton* (New York: Hill and Wang, 2009), 119–22.

25. Flexnor and Fitzpatrick, *Century of Struggle*, 137.

26. Ibid., 143.

27. Ginzberg, *Elizabeth Cady Stanton*, 125, and Flexnor and Fitzpatrick, *Century of Struggle*, 137–45.

28. Eric Foner, *A Short History of Reconstruction, 1863–1877* (New York: Harper and Row, 1990), 192.

29. Flexnor and Fitzpatrick, *Century of Struggle*, 145–46.

30. IWSA Minutes, 1869, and *Indianapolis Daily State Sentinel*, June 9, 1869.

31. *Indianapolis Journal*, June 9, 1869.

32. Ibid.

33. Ibid. For Professor A. C. Shortridge, see David Bodenhamer and Robert Barrows, eds., *Encyclopedia of Indianapolis* (Bloomington and Indianapolis: Indiana University Press, 1994), 1,259. Professor Shortridge, for whom Shortridge High School in Indianapolis is named, pushed for the Indianapolis School Board to hire women teachers at a time when Indianapolis public schools were in dire financial circumstances. He noted that women could be paid less than men and also should be hired because they were good teachers. He even opened a training school for women teachers on March 1, 1867, and hired "Nebraska Cropsay, as supervisor of primary instruction for the city." As early as 1836 Professor R. T. Brown advocated for woman suffrage and for women teachers to have equal pay with male teachers. He pushed for Northwestern Christian University to be open to women and taught classes there to both men and women. He then taught at Indiana Medical College in Indianapolis but resigned when the trustees decided to exclude women. This information on Brown is found in Elizabeth Cady Stanton, Susan B. Anthony, and Matilda Gage, eds., *History of Woman Suffrage*, vol. 3 (Rochester, NY: Susan B. Anthony, 1886), 550. For Wilhite see, H. W. Beckwith, *History of Montgomery County* (Chicago: H. H. Hill and N. Iddings Publishers, 1881), 168–69. Also, Karen Bazzani Zach, *Crawfordsville, Athens of Indiana* (Charleston, SC: Arcadia Publishing, 2003), 135. Doctor Mary H. Wilhite attended Penn Medical College. She graduated the same year as Thomas and practiced medicine in Crawfordsville, Indiana. She later held offices in the IWSA. Lizzy Boynton was involved in woman's rights in Crawfordsville even during the Civil War. After her marriage, she lived in Iowa and Illinois, working for woman suffrage in both states. She also wrote several books. See Steven M. Buechler, "Elizabeth Boynton Harbert and the Woman Suffrage Movement, 1870–1896" *Signs* 13 (Autumn 1987): 78–97 and Thomas E. Rodgers, "Hoosier Women and the Civil War Home Front," *Indiana Magazine of History* 97 (June 2001): 105–128.

34. *Indianapolis Journal*, June 9, 1869, for names of attendees. For Reverend Marshall, see B. R. Sulgrove, *History of Indianapolis and Marion County, Indiana* (Philadelphia: I. H. Everts and Company, 1884), 396; for Reverend Ingersoll, see Junius B. Roberts, "Plymouth Church, Indianapolis," *Indiana Magazine of History* 7 (June 1911): 52–60; for Reverend Mendenhall, see Sulgrove, *History of Indianapolis*, 403; and for Reverend Blanchard, see Sulgrove, *History of Indianapolis*, 389.

35. *Indianapolis Journal*, June 9, 1869, for quote by Way.

36. Ibid.

37. Ibid., and *Indianapolis Daily State Sentinel*, June 11, 1869.

38. *Indianapolis Journal*, June 10, 1869, carries the full text of the resolution as introduced with Julian's name. The IWSA minutes contain only the version with his name omitted and does not record the discussion found in both the *Journal* and the *Sentinel*. IWSA Minutes, June 1869.

39. IWSA Minutes, June 1869; *Indianapolis Journal*, June 10, 1869; *Indianapolis Daily State Sentinel*, June 10, 1869.

40. *Indianapolis Journal*, June 10, 1869, and IWSA minutes, June 1869.

41. *Indianapolis Journal*, June 10, 1869; IWSA minutes, June 1869; Ginzberg, *Elizabeth Cady Stanton*, 125, Lucy Stone said "that she would 'be thankful in my soul if *any* body can get out of the terrible pit.'"

42. *Indianapolis Daily State Sentinel*, June 10, 1869, and *Indianapolis Journal*, June 10, 1869. Information about the African American presence in Indiana prior to 1900 is found in Emma Lou Thornbrough, *The Negro in Indiana before 1900: A Study of a Minority* (Indianapolis: Indiana Historical Bureau, 1985).

43. IWSA Minutes, June 1869; *Indianapolis Journal*, June 10, 1869; *Indianapolis Daily Sentinel*, June 10, 1869, p. 4.

44. *Indianapolis Journal*, June 10, 1869, and *Indianapolis Daily State Sentinel*, June 10, 1869.

Chapter 3

1. Minutes, 1870, 1871, Indiana Woman's Suffrage Association Record Book, 1851–1886, Collection SC 1792/BV 2577, Indiana Historical Society William Henry Smith Memorial Library, Indianapolis (hereafter cited as IWSA Minutes); Eleanor Flexnor and Ellen Fitzpatrick, *Century of Struggle: The Woman's Rights Movement in the United States* (Cambridge, MA: Belknap/Harvard University Press, 1996), 145–46. Lori D. Ginzberg, *Elizabeth Cady Stanton* (New York: Hill and Wang, 2009), contains a concise introduction to the national suffragists.

2. Emma Lou Thornbrough, *Indiana in the Civil War Era, 1850–1880* (Indianapolis: Indiana Historical Society, 1995), 260. *Journal of the Indiana State Senate* (Indianapolis: State Printer, 1871), 235–36. The entire debate in the Senate can be found in *Brevier Legislative Reports*, 1871, vol. 12 (Indianapolis: W. H. Drapier, 1871), 292–93, 492–500. The IWSA minutes contain a one-page synopsis of Way's and Swank's visit to the legislature written by Thomas five years after the event.

3. Flexnor and Fitzpatrick, *Century of Struggle*, 158–63. Ellen Carol DuBois, "Outgrowing the Compact of the Fathers: Equal Rights, Woman Suffrage, and the United States Constitution, 1820–1878," *Journal of American History* 73 (December 1987): 836–62, for an explanation of the legal argument. Information about Cary and Douglass is found in Rosalyn Terborg-Penn, *African American Women in the Struggle for the Vote, 1850–1920* (Bloomington: Indiana University Press, 1998).

4. Flexner and Fitzpatrick, *Century of Struggle*, 158–60. Dubois, "Outgrowing the Compact of the Fathers," 860.

5. IWSA Minutes, 1871, November 1873, June 1873, May 1874. A discussion of the 1870s Prohibition movement in Indiana can be found in Thornbrough, *Indiana in the Civil War Era*, 262–65.

6. Ruth Bordin, *Woman and Temperance: The Quest for Power and Liberty, 1873–1900* (New Brunswick, NJ: Rutgers University Press, 1990) is a complete history of the WCTU.

7. For information on Wallace, see David Bodenhamer and Robert G. Barrows, eds., *Encyclopedia of Indianapolis* (Bloomington and Indianapolis: Indiana University Press, 1994), 1408–9; Linda C. Gugin and James E. St. Clair, eds., *Indiana's 200: The People Who Shaped the Hoosier State* (Indianapolis: Indiana Historical Society Press, 2015), 364–66; and Susan Vogelsang, "Zerelda Wallace: Indiana's Conservative Radical," *Traces of Indiana and Midwestern History* 4, no. 3 (Summer 1992): 35–41.

8. *Indianapolis News*, November 4, 1881. Wisconsin suffragists also suffered/benefited because of a close identification with temperance legislation. See Genevieve G. McBride, *On*

Wisconsin Women: Working for Their Rights from Settlement to Suffrage (Madison: University of Wisconsin Press, 1993), 94–99.

9. *Indianapolis News*, June 21, 1919.

10. Ray E. Boomhower, *"But I Do Clamor": May Wright Sewall, A Life 1844–1920* (Zionsville, IN: Guild Press of Indiana, 2001), Chapter 2 for Sewall's suffrage career. Elizabeth Cady Stanton, Susan B. Anthony, and Matilda Gage, eds., *History of Woman Suffrage*, vol. 3 (Rochester, NY: Susan B. Anthony, 1886), 535–36 for the formation of the Indianapolis suffrage group, quote on p. 535.

11. Erin K. Kelley, "'A Worthwhile Existence:' The Conservatism and Consciousness of Indianapolis's Clubwomen, 1875–1920" (master's thesis, IUPUI, 2003), Chapter 2 gives a thorough look at the creation of the Indianapolis Woman's Club and includes a description of the dustup between McKay and Sewall. See Theodore Lakin Steele Manuscript Collection, 1868–1913, MO263, box 1, folder 7, Indiana Historical Society for the many letters about the AWSA meeting. *Indiana State Sentinel*, November 20, 1878, details the meeting itself. The *Sentinel* could not help but note that Stone was very "motherly looking" and had no "expression of sternness." Boomhower, *"But I do Clamor,"* 34–36.

12. See Steele Manuscript Collection, box 1, folder 7, for the correspondence. It is difficult to find personal letters from Livermore and she destroyed much of her own personal correspondence. Her letters to McKay shed light on her effusive private personality and contain critiques of Hoosier suffragists. See also Kelley, "A Worthwhile Existence," 55–56.

13. *Indianapolis Indiana State Sentinel*, February 7, 1877, and Flexnor and Fitzpatrick, *Century of Struggle*, 165.

14. IWSA Minutes, 1880; Stanton, Anthony, and Gage eds., *History of Woman Suffrage*, 537.

15. Clifton Phillips, *Indiana in Transition: The Emergence of an Industrial Commonwealth, 1880–1920* (Indianapolis: Indiana Historical Bureau and Indiana Historical Society, 1968), 1–19 for the 1880 elections and 1881 legislative session. Charles Kettleborough, *Constitution Making in Indiana*, vol. 2, *1851–1916* (Indianapolis: Indiana Historical Bureau, 1975), 193. *Brevier Legislative Report*, vols. 19–20, Regular and Special Session 1881, pp. 191–93, 206. Stanton, Anthony, and Gage, eds., *History of Woman Suffrage*, 540.

16. *Brevier Legislative Report*, 1881, pp. 228–30; *Bloomington Progress*, March 9, 1881; Bodenhamer and Barrows, eds., *Encyclopedia of Indianapolis*, 683 for Hinton; *Indianapolis News*, February 26, 1881; Kettleborough, *Constitution Making in Indiana*, 193–94.

17. *Brevier Legislative Reports*, 1881, pp. 145–49; Kettleborough, *Constitution Making in Indiana*, 194–95; *Indianapolis News*, April 16, 1881.

18. *Indiana Tribune*, February 19, March 12, 1881.

19. Ibid., July 19, 1879, May 22, 1880.

20. Ibid., April 16, 1881.

21. Phillips, *Indiana in Transition*, 18–19.

22. IWSA Minutes, 1881. The newspaper cannot be found.

23. *Kokomo Weekly Dispatch*, June 16, 1881, and Nathan Gallagher, "'The Coming Storm': Women's Suffrage in Indiana 1851–1881" (unpublished undergraduate paper, IUPUI).

24. IWSA Minutes, 1881.

25. Ibid.

26. Ibid., Special October 1881 Meeting.

27. *Indianapolis News*, May 19, 20, 1882.

28. Stanton, Anthony, and Gage, eds., *History of Woman Suffrage*, 543.

29. Robert C. Kriebel, *Where the Saints Have Trod: The Life of Helen Gougar* (West Lafayette, IN: Purdue University Press, 1985), 85–87; *Indianapolis News*, November 29, 1882; *Terre Haute Saturday Evening Mail*, November 25, 1882.

30. Kriebel, *Where the Saints Have Trod*, 91–92, 94.

31. Ibid. 91; *Terre Haute Saturday Evening Mail*, April 14, 1883.

32. *Brevier Legislative Reports, 1883 Regular Session*, vol. 21, p. 142 for Foulke; *Bloomington Telephone*, February 3, 1883; and Kettleborough, *Constitution Making in Indiana*, 232–33. Information on Foulke found in William Dudley Foulke, *A Hoosier Autobiography* (New York: Oxford University Press, 1922).

33. Susan B. Anthony and Ida Husted Harper, eds., *History of Woman Suffrage*, vol. 4 (Rochester, NY: Susan B. Anthony, 1902), 614–15.

34. Ibid., 614; L. Alene Sloan, "Some Aspects of the Woman Suffrage Movement in Indiana" (PhD diss., Ball State University, 1982), 100–107; *Indiana Tribüne*, May 4, 1887.

35. *The Woman's Journal* (September 1, 1888); *Richmond Telegram*, August 23, 1888.

36. Doctor Mary Thomas to May Wright Sewall, November 14, 1887, and clipping about the statewide meetings found with the letter, box 1, folder 1, Grace Julian Clarke Manuscript Collection, L033, Indiana State Library, Indianapolis.

Chapter 4

1. Eleanor Flexnor and Ellen Fitzpatrick, *Century of Struggle: The Woman's Rights Movement in the United States* (Cambridge, MA: Belknap/Harvard University Press, 1996), 169–70, 214.

2. Susan B. Anthony and Ida Husted Harper, eds., *History of Woman Suffrage*, vol. 4 (Rochester, NY: Susan B. Anthony, 1902), 164 and Flexner and Fitzpatrick, *Century of Struggle*, Chapter 16.

3. Robert C. Kriebel, *Where the Saints Have Trod: The Life of Helen Gougar* (West Lafayette, IN: Purdue University Press, 1985) and Ray E. Boomhower, *"But I Do Clamor": May Wright Sewall, A Life 1844–1920* (Zionsville, IN: Guild Press of Indiana, 2001) are the most recent biographies. Elizabeth Boyton Harbert, a suffragist and native of Crawfordsville, Indiana, wrote a column for the Chicago-based *Inter-Ocean* at about the same time as these columns. More on Harbert is found in Steven Buechler, *The Transformation of the Woman Suffrage Movement: The Case for Illinois, 1850–1920* (New Brunswick, NJ: Rutgers University Press, 1986), especially Chapter 4.

4. Kriebel, *Where the Saints Have Trod*, 42–53, 66–67.

5. Ibid., 75–76. For the 1887 Indiana National Woman Suffrage Association request to Gougar see, National Woman Suffrage Association for Indiana Records, 1887–1893, Collection BV 2612, p. 3–5, Indiana Historical Society William Henry Smith Memorial Library, Indianapolis (hereafter NWSAI) and *Indianapolis News*, May 4, 1887, and May 5, 1887.

6. NWSAI, p. 10 for the notice of the 1887 meetings, p. 13 for the report, and pp. 14, 19 for the membership and financial results of the meetings. A newspaper clipping dated November 14, 1887, is also found in the Grace Julian Clarke Collection, L033, box 1, folder 1, Indiana State Library, Indianapolis.

7. Mike McCormick, "Historical Perspective: Women's Suffrage Convention 120 Years Ago," *Terre Haute Tribune Star*, December 29, 2007, and *Wabash Daily Express*, November 25, 1887.

8. *Bloomington Telephone*, November 15, 1887. Professors James A. Woodburn and William Lowe Bryan of Indiana University gave short speeches in favor of woman suffrage at this meeting.

9. *Indianapolis Journal*, May 16, 17, 1888, and NWSAI, pp. 27–29 for the meeting and p. 30 for presentation of the resolutions to the political parties.

10. NWSAI, 39–45, 48, and Anthony and Harper, eds., *History of Woman Suffrage*, 615–16.

11. *Indianapolis Journal*, October 12, 13, 15, 1889. Anthony and Harper, eds., *History of Woman Suffrage*, 615–16. List of the officers of each organization also found in NWSAI, 41.

12. Kriebel, *Where the Saints Have Trod*, 112–19.

13. NWSAI, 47–57; *The Woman's Journal* (June 1891); *Indianapolis Journal*, December 15, 16, 1891; NWSAI, 64.

14. Kriebel, *Where the Saints Have Trod*, 139, 148 for Gougar's comment on Anthony; Boomhower, *"But I Do Clamor,"* 94–97; *Indianapolis Journal*, May 20, 1893, for the headlines and comment about Gougar's use of "aggressive methods"; *Indianapolis News*, May 20, 1893, for the comment on enemies; and *Indianapolis News*, June 4, 1894, p. 6, for a letter Gougar had published that severely criticized Anthony. The Populist Party grew from the Farmer's Alliances, a political/social group that lobbied for changes in laws that would help farmers. Mary Lease and other women campaigned for the party.

15. *Indianapolis News*, November 6, 7, 1894, and *Indianapolis Journal*, November 7, 1894. The news stories may have been supplied by someone to the papers as they are very similar in wording.

16. *Indianapolis News*, November 6, 1894; *Indianapolis Journal*, November 7, 1894; *Crawfordsville Weekly Journal*, November 30, 1894.

17. *Indianapolis News*, January 10, 1895; *Crawfordsville Weekly Journal*, January 18, 1895 (p. 3, for Gougar in local court); *Indianapolis Journal*, February 20, 1897; *Terre Haute Semi-Weekly Express*, February 26, 1897; *Indianapolis Journal*, February 25, 1897 (p. 6, for Supreme Court decision against Gougar); Anthony and Harper, eds., *History of Woman Suffrage*, 621–23.

18. David Bodenhamer and Robert G. Barrows, eds., *Encyclopedia of Indianapolis* (Bloomington and Indianapolis: Indiana University Press, 1994), 1253–54; Elizabeth Cady Stanton, Susan B. Anthony, and Matilda Gage, eds., *History of Woman Suffrage*, vol. 3 (Rochester, NY: Susan B. Anthony, 1886), 556, for information about Sewall's newspaper work; Boomhower, *"But I Do Clamor,"* 85–89 (Sewall became the International Council president in 1899 at its London meeting).

19. Boomhower, *"But I Do Clamor,"* 92–3, and Karen J. Blair, *The Clubwoman as Feminist: True Womanhood Redefined, 1868–1914* (New York: Holmes and Meier Publishers, 1980), Chapter 6.

20. Genevieve G. McBride, *On Wisconsin Women: Working for Their Rights from Settlement to Suffrage* (Madison: University of Wisconsin, 1993), Chapter 5; Buechler, *Transformation of the Woman Suffrage Movement*, Chapter 4; Elizabeth Lindsay Davis, *Lifting as They Climb: An Historical Record of the National Association of Colored Women* (Washington, DC: National Association of Colored Women, 1933; New York: G. K. Hall and Company, 1996); and Erin K. Kelley, "'A Worthwhile Existence:' The Conservatism and Consciousness of Indianapolis's Clubwomen, 1875–1920" (master's thesis, IUPUI, 2003), especially Chapter 3.

21. Grace Gates Courtney, comp. and Arcada Stark Balz, ed. *History Indiana Federation of Clubs* (Indianapolis: Indiana Federation of Clubs, 1939), 25.

22. Courtney, comp. and Balz, ed., *History Indiana Federation of Clubs*, 27–30; Boomhower, *"But I Do Clamor,"* 66–70; McBride, *On Wisconsin Women*, 149–50.

23. Courtney, comp. and Balz, ed., *History Indiana Federation of Clubs*, 31–34, 58–61.

24. Ibid., 64–65.

25. Ibid., 66–79.

26. Ibid., 116–19.

27. Ibid., 224.

28. *Indianapolis News*, February 5, 1897; *Indianapolis Journal*, February 5, 6, 1897.

29. Susan B. Anthony to May Wright Sewall, August19, 1898, Clarke Collection.

30. Program from Plymouth Church meeting dated December 1899 and Dear Madam circular from Clarke and Peirce dated November 28, 1899, ibid.

31. *Indianapolis Journal*, December 7, 1899; *Bloomington Progress*, December 8, 1899; Gougar to McWhirter, December 28, 1899, box 5, "Woman's Suffrage" folder, Mrs. F. T. (Luella) McWhirter Papers, Lilly Library, Indiana University, Bloomington; Kriebel, *Where the Saints Have Trod*, 179–82 for Gougar's activities in 1899.

32. *Indianapolis Journal*, December 8, 1899.

33. *Indianapolis News*, December 8, 1899; *Indianapolis Journal*, December 9, 10, 1899.

34. Susan B. Anthony to Grace Julian Clarke, December 18, 1899, Anthony to Clarke, January 11, 1900, and Anthony to Clarke, January 20, 1900, box 1, folder 2, Clarke Collection. See also, Anthony and Harper, eds., *History of Woman Suffrage*, 616.

35. Anthony to Clarke, December 18, 1899, Anthony to Clarke, January 11, 1900, and Anthony to Clarke, January 20, 1900, box 1, folder 2, Clarke Collection.

36. Anthony and Harper, eds., *History of Woman Suffrage*, 617.

Chapter 5

1. Genevieve G. McBride, *On Wisconsin Women: Working for Their Rights from Settlement to Suffrage* (Madison: University of Wisconsin, 1993), 210–13 for similar tactics in Wisconsin; Steven Buechler, *The Transformation of the Woman Suffrage Movement: The Case for Illinois, 1850–1920* (New Brunswick, NJ: Rutgers University Press, 1986), 174–75 for a similar tactics in Illinois; Eleanor Flexnor and Ellen Fitzpatrick, *Century of Struggle: The Woman's Rights Movement in the United States* (Cambridge, MA: Belknap/Harvard University Press, 1996), 241–47 for New York.

2. Ida Husted Harper, ed., *History of Woman Suffrage*, vol. 6 (Salem, New Hampshire: Ayer Company Publishers, 1984), 166–68, and Barbara Anne Springer, "Ladylike Reformers: Indiana Women and Progressive Reform, 1900–1920" (PhD diss., Indiana University, 1985), 76–77.

3. Harriet Taylor Upton to Clarke, September 20, 1909 and Mrs. M. D. Breckinridge to Clarke, July 13, 1910, box 1, folder 3, Grace Julian Clarke Collection, Indiana State Library, Indianapolis; Springer, "Ladylike Reformers," 77; Flexnor and Fitzpatrick, *Century of Struggle*, 168–69 for school suffrage elsewhere.

4. Scrapbook 422-06, newspaper article with no date or name of newspaper for information on the school board election and the remark by Keller, Clarke Collection; *Indianapolis News*, November 3, 1909, contains remarks on wives' influence; and *Indianapolis Star*, November 3, 1909, for number of votes cast.

5. *Indianapolis Star*, February 7, 1910.

6. Springer, "Ladylike Reformers," 79–81 (p. 79 for membership numbers); *Indianapolis Star*, September 9, 1910; *Indianapolis Sun*, January 18, 1911, Scrapbook 422-06, Clarke Collection.

7. Scrapbook, 422-06; *Indianapolis Sun*, January 18, 1911, for an article about the desks. *Indianapolis Star*, February 3, 1911; *Indianapolis News*, February 3, 1911; Springer, "Ladylike Reformers," 88–90.

8. Clarke to Ida Husted Harper, April 1, 1911, box 1, folder 4, Clarke Collection. Clarke also noted that English suffragette Sylvia Pankhurst had just visited Indianapolis. The *Indianapolis News* reported that a crowd of 600 to 700 heard her speak on March 23, 1911. Men who heard her speak included authors Meredith Nicholson and Booth Tarkington. *Indianapolis News*, March 24, 1911, and *Indianapolis Star*, March 24, 1911. Flexner and Fitzpatrick, *Century of Struggle*, 243–44, briefly discusses suffragettes.

9. Series of circulars from the Woman's Franchise League, beginning in June 1911, box 1, folder 4, Clarke Collection, and *Indianapolis News*, April 22, 1911.

10. Clifton Phillips, *Indiana in Transition: The Emergence of an Industrial Commonwealth, 1880–1920* (Indianapolis: Indiana Historical Bureau and Indiana Historical Society, 1968), 110–14.

11. *Indianapolis Star*, April 2, 3, 4, 5, 1912, and *Indianapolis News*, April 4, 1912. The *News* ran a series of front-page editorial cartoons about suffrage from April 4–6, 1912, including a very pointed jab at the proposed Marshall constitution.

12. *Indianapolis News*, April 4, 1912; *Indianapolis Star*, April 4, 1912.

13. Salvation Army speech found in *Indianapolis News*, February 19, 1912; *Indianapolis Star*, April 24, 1912; and *Indianapolis News*, April 24, 1912.

14. See August 10, p. 28 for leaflets and August 14, 1912, p. 30, September 6, 1912, p. 31, September 21, 1912, p. 32, September 28, 1912, p. 35 for arranging for candidate talks, Woman's Franchise League of Indiana Minute Book, box 1, folder 1, League of Women Voters of Indiana Collection, M612, Indiana Historical Society William Henry Smith Memorial Library, Indianapolis (hereafter cited as LWVIC).

15. May 25, 1912, p. 7 for baseball game and auto tour and June 1, 1912, p. 9 for more on the auto tour plans, box 1, folder 1, LWVIC.

16. June 15, 1912, p. 15 and June 22, 1912, p. 17 for baseball game, box 1, folder 1, ibid.

17. *Indianapolis News* June 6, 1912, and *Indianapolis Star*, June 6, 1912.

18. *Indianapolis Star*, June 13, 1912.

19. *Indianapolis News*, June 18, 1912, for an earlier postponement of the event. *Indianapolis Star*, June 22, 1912, and *Indianapolis News*, June 22, 1912.

20. *Indianapolis Star*, June 22, 1912; *Indianapolis News*, June 22, 1912; June 21, 1913, p. 114 for the fete held at Clarke's the following year, box 1, folder 1, LWVIC. The lyrics for "The Blue Lady" cannot be found.

21. June 22, 1912, p. 17–18, box 1, folder 1, LWVIC.

22. *Indianapolis News*, June 18, 1912, and *Indianapolis Star*, June 22, 1912.

23. *Indianapolis News*, June 25, 1912. Barnes quote found in *The Crisis* 4, no. 5 (September 1912). *Indianapolis News*, July 1, 1916, for more about Barnes.

24. Flanner House meeting, *Indianapolis Recorder*, June 29, 1912; July meeting, *Indianapolis News*, July 9, 1912; Second Christian Church meeting, *Indianapolis Star*, August 1, 4, 1912; information on Garrison, *Muncie Star Press*, January 22, July 22, 1912; and Mount Zion Church meeting, *Indianapolis Star*, October 6, 1912. Information about Flanner House is found in David Bodenhamer and Robert G. Barrows, eds., *Encyclopedia of Indianapolis* (Bloomington and Indianapolis: Indiana University Press, 1994), 577.

25. Phillips, *Indiana in Transition*, 117–20.

26. *Indianapolis News*, January 28, 1913, and *Indianapolis Star*, January 28, 1913.

27. *Indianapolis News*, January 28, 1913, and *Indianapolis Star*, January 28, 1913.

28. *Indianapolis Star*, January 31, 1913; *Woman's Journal* 44, no. 6 (February 8, 1913); *Indianapolis News*, March 1, 1913, January 4, 1913, p. 59–60, and February 1, 1913, p. 69, box 1, folder 1, LWVIC.

29. A concise summary of the Washington, DC, parade is found in Flexnor and Fitzpatrick, *Century of Struggle*, 256–57. *Indianapolis Star*, March 3, 1913, for what the women hoped would happen in Washington, DC. *Richmond Palladium*, March 1, 1913, mentions Harriet Noble and Mary (Mrs. Ovid Butler) Tarkington Jameson and the banner as they made their way to Washington. February 26, 1913, p. 78 and March 1, 1913, p. 79–80 for the Indiana event, box 1, folder 1, LWVIC.

30. *Indianapolis Star*, March 4, 1913, which includes a photo of the suffragists; *Indianapolis News*, March 4, 1913, includes a photo of the women before they entered the building, which

the newspaper stated, they "besieged." At the start of the legislative session Governor Samuel Ralston had received a letter from a Colorado man who stated, "women are trouble makers" and suggested that Ralston have the legislature enact a "woman suffrage county option" law similar to county option laws for alcoholic drinks. There is no indication if Ralston responded. The letter is found in Correspondence Woman Suffrage, box 28, folder 28, Samuel M. Ralston Papers, 1913–1917, Indiana State Archives, Commission on Public Records, Indianapolis.

31. *Indianapolis News*, May 2, 1913, for Keller's comment and the meeting. Another report on the meeting is found in *Richmond Palladium*, May 2, 1913. Events for the year are seen in May 17, 1913, p. 99–100; May 31, p. 104–06; June 7, 1913, p. 107–08; July 12, 1913, p. 116–17; December 6, p. 157–58; December 13, 1913, p. 159, Box 1, Folder 1, LWVC. Speakers Bureau flyer found in Scrapbook 422–07, Clarke Collection.

32. *Indianapolis Star,* May 2, 3, 1914, and *Indianapolis News*, May 2, 1914, for a photo of the street meeting. Information about W. D. Headrick is found in Carl Painter, "The Progressive Party in Indiana," *Indiana Magazine of History* 16 (September 1920): 173–283.

33. *Indianapolis News*, May 2, 1914; *Indianapolis Star*, May 3, 1914.

34. *Indianapolis News*, May 2, 1914.

35. Flexnor and Fitzpatrick, *Century of Struggle*, 183–84 and Karen Blair, *The Clubwoman as Feminist: True Womanhood Redefined, 1868–1914* (New York: Holmes and Meier Publishers, 1980), 108–10 for an introduction to friction between clubs. *Indianapolis Recorder*, August 15, 1914, discusses the "echo meeting" in Indianapolis following the National Association of Colored Woman's Clubs annual meeting held at Wilburforce University. *Indianapolis Recorder*, February 7, 1914, March 28, 1914, September 19, 1914, October 17, 24, 1914, April 10, 1915, June 24, 1916, August 19, 1916, October 7, 21, 1916, and November 18, 1916. For Terre Haute, *Terre Haute Daily Tribune*, October 31, 1918. McBride, *On Wisconsin Women*, 214, suggests that both low population and the absence of an African American newspaper led to less organization among African American women there, but that was not the circumstances in Indianapolis. Carrie Barnes Ross and her husband settled in Boston, but their marriage was very short. In 1918 Carrie gave birth to their son Hubert Barnes Ross and died a few weeks later leaving her infant and husband behind. Madame Walker went to Boston and found that Barnes had surgery and never recovered from the trauma. Her husband later enlisted in World War I, survived, and died from unknown causes in 1921. Their son went to live with his father's sibling and became a well-known anthropologist in later life. Walker left the child $10,000 in her will. Barnes's life can be traced through the Federal Population Census for Marion County, Indiana; *Indianapolis News*, July 1, 1916; and Walker to F. B. Ransom, April 27, 1918, about the baby's birth, April 30, 1918, about Ross's death, box 1, folder 10, about Madame C .J. Walker leaving $10,000 to the baby in her will, box 1, folder 15, Madame C. J. Walker Collection, M 399. Ross's son's career is found in Ira E. Harrison, "Hubert B. Ross, the Anthropologist Who Was," in *African-American Pioneers in Anthropology*, Ira E. Harrison and Faye V. Harrison, eds. (Chicago: University of Illinois Press, 1999), 265–73.

36. *Indianapolis Star*, September 6, 1914; August 15, 29, pp. 234–39, box 1, folder 1, LWVIC. *Logansport Pharos-Reporter*, March 13, 1915; and article by Clarke, Scrapbook, 422–08, Clarke Collection.

37. Spring, "Ladylike Reformers," 142–43.

38. Clarke to Luella McWhirter, November 12, 1914, McWhirter to "My dear Mrs. President," January 28, 1915, for McWhirter's reference to herself as "Acting President," miscellaneous correspondence and especially postcards dated, February 10, 11, 12, 15, 25, 26, 1915, box 2, folder

labeled "Legislative Council of Indiana Women," Mrs. F. T. (Luella) McWhirter Papers, Lilly LIbrary, Indiana University, Bloomington. See also, Springer, "Ladylike Reformers," 140–53.

39. Helen Benbridge to Clarke, July 7, 1915, September 3, 1915, box 1, folder 8, Clarke Collection.

40. Helen Baumgartner to Clarke, July 22, 1915, August 5, 1915, Benbridge to Clarke, August 13 and 17, 1915, Bacon to Clarke, August 14, 1915, Clarke to McWhirter, August 14, 1915, Kehrer to Clarke, August 13, 1915, McWhirter to Clarke, August 23, 1915, box 1, folder 8, Clarke Collection. Carrie D. Hageman to McWhirter, July 11, 1915, box 5, folder labeled "Woman's Suffrage," McWhirter Collection.

41. Clarke to Stimson, August 28, 1915, Clarke to Virginia Meredith, August 30, 1915, box 1, folder 8, Clarke Collection.

42. A series of editorial cartoons about the Federation of Clubs meeting ran in the *Fort Wayne Daily News*, October 17, 1914, October 28, 30, 1915. Articles include *Fort Wayne Daily News*, October 29, 30, 1915. *Terre Haute Tribune*, October 29, 1915, for Fairbanks and beer.

43. Letter from the WFL dated November 20, 1915 and minutes from the board meeting and the vote to oust Stimson dated November 18, 1915, box 1, folder 9, Clarke Collection. *Indianapolis News*, November 9, 1915, and *Indianapolis Star*, November 9, 1915.

Chapter 6

1. Handwritten speech by Doctor Keller, no date, box 3, folder 2, Grace Julian Clarke Collection, Indiana State Library, Indianapolis. Voters in Warren County and Porter County are found in the *Hoosier Suffragist*, August 22, October 26, 1917. Also for Warren County, *Indianapolis News*, June 6, 1917.

2. Eleanor Flexnor and Ellen Fitzpatrick, *Century of Struggle: The Woman's Rights Movement in the United States* (Cambridge, MA: Belknap/Harvard University Press, 1996), 255–68, quote on 266.

3. Ibid.

4. Both major newspapers carried reports of the suffrage events: *Indianapolis News*, February 5, March 18, 1916, for the quote from Barker; March 20, 31, 1916; April 6, 14, 1916, for vote total and for partial or full suffrage. *Indianapolis Star*, March 18, April 14, 15, 1916. The Chicago parade coverage includes *Indianapolis News*, May 20, 1916; *Indianapolis Star*, June 7, 1916 (complete with photos of some suffragists who attended); and June 8, 1916, for the list of the women who braved the fierce storm and more photos. League of Women Voters of Indiana Collection, M612, Indiana Historical Society William Henry Smith Memorial Library, Indianapolis (hereafter cited as LWVIC). "Why Parade?" broadside, box 3, folder 6, Grace Julian Clarke Collection, Indiana State Library, Indianapolis. The Wisconsin delegation is described in Genevieve G. McBride, *On Wisconsin Women: Working for Their Rights from Settlement to Suffrage* (Madison: University of Wisconsin, 1993), 265–66. Information on Eleanor Barker is found in Logan Esarey, *History of Indiana from Its Exploration to 1922*, vol. 4 (Dayton: Dayton Historical Publications, 1924), 388–89.

5. "Congressional Conference" and May 18, 1916, League Circular, box 1, folder 4, June 13, 1916, LWVIC. For the complete history of the repeated attempts at amalgamation see, box 3, folder 2, Clarke Collection. For Catt in Iowa, Louise R. Noun, *Strong-Minded Women: The Emergence of the Woman-Suffrage Movement in Iowa* (Ames: Iowa State University Press, 1969), 252–57.

6. News of the upcoming meeting is found in *Indianapolis News*, June 14, 1916, and *Indianapolis Star*, June 14, 1916. *Indianapolis Star*, June 18, 23, 24, 25, 1916, for more on the Congressional Union. *Indianapolis News*, June 17, 1916, for photos of some suffragists; June 20, 1916, has a brief report on the WFL/ESA meeting; June 21, 1916, for the "harmony flies out the window" report; and June 24, 1916, for reports on the automobile parade complete with a photo. The *Richmond Palladium*, June 27, 1916, has details about a street meeting in Richmond, apparently the biggest to that day, led by Barker and Hill.

7. *Indianapolis Recorder*, June 24, 1916, for hearing Catt speak, and August 19, October 7, 1916, for meetings. The letter from Sickler is found in November 18, 1916.

8. *Indianapolis News* September 25, 1916. *Indianapolis Star*, September 24, 1916, for a photo of the rally with suffragists prominently placed in the balcony. In the *Indianapolis Recorder* November 18, 1916, Alma Sickler stressed that women who participated in the parade and rally did so as individuals and not as members of the WFL.

9. *Indianapolis Star*, July 2, 1916. Franchise League Circular, October 6, 1916, box 1, folder 4, and Franchise League Circular, January 12, 1917, box 1, folder 5, LWVIC. James P. Goodrich to Luella McWhirter, January 13, 1917, box 5, folder "Woman's Suffrage," Mrs. F. T. (Luella) McWhirter Papers, Lilly Library, Indiana University, Bloomington.

10. Jennifer M. Kalvaitis, "Indianapolis Women Working for the Right to Vote: The Forgotten Drama of 1917" (master's thesis, IUPUI, 2013), 17–18. Letter dated April 24, 1917, mentions their location in the statehouse, box 5, folder "Woman's Suffrage," McWhirter Papers, as does an extensive, in-depth article complete with a history of the Woman's Legislative Council in the *Indianapolis News*, February 24, 1917. The *News* stated that granting women lobbyists a room in a statehouse had been done in only one other state. *The Woman's Journal*, February 27, 1917, mentions that the council shared the room with the press. *Terre Haute Star* , February 27, 1917, for more on the staff. The ESA and WFL had an agreement to merge in December 1916, but the merger ever took place. See *Indianapolis News*, December 8, 1916.

11. *Indianapolis News*, January 20, 1917, for antisuffragists, and January 22, 1917, for the response from Charity Dye and from a suffragist known as H. T. J.

12. *Indianapolis News*, January 23, 1917, for stenographers and librarians; *Indianapolis News*, January 24, 1917, for Vassar graduates; *Indianapolis News*, January 25, 1917, for physicians; *Indianapolis Star*, January 23, 1917, for a fictionalized account of the nineteen women and for a letter to the editor from Grace Julian Clarke, another prosuffrage response from "HJT," and a sarcastic missive to the nineteen antisuffragists from Clara Nixon Bates; and *Indianapolis Star*, January 24, 1917, for a response from an "anti."

13. Flexner and Fitzpatrick, *Century of Struggle*, Chapter 22 for a concise and thorough analysis of antisuffrage.

14. Letter dated January 27, 1917 and letter dated January 29, 1917, box 1, folder 5, LWVIC.

15. Franchise League Circular, February 9, 1917, box 1, folder 5, ibid.; Sara Messing Stern to Luella McWhirter, no date, but details indicate 1917, box 5, folder "Woman's Suffrage," McWhirter Collection.

16. *Indianapolis News*, February 14, 1917, and *Indianapolis Star*, February 14, 15, 1917, for an antisuffrage letter to the editor.

17. *Indianapolis News*, February 16, 1917.

18. Ibid., February 17, 1917.

19. Kalvaitis, "Indianapolis Women Working for the Right to Vote," 34–35; Charles Kettleborough, *Constitution Making in Indiana*, vol. 3 (Indianapolis: Indiana Historical Bureau, 1977), 40–42; *Indianapolis Star*, February 23, 1917.

20. *Indianapolis Star*, February 28, 1917, for the suffrage celebration; *Indianapolis News* , February 28, 1917, for the signing of the bill; Kalvaitis, "Indianapolis Women Working for the Right to Vote," 35–36; Kettleborough, *Constitution Making*, 40–42.

21. Kalvaitis, "Indianapolis Women Working for the Right to Vote," 36–37; Kettleborough, *Constitution Making*, 24–27.

22. Clifton Phillips, *Indiana in Transition: The Emergence of an Industrial Commonwealth, 1880–1920* (Indianapolis: Indiana Historical Bureau and Indiana Historical Society, 1968), 497; Jason Lantzer, *Prohibition Is Here to Stay: The Reverend Edward S. Shumaker and the Dry Crusade in America* (South Bend, IN: University of Notre Dame, 2009), 80–83; *Indianapolis News*, February 9, 1917, for bill signing.

23. League Circular, March 6, 1917, box 2, folder 1, Clarke Collection. *Terre Haute Daily Tribune*, March 18, 1917. Mabel Curry was on a speaking tour of the state and by April 1 she had rallied suffragists in Lafayette and Indianapolis. *Terre Haute Daily Tribune*, April 1, 1917.

24. *Terre Haute Daily Tribune*, April 19, 1917; *Indianapolis News*, April 19, 1917; *Indianapolis Star*, April 19, 1917.

25. *Indianapolis News*, March 28, April 7, August 9, 1917, for Barker leaving the Woman's Party; *Indianapolis Star*, September 19, 1917, for Barker and Republican Party office; *Indianapolis Star*, July 22, 1917, for Clarke's comments; Flexnor and Fitzpatrick, *Century of Struggle*, 275–80 for the Woman's Party and picketing the White House.

26. Examples of women's war work can be found in *The Hoosier Suffragist*, August 22, October 26, 1917, February (no day), April (no day), and other issues. On a larger scale, see Flexnor and Fitzpatrick, *Century of Struggle*, 280–81.

27. *The Indiana Forum*, May 12, 1917, V422-10, Clarke Collection; Allison Stuart to Marie Edwards, April 23, 1917, box 1, folder 5, LWVIC.

28. Barbara Anne Springer, "Ladylike Reformers: Indiana Women and Progressive Reform, 1900–1920" (PhD diss., Indiana University, 1985), 200 for Bennett; Kettleborough, *Constitution Making*, 43–65; Kalvaitis, "Indianapolis Women Working for the Right to Vote," 60–65; and Marie Edwards to William Thornton, June 30, 1917, and Thornton to Edwards, July 2, 1917, box 1, folder 5, LWVIC.

29. *Indianapolis News*, June 23, 1917, and Flexnor and Fitzpatrick, *Century of Struggle*, 282

30. *Indianapolis Star*, March 25, 1917, announced the "Home Study Class" that ran in the paper until June 3, 1917; *Indianapolis News*, May 24, 1917, for Keller and Goodrich; *Indianapolis News* June 6, 1917, for Frances Berry Coston article; and Darlene Clark Hine, *When the Truth Is Told: A History of Black Women's Culture and Community in Indiana, 1875–1950* (Indianapolis: National Council of Negro Women, Indianapolis Section, 1981), 44. More information about Coston is found in William Henry Harrison, Jr., *Colored Girls and Boys' Inspiring United States History and A Heart to Heart Talk about White Folks* (Allentown, PA: Searle and Dressler Company, 1921), 138–39. Her obituary is found in *Indianapolis Recorder*, July 23, 1960. A graduate of Berea College, she also did graduate coursework at Butler University, Indiana University, Harvard University, Columbia University, and the University of Chicago.

31. *Indianapolis News*, June 30, 1917, displays photographs of the first women to register to vote in many counties; telegrams to Marie Edwards from A. E. Stuart, June 25, 1917, and from Ele Stansbury, June 28, 1917, box 1, folder 5, LWVIC.

32. *Indianapolis News*, June 30, 1917.

33. Ibid. Elizabeth Hubbard was probably the fifty-year-old laundress and wife of Bluford Hubbard found in the1920 Federal Census for Bartholomew County, Indiana. It is not possible to clearly identify Fanny Davis.

34. For Curry, *Terre Haute Daily Tribune*, June 17, 1917, and *Indianapolis News*, June 30, 1917. More news on hundreds of women registering to vote found in *Indianapolis News*, June 28, 1917.

35. Springer, "Ladylike Reformers," 201–3.

36. Kalvaitis, "Indianapolis Women Working for the Right to Vote," 66; Springer, "Ladylike Reformers," 203; and *The Hoosier Suffragist*, August 22, 1917, for the quote on the ballot boxes. A detailed article in the *Indianapolis Star* explained how women must have separate ballot boxes in case the law was challenged and it was decided that women could not vote. With separate ballot boxes, the women's votes could be easily discarded, and the entire election would not be invalidated. The bipartisan committee that created this interpretation included the state attorney general, the Republican and Democratic state chairs, and one other Republican and Democrat. The article is also extremely useful to see the citizenship rules for women who married foreign-born men or who were the foreign-born wives of foreign-born men. See *Indianapolis Star*, April 3, 1917.

37. Kettleborough, *Constitution Making*, 65–108; Kalvaitis, "Indianapolis Women Working for the Right to Vote," 67–72; Stuart to Edwards, August 17, 1917, Edwards to Stuart, September 14, 1917, Stuart to Edwards, September 24, 29, 1917, box 1, folder 6, Edwards to Thompson, October 18, 1917, Edwards to Hays October 19, 1917 (for Will Hays's covert involvement), November 5, 1917, box 1, folder 7, LWVIC. Edwards thanked Hays and stated, "Probably no one but myself realizes quite how much you have done, partly because of the fact that all direct political help had to come from Mr. Henly." In his autobiography, Hays said that his Aunt Sally, who had to pay taxes on several houses she owned and who could not vote on a referendum about placing sidewalks in front of those houses, was the motivation for his strong belief in woman suffrage. Will H. Hays, *The Memoirs of Will H. Hays* (Garden City, NY: Doubleday,1955), 57. Catt's visit is mentioned in Report of the President Woman's Franchise League of Indiana 1917–1918, box 2, folder 2, LWVIC. Petition by the WFL and the Woman's Party is found in *Indianapolis Star*, September 5, 1917.

38. Quote found in Kalvaitis, "Indianapolis Women Working for the Right to Vote," 71. Abram Simmons (one of the WFL's lawyers) to Edwards, September 18, 1917, box 1, folder 6, LWVIC.

39. McWhirter and Edwards comments found *Indianapolis News*, September 17, 1917.

40. *The Hoosier Suffragist*, September 21, 1917. Cast members and a photograph of "Sir Dark the Knight" and "Bill Suffrage" are found in the *Indianapolis News*, September 22, 1917. *Indianapolis News*, September 29 1917, identified the authors of the play as Mrs. Kin Hubbard, Mrs. Walter Greenough, Mrs. Lydia Parry Teasdale, Alma Sickler, and Sara Lauter (who also acted the role of Sir Dark the Knight). Also, *Indianapolis Star*, September 29, 1917.

41. *Indianapolis News*, October 26, 1917; *Indianapolis Star*, October 27, 1917; *Hoosier Suffragist*, October 26, 1917. The *Indiana Tribune*, covered the events in the October 3, 9, 27, 29, 1917, issues and reported the case facts, without any commentary on its preference on the question of woman suffrage.

42. Kalvaitis, "Indianapolis Women Working for the Right to Vote," 82–84; Simmons to Edwards, October 29, 1917, box 1, folder 7, report dated November 21, 1917, box 1, folder 7, LWVIC.

43. *Hoosier Suffragist*, February 1918.

44. *Indianapolis News*, August 9, 1917. *Indianapolis News*, November 8, 1917, for Nellie Barnes leaving for Washington. *Indianapolis Star*, November 11, 1917, for her arrest and her husband's

first notice, from the *Star* reporter, of her arrest, November 13, 1917, for Barnes quote about her reason to picket. Her arrest was also reported in the *Indianapolis News*, November 12, 13, 1917. *Indianapolis Star*, November 26, 1917, for her unfavorable views on the experience reported while she was still in Washington. *Indianapolis News*, November 26, 1917, for Barnes' favorable report on her experience. *Indianapolis News*, November 20, 1917, for the organizers in Indianapolis. *Indianapolis Star*, November 30, 1917, for Barnes's recanting. For even more problems, the *Indianapolis Star,* November 18, 1917, noted that longtime suffragist Mrs. W. T. Barnes, was not the same person as Mrs. Charles W. Barnes, who was arrested. Evidently people in the city were confusing the two women with each other.

45. Edwards to "Dear Near Voter," November 3, 1917, box 2, folder 1, Clarke Collection.

Chapter 7

1. *Indianapolis News*, November 17, 1917.

2. The most recent study of the part U.S. women played in World War I is Lynn Dumenil, *The Second Line of Defense: American Women and World War I* (Chapel Hill: University of North Carolina Press, 2017). Broad overviews of Indiana during World War I are found in Cedric C. Cummins, *Indiana Public Opinion and the World War* (Indianapolis: Indiana Historical Bureau, 1945) and Clifton Phillips, *Indiana in Transition: The Emergence of an Industrial Commonwealth, 1880–1920* (Indianapolis: Indiana Historical Bureau and Indiana Historical Society, 1968). See also, Genevieve G. McBride, *On Wisconsin Women: Working for Their Rights from Settlement to Suffrage* (Madison: University of Wisconsin, 1993), 278–80. *Indianapolis Star*, August 14, 1914, for both quotations and more comments from Grace Julian Clarke, August 23, 1914.

3. Phillips, *Indiana in Transition*, 589; Cummins, *Indiana Public Opinion*, 157; Dumenil, *Second Line of Defense*, 34–35. Eleanor Flexnor and Ellen Fitzpatrick, *Century of Struggle: The Woman's Rights Movement in the United States* (Cambridge, MA: Belknap/Harvard University Press, 1996), 280–81, discusses suffragists' reasons to support the war. *Jasper Weekly Courier*, December 14, 1917, emphasis in the original. Betty Blythe was the penname of Marie Chomel. She also helped with the publicity of the Woman's Committee of the Indiana State Council of Defense. Blythe was known for "stunt reporting" such as her ride in an Indianapolis race car around the Speedway track in 1909. See Hoosier State Chronicles blog for March 8, 2016.

4. Dumenil, *Second Line of Defense*, 35, 60–62. Some states' League for Woman's Services group had trouble cooperating with the official, state government woman's group. For Indiana's council, see Phillips, *Indiana in Transition*, 597–98. Will H. Hays, *The Memoirs of Will H. Hays* (Garden City, NY: Doubleday,1955), Chapter 8, has a good overall view of the state council. *Report of Julia E. Landers Chairman of the Indiana League for Woman's Service*, found at the Indiana State Library digital collections. At the national level, the League for Women's Services and NAWSA did not cooperate apparently because the LWS was staffed by, mostly, antisuffragists. That was not the case in Indiana. Julia Landers was both a suffragist and a Democrat. For the national LWS see, Barbara Steinson, *American Women's Activism in World War I* (New York: Garland Publishing, 1982), 304–10.

5. Phillips, *Indiana in Transition*, 597–98. *Report of the Woman's Section of the Indiana State Council of Defense* (Indianapolis: Wm. B. Burford, 1919), 6–9 explains the formation of the committee and lists the members. In a May 1918 speech, Anne Studebaker Carlisle noted that her daughter worked for the Red Cross in France, two sons were in the navy, and another son was about to join the armed services. Information about her daughter's service is found in *Indiana Women in the World War*, vol. 1 (Indianapolis: American Legion Auxiliary, 1936 (revised 1938),

76. Her comments are found in *Hammond Times*, May 27, 1918. Will Hays praised Hoosier women for their war work, especially in food conservation and the efficient organization the suffragists had devised. Hays, *Memoirs of Will H. Hays*, 129–30.

6. The comprehensive report of the national committee is Emily Newell Blair, *The Woman's Committee United States Council of National Defense: An Interpretative Report April 21, 1917 to February 27, 1919* (Washington, DC: Government Printing Office, 1920). For the new Indiana committees, *Report of the Woman's Section of the Indiana State Council of Defense*, 6.

7. Eleanor Barker spoke as far away as South Dakota, see *Daily Deadwood Pioneer Times*, March 1, 1918. Reports for the Women in Industry committee are found at Women in Industry, Indiana State Council of Defense Papers and Correspondence Woman's Section, bound volume and Women in Industry and Woman's Section Miscellaneous papers, bound volume, Indiana State Archives, Indianapolis. Mabel Many, finally, after many previous attempts to do so, stepped down due to her busy work schedule. *Indianapolis News*, July 8, 1918, and *Indianapolis Star*, July 7, 1918, for information and a photograph of Many. *Indianapolis News*, October 8, 1918, for Jennie Ralston's involvement. Cora Goodrich's comment on working conditions and the factory inspector are found in *Journal of the Indiana State Senate* (Indianapolis: Wm. B. Buford, 1919), 18. *Report of the Woman's Section of the Indiana State Council of Defense*, 35–36. For correspondence about appointing a woman factory inspector see Keller to Goodrich, January 7, 1918, and Goodrich to Keller, January 8, 1918, Keckly-Keller box 139, folder 1, James P. Goodrich Manuscript Collection, Indiana State Archives. The only study of women in industry during World War I for Indiana is Peggy Seigel, "Industrial 'Girls' in an Early Twentieth-Century Boomtown: Traditions and Change in Fort Wayne, Indiana, 1900–1920," *Indiana Magazine of History* 99 (September 2003): 246–53.

8. *Terre Haute Daily Tribune*, April 19, 1917, for Henderson's retirement. *Report of the Woman's Section of the Indiana State Council of Defense*, 37–39, gives the Fourteen Minute Women report. Information about the Fourteen Minute Women's work is found in *Indianapolis News*, November 22, 1917, May 10, 11, 1918. *Indianapolis Star*, May 5, 1918, for the rousing speeches and woman's train trip, also May 11, July 31, 1918. *Richmond Palladium*, January 21, May 14, 1918. *Terre Haute Daily Tribune*, March 17, 1918. No texts of any speeches have been found. Henderson most likely got the idea from the federal government's Committee on Public Information Four Minute Men who gave similar speeches across the country.

9. *Report of the Woman's Section of the Indiana State Council of Defense*, 27–30.

10. Ibid., 18–21. Vida Newsom to Clarke, October 13, 1920, box 2, folder 4, Grace Julian Clarke Collection, Indiana State Library, Indianapolis, referred to Albion Fellows Bacon as someone "who has never done any active work for suffrage or been an 'out loud suffragist.'"

11. Reasons for registration found in *Richmond Palladium*, March 27, 1918. Steinson, *American Women's Activism in World War I*, 324, citing Blair, *Woman's Committee United States Council of National Defense*, 73, for the comment on the importance of volunteers. *Woman's Section Indiana State Council of Defense Manual for Registrars*, Indiana State Library digital collections. Dumenil, *Second Line of Defense*, 66, for women and men who feared registration was somehow tied to woman suffrage registration. *Report of the Woman's Section of the Indiana State Council of Defense*, 12–13, for registration. *Hammond Times*, September 10, 1918, for Lake County and Henry County totals. The totals given here combine the newspaper report with the official reports as found in *Report of the Woman's Section of the Indiana State Council of Defense*, 80 for Lake County and 70 for Henry County. *Indianapolis News*, December 8, 1917, for wages.

12. *Report of the Woman's Section of the Indiana State Council of Defense*, 39–40. *Indianapolis Star*, June 23, 1918, June 21, 1918, for "kitchen on wheels." The Indiana Federation of Clubs also encouraged Americanization work, *Indianapolis Star*, June 21, 1918.

13. *Report of the Woman's Section of the Indiana State Council of Defense*, 117, (Saint Joseph County), 136 (Wayne County). Quote from Dumenil, *Second Line of Defense*, 70–71. For Americanization activities west of Indiana, see Sara Egge, *Woman Suffrage and Citizenship in the Midwest, 1870*–1920 (Ames: University of Iowa Press, 2018), 162–65.

14. Egge, *Woman Suffrage* 9–10 for a discussion of naturalization and citizenship.

15. Cummins, *Indiana Public Opinion and the World War*, 45 and n5.

16. David Bodenhamer and Robert G. Barrows, eds., *Encyclopedia of Indianapolis* (Bloomington and Indianapolis: Indiana University Press, 1994), 618 and George Theodore Probst, *The German in Indianapolis, 1840–1918* (Indianapolis: German American Center and Indiana German Heritage Society, 1989), 90. Jacob Piatt Dunn Jr., *Indiana and Indianans: A History of Aboriginal and Territorial Indiana and the Century of Statehood*, 5 vols. (Chicago: American Historical Society, 1918), 4:1881, and *Central States Medical Monitor* 10, no. 1 (January 15, 1907): 29–30 for Keller. William A. Fritsch, *German Settlers and German Settlements in Indiana* (Evansville, IN: No publisher, 1915), 26, for Keller's father. For Lauter, *Indianapolis Star*, June 9, 1907, for obituary and Dunn, *Indiana and Indianans*, 5:1944–45. Lauter's factory still stands today and has been converted into condominiums.

17. Cummins, *Indiana Public Opinion and the World War*, 224–34. Dane Starbuck, *The Goodrichs: An American Family* (Indianapolis: Liberty Fund, 2001), 98–99, 101–3. Philips, *Indiana in Transition*, 595–96, for information on Lieber. In contrast to Goodrich, Iowa's governor banned using a language other than English in churches or on the telephone, see Egge, *Woman Suffrage*, 156. Dunn, *Indiana and Indianans*, 3:1491–93, for information about the Riesenbergs. Meetings of the Friends of German Democracy are found throughout the Indianapolis newspapers including: *Indianapolis News*, March 1, 20, April 12, 16, May 7, July 18, August 8, October 4, 1918; and *Indianapolis Star*, May 7, June 23, 1918. Egge, *Woman Suffrage*, 155, for quote on nativism. See also, Phillips, *Indiana in Transition*, 603.

18. *Hoosier Suffragist*, August 22, 1917, for quote. Fairbanks's committee comment in Hays, *Memoir of Will H. Hays*, 130.

19. *Hoosier Suffragist*, August 22, 1917, for the WFL war committees and February, April, June 1918 for articles concerning Red Cross and Liberty Loans. *Indianapolis News*, March 2, 1918, for Liberty Loan and Red Cross work.

20. *Hoosier Suffragist*, April 1, and May 1918. Greenough's husband later wrote Walter Sidney Greenough, *The War Purse of Indiana* (Indianapolis: Indiana Historical Commission, 1922).

21. *Hoosier Suffragist*, May, October 1918, for hospitals.

22. *Report of the Woman's Section of the Indiana State Council of Defense*, 47.

23. Ibid., 49, 50, 61, 81.

24. Ibid., 8–9. Nina Mjagky, ed., *Organizing Black America* (New York: Routledge, 2013), 219. Tamara L. Brown, Gregory S. Parks, and Clarenda M. Phillips, eds., *African American Fraternities and Sororities: The Legacy and the Vision* (Lexington: University of Kentucky Press), 81. Theda Skocpol, Ariane Liazos, and Marshall Ganz, eds., *What a Mighty Power We Can Be: African American Fraternal Groups and the Struggle for Racial Equality* (Princeton, NJ: Princeton University Press, 2006), 21–60. Dumenil, *Second Line of Defense*, 44, 58–60, 84–94 for African Americans on state councils. *Report of the Woman's Section of the Indiana State Council of Defense*, 126, 135.

Indiana War Records Colored Section (Indianapolis: No publisher or date), Indiana State Library digital collection, no pagination, and *Indianapolis News*, June 22, 1918. Some of the information in the newspaper does not match the *Indiana War Records, Report of the Woman's Section of the Indiana State Council of Defense*, 86–88, or the *Indiana War Records Colored Section*.

25. *Report of the Woman's Section of the Indiana State Council of Defense*, 86–88. *Indianapolis News*, July 20, 1918, for the women who will speak. In the *Indianapolis News*, July 12, 1918, Frances Berry Coston reported on almost those exact words as in the July 1918 issue of W. E. B. DuBois's *The Crisis* when he stated, "That which the German power represents today spells death to the aspirations of the negroes and all darker races for equality, freedom and democracy. Let us not hesitate. Let us while this war lasts forget our special grievances and close our ranks shoulder to shoulder with our own white fellow citizens and the allied nations that are fighting for democracy."

26. For more examples of war work, *Indianapolis News*, July 13, September 14, 21, October 19, 1918. For the parade, *Indianapolis Star*, August 21, 1918, and *Indianapolis News*, August 19, 1918.

27. *Indianapolis News*, April 17, 18, 1918, (photo of WFL dinner at the Claypool); April 19, April 20, 1918. The quotes from Catt about democracy and Edwards on the membership drive are found in *Indianapolis Star*, April 18, 1918. *Indianapolis News*, April 17, 1918, for Shaw speaking at the state council of defense meeting.

28. "Report of the President Woman's Franchise League of Indiana 1917-18" for Edwards quote, box 2, folder 2, League of Women Voters of Indiana Collection, M612, Indiana Historical Society William Henry Smith Memorial Library, Indianapolis (hereafter cited as LWVIC).

29. *Terre Haute Daily Tribune*, March 17, 1918.

30. Barbara Anne Springer, "Ladylike Reformers: Indiana Women and Progressive Reform, 1900–1920" (PhD diss., Indiana University, 1985), 238–39. For psychological moment quote, see *Indianapolis News*, July 18, 1918. Column by Grace Julian Clarke, *Indianapolis Star*, August 29, 1918. Marie Edwards quote also found in another Clarke newspaper column, *Indianapolis Star*, August 11, 1918.

31. See box 1, folder 2, Woman's Franchise League of Indiana 1899–1919, SC 1761, Indiana Historical Society William Henry Smith Memorial Library (hereafter cited as WFL). Also see *Fort Wayne Sentinel*, December 5, 1917, where the idea that suffrage was a "war measure" that would counteract the votes of "ignorant foreigners" can be seen at a meeting of the Indiana State Council of Defense when Mrs. Henry Jameson, Mrs. John Barnhill, Julia Landers, and Doctor Amelia Keller "invaded" the council (according to the newspaper) and presented the idea.

32. Emphasis in the original, box 1, folder 2, WFL. The mayor referred to here is most likely Michigan City mayor Fred C. Miller, who became mayor with some doubting his American citizenship. *Indianapolis Star*, January 8, 9, 1918.

33. Emphasis in the original, box 1, folder 2, WFL.

34. *Indianapolis Star*, November 12, 1918, and *Indianapolis News*, November 11, 1918, for the man on the street.

35. Springer, "Ladylike Reformers," 224–25. For McWhirter and the General Federation see *Terre Haute Daily Tribune*, October 6, 1918. Grace Gates Courtney, comp. and Arcada Stark Balz, ed. *History Indiana Federation of Clubs* (Indianapolis: Indiana Federation of Clubs, 1939), 257, 268.

36. The quote from Goodrich is found in the *Indianapolis Star* June 2, 1918, and *Indianapolis News*, May 29, 1918. Circular, December 10, 1918, January 3, 1919, box 1, folder 1, WFL. Springer, "Ladylike Reformers," 239.

37. *Indianapolis Star*, January 10, 1919. The U.S. House of Representatives had approved the Nineteenth Amendment in January 1918. In a dramatic turn of events, Indiana congressman Henry A. Barnhart had to be taken to the House chamber from a Washington hospital, where he was recuperating from an operation. After his affirmative vote, he returned to the hospital. House Republican leader James R. Mann had been in the hospital at Baltimore and was also taken to the chamber for the vote. See *Indianapolis Star*, January 11, 1918, for the House vote.

38. Springer, "Ladylike Reformers," 240. For the legislators' comments, *Indianapolis Star*, February 6, 1919. For the pen and gavel, *Indianapolis News*, February 7, 1919.

39. Springer, "Ladylike Reformers," 240–41. *Indianapolis News*, January 14, 1919, for the early agreement between Beardsley, the WFL, and the Woman's Legislative Council to pull the original Beardsley Amendment. *Indianapolis News*, January 16, 1919, for introducing the new amendment. *Indianapolis Star*, February 11, 1919, for the new Beardsley Amendment passing unanimously.

40. *Indianapolis News*, June 4, 1919, for governor's comments and June 5, 1919, for White and Lauter. The *News* kept the pressure on the legislature the next day with a front-page editorial cartoon, June 6, 1919. *Indianapolis Star*, June 5, 1919. *Indianapolis News*, June 19, 1919, reported on the cost of voting under partial versus full suffrage. *Indianapolis Star*, June 6, 1919, for a less favorable response to a special session. Springer, "Ladylike Reformers," 241. Governor Goodrich to Sara Lauter, August 4, 1919, box 1, folder 8, Correspondence 1918–1919, LWVIC.

41. See the following for celebrations: *Indianapolis News*, June 6, 7, 1919; *Indianapolis Star*, June 8, 1919; *Indianapolis News*, June 21, 1919, for the tea, complete with photographs of some of the suffrage pioneers. *Indianapolis News*, June 23, 1919. Lauter to League Member, September 11, 1919, for the citizenship school, box 1, folder 8, Correspondence 1918–1919, LWVIC.

42. See, *Handbook of NAWSA Proceedings of the Victory Convention National American Woman Suffrage Association (1869–1920) and First National Congress League of Women Voters* (Chicago, IL: League of Women Voters, 1920), 146, for the governor's pet projects and the special session, box 2, folder 11, LWVIC. *Indianapolis News*, November 18, 1919, for letters presented to Lieutenant Governor Bush. Goodrich to Helen Benbridge, December 30, 1919, box 1, folder 8, LWVIC; Benbridge to Dear Sir, January 3, 1920, to ask about the special session, box 1, folder 9, LWVIC; Benbridge to Mrs. J. G. McNutt, January 6, 1920, and James M. Knapp to Benbridge, January 6, 1920, for responses from legislators to the call for a special session, box 1, folders 9 and 10, LWVIC. See also, The Presidents Report (no date), box 2, folder 2, LWVIC. In spite of Goodrich's expressed desire to ratify the Nineteenth Amendment and his wife's suffrage activities, he apparently later stated in his autobiography that he never really thought suffrage would do much good for politics as women would act the same as men. Starbuck, *Goodrich Family*, 113. Clark to Benbridge, January 14, 1920, box 1, folder 10, LWVIC.

43. *Indianapolis News*, January 16, 1920. *Indianapolis Star*, January 17, 1920, for Goodrich's opening comments. Comment about signing the Maston-McKinley bill found in *Indianapolis News*, February 28, 1917.

44. The Presidents Report (no date), box 2, folder 2, and Lauter to Madam President, March 6, 1920, box 1, folder 10, LWVIC. The creation of the League of Women Voters is found in Jean

H. Baker, ed., *Votes for Women: The Struggle for Suffrage Revisited* (New York: Oxford University Press, 2002), 141, and Dumenil, *Second Line of Defense*, 260. The criticism of the league is found in Flexnor and Fitzpatrick, *Century of Struggle*, 320. Quote from Catt, *Indianapolis News*, August 18, 1920.

45. *Indianapolis News*, August 18, 1920, includes quotes from Indiana suffragists and Catt quote about slackers. Watson quote from *Indianapolis Star*, August 19, 1920. Hays quote *Indianapolis Star*, August 19, 1920.

46. *Indianapolis News*, August 27 (page 1 has a wonderful editorial cartoon), 28, September 14, 1920, for Shelbyville festivities. *Indianapolis Star*, August 27, 1920. *Indianapolis Star*, August 29, 1920, noted that Laura Donnan no doubt dampened the spirits when she told the crowd, "Though we are on the heights, let us not get dizzy. We have just begun our emancipation. Each woman must emancipate herself."

47. *Indianapolis Star*, October 4, 1920, and *Indianapolis News*, September 28, 1920. *Indianapolis News*, March 7, 1918, listed women associated with the Democratic Party when Mrs. George Bass, Secretary of the Liberty Loan Committee and chair of the women's section of the Democratic Party (national) spoke to "the Democratic women of Indianapolis."

48. *Indianapolis News*, October 11, 1920, for Barker comment. Damn fool letter, box 2, folder 4, November 1920, Clarke Collection. Her speech found in the *South Bend News Times*, September 22, 1921. *Indianapolis News*, September 28, 1920, for Clarke's views on Harding. An example of the "Women in Politics" column is *Indianapolis Star*, October 10, 1920.

49. *Indianapolis News*, November 2, 1920, and *Indianapolis Star*, November 3, 1920.

50. *Indianapolis News*, November 2, 1920; *Lafayette Journal and Courier*, November 2, 1920; *Richmond Palladium*, November 2, 3, 1920.

51. *Indianapolis News*, November 2, 1920, for women on the ballot around the state; *Indianapolis News*, November 3, 1920, for Nelson's election; *Indianapolis News*, November 6, 1920, for interview with Nelson. More on Nelson is found at https://www.in.gov/icw/files/20160319_Nelson_Julia.pdf. *Indianapolis Star*, November 5, 1920, for Ada Bush.

52. Flexnor and Fitzpatrick, *Century of Struggle*, 317.

53. *Indianapolis News*, November 6, 13, 1920, for remarks about the effects of the vote on women.

54. *Indianapolis News*, December 11, 1920, for constituent comment.

Index

abolition, 15, 19, 30, 31, 41, 43, 52
African Americans: and suffrage, 2, 6–7, 8, 11, 44–47, 51, 56, 58, 76, 101, 106, 112, 117–18, 125–27, 142, 156–57; attend white schools, 7; population of in Indianapolis, 7–8, 53; women included in Indiana suffrage efforts, 52, 72; women attempt to vote, 58; and women's suffrage organizations, 61; and women's clubs, 91; community in Indianapolis, 101; women register to vote, 158; women and World War I work, 184–87; voter turnout for, 204,
Alexander, Georgia, 124
Alldredge, John S., 195, 196
American Equal Rights Association, 44, 45, 46, 47, 51
American Federation of Labor, 135
American Woman Suffrage Association (AWSA), 4, 5, 32, 47, 49, 51, 52, 53, 56, 61, 62, 63, 75, 76, 79, 80, 88, 90, 197
Americanization, 171, 175–76
Anderson, IN: women attempt to vote in, 88
Anthony, Susan B., 5, 10, 22, 35, 45, 46, 47, 55, 58, 62, 64, 74, 76, 79, 82, 83, 84, 85, 86, 88, 90, 95, 96, 97, 98, 99, 102,149, 203; (illus.), 17, 26
Armstead, Mrs. W. H., 187
Art Association of Indiana, 90
Association of College Alumnae, 128
Atkins, Mrs. E. C., 162
Atlas of Iowa (book), 4
Automobile: use of in suffrage movement, 101, 114–16, 127; (illus.), 108, 109, 130
Avery, Rachel Foster, 87, 90; (illus.), 89

Bacon, Albion Fellows. 132, 172–73
Barker, Eleanor P., 139, 153, 162, 171, 172, 203; (illus.), 169
Barnes, Carrie. *See* Ross, Carrie Barnes
Barnes, Corinne Emma Robbins (Mrs. W. T.), 105, 114, 124; (illus.), 109
Barnes, Mrs. Charles W. *See* Barnes, Nellie
Barnes, Mrs. W. T. *See* Barnes, Corinne Emma Robbins
Barnes, Nellie, 163–64
Barnes, W. T., 121
Barnhill, Celeste, 108, 115, 124; (illus.), 110
Barnhill, John F., 121
Barnhill, Mrs. J. F. *See* Barnhill Celeste
Barr, Daisy Douglas, 124
Baughman, Mrs. Charles, 187
Baumgartner, Helen, 131
Beardsley, Mrs. A. H., 198, (illus.), 149
Beardsley Full Suffrage Amendment, 151, 159, 189, 196
Beeson, Othniel, 56
Belleville, Mr. _______, 49, 50
Benbridge, Helen, 124, 127, 131–32, 172, 191, 197, 198, 199
Bennett, Henry W., 155–56, 157, 159, 160
Beveridge, Albert, 80, 114
"Big Lobby," 151
Birdsall, Mary, 25, 27, 28, 29, 32, 39
Blackwell, Henry, 46, 47, 55, 56, 62, 71, 79
Blanchard. Reverend, ______, 49
Bloomer, Amelia, 25, 39, 40
Bloomington Progress, 97
Blythe, Betty. *See* Chomel, Marie
Bolton, Sarah, 18
Bosart, Dora, 163; (illus.), 149, 150
Boyd, Helen, 169
Boyd, Mrs. James A. *See* Boyd, Catherine
Boynton, Lizzie. *See* Harbert, Elizabeth Boynton
Brabham, Daisy, 184
Brabham, Reverend ______, 184
Breckinridge, Mrs. M. D., 102, 104
brewers and breweries, 3, 10, 68, 87, 180
Brewster, Belinda, 128
Brooks, Virginia, 112
Brookville, IN, 16
Bross, Ernest, 121
Brown, Jason B., 75
Brown, R. T., 48
Bryan, William Jennings, 152
Buehler, Eugene, 121
Bull Moose Party, 124
Bunnell, Lizzie. *See* Read, Lizzie Bunnell

Burns, Lucy, 138
Burns, Mrs. _____, 51
Bush, Adah, 205
Bush, Edgar D., 198
Butler, Ovid, 197

Cable, Mary E., 184
Cadets of Temperance, 16
Cannon, Sarah, 205
Cardwell, Mary, 86
Carey, Angeline, 185
Carey, Martha: (illus.), 149
Carlisle, Anna Studebaker, 170, 171, 188
Carmel, IN, 115
Carrington, H. B., 49
Carter, Mrs. Fred, 205
Cary, Mary Ann Shad, 58
Catt, Carrie Chapman, 96, 97, 138, 140–41, 142, 144, 160, 187, 188, 189, 200, 201, 203, 205; (illus.), 134
Central Labor Union, 108, 112, 120
Charles, Mrs. Arthur, 175
Chicago, 87, 91
Chicago Inter-Ocean, 4
Child, Lydia Maria: (illus.), 26
Child Welfare Committee, 173, 183
Chomel, Marie, 115, 168, 169
Christian, Mrs. Wilmer, 201
Christian Commission, 36
Citizenship School, 198
City Belle (riverboat), 38, 39
Civil Rights Acts of 1866, p. 44
Civil War: women work for Union victory in, 9, 12, 30, 35–39, 43, 44, 54, 56, 154, 167
Clark, Dora, 199
Clarke, Charles, 120, 121, 122, 129
Clarke, Grace Julian, 1, 3, 5, 6, 11, 79, 94, 95, 96, 98, 101, 104, 105, 106, 108, 111, 114, 115, 117, 120, 121, 123, 124–25, 126, 128, 129, 131, 132, 134, 135, 139, 144, 153, 154–55, 162, 168, 172, 191, 203, 204; (illus.), 107, 109, 123
Clarke, Mrs. M. A., 184
Clay, Ella, 184, 186, 187
Coburn, John, 49
Cohee, Adie, 158
College Corner Club, 92
Collegiate Alumnae Association of Indiana, 170
Colorado: women vote in, 88, 96
Columbia City, IN, 43
Columbian Exposition, 87, 91
Committee on Public Information, 179
Compton, Lizzie, 142
Congressional Union, 138, 139, 140, 141–42, 148, 153, 171
Constitutional Convention, 152, 163
Consumer League, 128
Cook, Agnes, 15, 27, 29
Cooper, Elizabeth, 199
Coston, Frances Barry, 1, 156–57, 184, 187; (illus.), 173
Coulter, Stanley, 124
Council of Jewish Women, 114, 117, 128; Terre Haute, 147
Council of National Defense, 169, 172, 179, 187
Cox, Lenore, 105, 131–34, 135, 191
Cox, Mrs. Arthur T., 171
Cox, Mrs. Lewis J. *See* Cox, Lenore
Cravens, Joseph, 199
Crawfordsville, IN: women attempt to vote in, 88
Criley, J. B., 49
Croly, Jane Cunningham, 91
Curry, Mabel, 124, 152, 158
Curry, Margaret: (illus.), 177
Curry, Mrs. C. M. *See* Curry, Mabel

Daughters of Temperance, 16
Daughters of the American Revolution, 169
Davis, Chester, 148
Davis, Fanny, 158
Davis, Joel P., 15
Davis, Lydia, 15
Davis, Sarah, 102
Day, T. C., 121
Debs, Eugene V., 111, 152
Debs, Kate, 153
Declaration of Sentiments, 21, 22
Democratic Party, 114, 118, 141, 179, 195, 203; and prohibition, 68, 70; and suffrage, 84, 85, 86, 142
Dickenson, Anna, 86; (illus.), 26
Diggs, M. J., 15
Dix, Dorothy, 41
Dodge, Mrs. Arthur, 145
Donnan, Laura, 1, 61, 126, 127, 197
Donnell, Daneva, W., 184
Donnell, Miss _____, 187
Douglass, Frederick, 46–47, 51, 58
Du Valle, Mrs. Alfred, 197

Dublin, IN, 9, 15, 19
Duvalle, Emma, 184, 187
Duvalle, Mrs.______, 184
Dye, Charity, 1, 108, 145, 168, 197, 203
Dye, Mrs. John T., 197

Eaglesfield, Carina, (illus.), 133
Edwards, Betsy, 140
Edwards, Marie, 1, 152, 155–56, 158, 161, 163, 164–65, 169, 188, 189–90, 191, 197, 199, 200, 204; (illus.), 194
Elder, Mrs. William L., 184
Emancipation Proclamation, 35
Equal Rights Amendment, 200
Equal Rights Association, 51, 52
Equal Suffrage Association (ESA), 11, 101, 102, 103, 106, 108, 109, 111, 112, 114, 117, 118, 119, 120, 121, 122, 125–26, 127, 128, 138, 139, 140, 141, 143–44, 147, 148, 152; Branch Number 6, p. 112; Branch Number 7, pp. 1, 117, 118, 125–26, 127
Erskine, John, 196, 199
Evansville, IN: women march in, 124

Fairbank, Caroline 134, 169, 170
Fairbanks, Charles W., 11, 13, 101, 112, 116, 143, 180
Fairmount, IN: women attempt to vote in, 88
Fenton, Mrs. C. O.: (illus.), 149
Ferguson, Mrs.______, 28
Fifteenth Amendment, 44, 46, 47, 48, 49, 50, 51, 56, 58, 64, 155
First Colored Woman's Suffrage Club, 1, 127, 156
Flanner House, 118, 187
Flint, Lucy, 118
Forrest, Albertina A., 98
Fort Wayne, IN, 183; women meet in, 59
Foster, Blanche: (illus.), 150
Foulke, William Dudley, 5, 75, 80, 112, 197, 171–72, 186–87
Fourteenth Amendment, 44–47, 48, 49, 58, 64, 155
Furnas, John H., 65, 199

Gage, Frances Dana, 25, 44, 75
Garrison, S. C., 118
Garrison, William Lloyd, 153
Gavit, Frank N., 122
General Federation of Women's Clubs, 5, 81, 91, 94, 95, 194
Germans: and temperance, 10; prohibition, 55, 67–68; women's suffrage, 55, 67–68; brewers, 68
Giddings, Joshua, 96
Gilliam, Nellie, 156
Girls' Classical School, 90
Goodrich, Cora, 13, 150, 156, 171, 173, 189, 194, 195, 199, 200
Goodrich, James P., 2, 12, 13, 143, 144, 150, 157, 159, 169, 171, 179, 187, 194, 195, 196, 197, 198, 199, 200
Gougar, Helen, 1, 10, 65, 66, 67, 71, 73–74, 75, 76, 79, 80, 81, 82, 83, 85–88, 89–90, 91, 95, 96, 97, 98, 125, 131, 160; (illus.), 57
Gougar v. Timberlake, 89
Graham, Hannah, 1, 11, 108, 109, 112, 114, 117, 118, 120, 121, 122, 126, 140, 203; (illus.), 105
Greenback Party, 71
Greencastle, IN, 152
Greene, John, 49
Greenough, Mrs. Walter, 183
Greenwood, Grace: (illus.), 26
Griffin, Martha, 88
Grover, Mrs. Arthur, 197

Hagerty, Charles, 196, 199
Haggart, Mary, 65, 66, 67, 70, 71, 73, 75, 82
Hanley, Rhoda, 184
Hannaman, William, 48
Harbert, Elizabeth Boynton, 4, 48, 71
Harding, Warren G., 204, 205
Harper, Ida Husted, 5, 73, 74, 79, 82, 83, 85, 86, 90, 106, 108, 111, 156, 206; (illus.), 84
Harrison, Benjamin, 79, 80
Hart, Hester Moore, 98
Hay, Mary Garret, 5, 152; (illus.), 81
Hays, Will, 160, 169, 170, 179, 180, 201
Headrick, W. D., 124
Hedrick, James W., 105
Hedrick Bill, 105, 106
Heilman, Rose, 139
Henderson, Julia C., 108, 114, 117, 171–72, 203 ; (illus.), 110
Henderson, Mrs. G. H. *See* Henderson, Julia C.
Henrotin, Ellen, 87–88
Hiatt, Fanny, 15, 22
Hiatt, Hannah, 71
Hiatt, Henry, 15, 22
Highbaugh, Minnie, 142

Hill, Elsie, 141–42
Hilles, Florence Bayard, 153
Hinton, James, 66, 67
History of Woman Suffrage (book), 5, 29, 30, 99, 102
Hodgin, Caroline C., 86
Homestead Bill, 43
Hoosier Suffragist, The, 160, 170
Hoover, Herbert, 160
Household of Ruth, 184, 187
Hubbard, Elizabeth, 158
Hubbard, Mrs. Kin, 203
Hudson, Mrs.______, 118
Hughes, Charles Evans, 12, 142–43, 206
Hummons, Mrs. ______, 187
Hurrell, Mrs. Arthur S., 175
Hutchins, Mrs. Frank: (illus.), 149

Idaho: women vote in, 96
Iliff-Davis, Sarah, 25, 41
Immigrants, 179, 190, 192–93; voting rights of, 8–9, 167, 188, 190, 192; nativism, 176, 188; naturalization, 175
Indiana: women vote in, 12; women's club movement in, 79, 81, 91, 92–93; Germans in 176–77, 179–80; three suffrage groups operate in, 137–45, 153–54; women register to vote, 201
Indiana Club Union. *See* Indiana Union of Literary Clubs
Indiana Constitution: amending of, 10, 12, 55, 56, 64, 75, 111, 123, 125, 139, 163; and women's property rights, 15, 18, 28; woman suffrage, 44, 120, 154–55, 157, 163, 189; moves to rewrite, 137, 139, 147, 150, 152, 153, 154–55, 157, 163
Indiana Dry Federation, 151, 152
Indiana Equal Suffrage Association, 170
Indiana Federation of Clubs, 11, 94, 104, 105, 109, 110, 117, 124, 128, 131, 135, 141, 145, 168, 169, 170, 172, 191
Indiana Federation of Labor, 104
Indiana Forum, 155
Indiana General Assembly, 2, 3, 9, 10, 12; and amending of Indiana constitution, 10, 55, 56; suffrage bills, 12, 19, 27–29, 55, 56, 60, 64, 65–66, 67, 68, 71, 73, 74–75, 82, 95, 104–6, 107, 118–23, 127, 128, 137, 138, 146–49, 151–52, 167, 170, 189–90, 194, 195; prohibition bills, 55, 60, 67, 68, 73; special session of, 67, 68, 70, 159, 197, 198–99; women petition and lobby, 140, 142, 144, 149; Nineteenth Amendment, 195–200
Indiana Historical Commission, 145
Indiana Industrial Board, 171
Indiana League for Woman's Service, 169, 170
Indiana National Woman Suffrage Association, 76, 82, 83, 84, 85, 86
Indiana State Council of Defense, 169–70, 179, 180, 187
Indiana State Suffrage Association, 98
Indiana State Teachers' Association, 145, 170
Indiana Supreme Court, 189; and suffrage bills, 137, 159, 160, 161–63, 196
Indiana Tribüne, 67, 76
Indiana Union of Literary Clubs, 93, 94, 101
Indiana War Records Colored Section, 187
Indiana Woman's Rights Association, 1, 5, 6, 9, 19, 23–25, 27, 28, 29, 30, 31, 32, 33, 36, 37, 44, 47, 48, 49, 52, 71, 72, 76
Indiana Woman's Suffrage Association, 1, 7, 50, 51, 52, 53, 55, 56, 58, 59, 61, 62, 63, 64, 65, 67, 70, 71, 72, 75, 76, 82, 84, 85, 86–87, 88, 95, 96, 97
Indiana Women's Committee, 169, 170
Indianapolis, 6, 11; African American population of, 7–8, 53; German community in, 8, 177, 179–80; women's conferences in, 47–51, 52, 55, 56, 63, 64, 72, 76, 96–98, 101, 126, 141, 148, 188–91, 200; women's clubs in, 61, 62, 93–94, 126, 127; African Americans in, 101; women on school board ballot, 102; women march in, 122, 123
Indianapolis Colored Women's Mutual Society, 66
Indianapolis Council of Women, 105
Indianapolis Daily Journal, 28, 29
Indianapolis Daily State Sentinel. See *Indianapolis Sentinel*
Indianapolis Equal Suffrage Society, 62, 65, 67
Indianapolis High School. *See* Shortridge High School
Indianapolis Journal, 85–86, 87, 97
Indianapolis News, 60, 112, 121, 135, 145, 147, 148, 150, 153, 156, 157, 158, 162, 164, 167, 188, 194, 197, 199, 204
Indianapolis Recorder, 142
Indianapolis Sentinel, 48, 49, 50, 52, 64
Indianapolis Star, 111, 115, 128, 137, 148, 156, 162, 164, 188, 191, 204
Indianapolis State Sentinel. See *Indianapolis*

Sentinel
Indianapolis Suffrage Society, 61, 197
Indianapolis Times, 80
Indianapolis Woman's Club, 63, 64, 87, 93, 94, 96
Ingersoll, E. P., 49
International Council of Women, 90

Jameson, Mary Tarkington, 2–3, 122, 140, 172, 199
Jameson, Mrs. Ovid Butler. *See* Jameson, Mary Tarkington
Jewett, Charles W., 189
Jewett, Mrs. Charles W., 189
Johnson, Francis, 73
Johnson, Harriet, 142
Johnson, Mrs. Kizzzie, 76
Jones, Pearl, 184
Judah, Mary Jameson, 98
Judah, Mrs. John M., 197
Julian George W., 42, 46, 50, 51, 72, 93, 96, 97
Julian, Grace Giddings, 51, 72, 75
Julian, Laura Giddings, 51, 93, 96

Kealing, Mrs. Joseph B., 201, 204
Keegan, John J., 105
Keegan Bill, 105, 106
Keller, Amelia, 1, 8, 11, 102, 103, 104, 105, 106, 108, 121, 122, 123, 124, 127, 137, 139, 140, 142, 156, 170, 171, 172, 177, 179, 194, 195, 199, 203; (illus.), 134
Ketcham, Lila M. D., 98
Ketcham, Mrs. John L. *See* Ketcham Lila M. D.
Kinley, Isaac, 49
Kline, Oliver, 196, 199
Knapp, James M., 199
Knight, William W., 159–60, 161
Kokomo, 96, 98; women attempt to vote in, 88–89; women meet in, 102
Kokomo Equal Suffrage Club, 88
Kokomo Weekly Dispatch, 70
Kregelo, Mrs. Charles E., 197

Lafayette, IN, 125; women attempt to vote in, 88, 89
Lafayette Courier, 80
Lafayette Morning Journal, 86
Landers, Julia, 169, 170, 174, 201, 203; (illus.), 149
Landgraf, William, 120
Lasselle, Charles B., 44
Lauter, Eldena, 1, 8, 162, 179; (illus.), 113
Lauter, Sara, 1, 8, 114, 115, 179, 197, 200, 201; (illus.), 109, 146
Leach, Antoinette, 106, 120
League of Nations, 203–4, 205
League of Women Voters, 200, 201, 203
Lease, Mary, 88
Lebanon, IN, 115
Leck, Ada B., 98
Legislative Council, 128
Lesh, Imogene Taft: (illus.), 149
Lesh, U. G., 160
Lewis, Olive Beldon, 203
Liberty Loans, 170, 172, 180, 183, 187, 191
Lieber, Richard, 179
Lily, The, 25, 28, 32, 39, 40
Lincoln, Abraham, 33, 35, 36, 41, 42
Lincoln, Mary, 42
Lively, Chaney, 7
Livermore, Mary, 6, 50, 51, 52, 53, 54, 63, 64; (illus.), 26
Local Council of Women, 128
Logansport, IN, 125; women meet in, 102
Lundy, Benjamin, 31

Mandler, Henry, 73, 74
Many, Mabel, 171
Marion, 6; women attempt to vote in, 88
Marion County Superior Court, 155, 160
Marshall, C. H., 48
Marshall, Lois, 104, 106
Marshall, Thomas R., 106, 108, 111, 118
Martindale, Charles, 49, 52
Mason, Mrs. M. A., 76
Maston, Marion, 130, 148, 150
Maxey, Celia, 184
Mayflower, The (newspaper), 4, 39–44
Mays, Elizabeth, 127
McClintock, Lizzie, 21, 22
McCloud, J. E., 137
McCray, ______, 199
McCray, Warren T., 205
McCulloch, Catharine, 160
McCullough, Alice Foster, 180, 183, 199, 203
McDonald, David, 49
McKay, Horace, 61, 62
McKay, Martha, 1, 61, 62, 63, 88, 92, 93, 94, 103, 197; (illus.), 64
McKinley, Arthur, 148, 150
McKinley, Clark D., 205

McNutt, Mrs. J. G., 199
McPhetridge, Lannes, 108
McWhirter, Luella, 1, 3, 6, 95, 97, 108, 122, 124, 128, 129, 132, 135, 144, 145, 151, 161, 194, 201, 203; (illus.), 149, 150
McWhirter, Mrs. Felix. *See* McWhirter, Luella
Meara, Myrtle, 205
Meier, Mrs. George Philip, 98
Mendenhall, M. H., 49
Meredith Virginia Claypool, 93, 94, 101, 132
Merrill, Hattie E., 86
Merritt, Paulina T., 66
Miller, Mrs. Harry, 114, 124; (illus.), 109
Miller, Mrs. Walter McNabb: (illus.), 134
Milliken, Mrs. Henry, 187
Minor, Virginia, 58, 59, 60, 64
Minor v. Hapersett, 59
Moore, Hortense Tap, 203
Morton, Oliver P., 38, 41
Motor Corps, 171, 175
Mott, Lucretia, 21, 22, 26, 32; (illus.), 23, 26
Mount, Catherine Boyd (Mrs. James A.), 98
Mount, James A., 98
Mulky, Major ______, 83
Muncie, IN, 6
Murrow, Jane, 25, 29
Myers, Carlin, 121
Myers, Mary, 31
Myers, Samuel, 31

Nashville, TN, 38, 39
Natchez, MS, 39
National American Woman Suffrage Association (NAWSA), 5, 11, 56, 79, 83, 87, 88, 96, 98, 102, 108, 123, 124, 169, 171, 180, 183, 187, 188, 189, 191, 192, 195, 200, 203, 205, 206
National Association of Colored Women, 91, 170, 184
National Association of Colored Women's Clubs, 126
National Association Opposed to Woman Suffrage, 145
National Council of Jewish Women, 1
National Council of Women of the United States, 90, 91
National League for Women's Service, 169
National Woman Suffrage Association (NWSA), 4, 47, 49, 51, 55, 56, 58, 61, 62, 63, 64, 71, 75, 76, 79, 80, 83, 84, 90, 96, 137, 138, 139, 140, 154
National Woman's Loyal League, 35
National Women's Party, 200
nativism, 176, 179
naturalization, 175
Negley, Harry, 199
Nelson, Julia, 205
New, Mrs. John C., 197
New York Tribune, 206
Newsom, Vida, 95, 97, 172; (illus.), 150
Nicholson, Elizabeth, 93; 197
Nicholson, Eugenie, 106, 108, 121, 123, 139, 203
Nicholson, Mary, 103, 197
Nicholson, Meredith, 181, 105–6, 108
Ninde, E. M., 49
Nineteenth Amendment, 2, 12, 13, 64, 123, 124, 140, 141, 142–43, 159, 164, 165, 180, 188, 191, 192, 195, 198–99, 200, 206; ratification of, 199–201, 203, 206
Noble, Harriet, 1, 93, 108, 122, 124, 140, 145
Noblesville, IN, 115
Noe, Mrs. A. M., 112, 120
Noland, Anna Dunn, 102, 140, 152; (illus.), 134
Nutter, G. W., 115

O'Hair, Belle, 105, 106, 124, 172
Occpquan, 164
Order of Templars, 41, 42
Our Herald, 80, 82
Owen, Robert Dale, 18

Page, William, 31
Palmer, Bertha, 88
Pankhurst, Sylvia, 108
partial-suffrage bill, 104–6, 118–20, 130, 137, 139, 144, 147, 148, 155, 156, 159, 195–96, 197
Patterson, Virginia S., 98
Paul, Alice, 138, 141
Payne, Catherine Curry, 177
Peirce, Alice Wheeler, 96, 98
Perkins, Edgar, 104, 108, 121
Perkins, Mrs. Edgar, 108, 121
Perkins, Mrs. Samuel, 184, 203
Peru, IN, 39
Phillips, Sallie, 184
Pierce, H. D., 121
Pierce, Mrs. Henry D., 197
Pomeroy, Samuel C., 45, 46
Populist Party, 88

Porter, Albert G., 65, 72, 74
Porter, Hattie, 184
Portland, IN: women attempt to vote in, 88
Pratt, W. D., 121
Price, Mrs. Walter, 187
Profit, Laura, 184
Progressive Party, 110, 118, 122, 124
prohibition, 2, 3, 11, 55, 67, 68, 70, 72, 73, 74, 82, 83, 86, 90, 130, 131–32, 135, 137, 144, 151–52, 154; and suffrage, 140, 151–52
Prohibition Party, 83, 84, 85, 86
Propylaeum, 93; (illus.), 92
public relations, 108–9, 110, 112, 114–17, 121–22, 124–25, 127

Quakers, 6, 7, 9, 16, 21, 22, 30, 31, 32, 33, 48

Ralston, Alexander, 7
Ralston, Jennie, 171, 173, 189, 203
Ralston, Samuel, 118, 122, 123, 130, 144, 171
Ransom, F. B., 112, 114, 117, 127, 187
Ratliff, Mrs. R. F.: (illus.), 149
Read, Lizzie Bunnell, 4, 39–40, 42, 43
Read, S. G. A., 43
Red Cross, 180–81, 183, 187, 191, 193
Redpath Bureau, 82, 86
Reed, Mrs. F. T., 204
reforms and reformers, 2, 3, 5, 11, 15, 16, 18–19, 27, 28, 30, 41
Religion: and slavery, 15, 16
Report of the Women's section of the Indiana State Council of Defense, 183
Republican Party, 82, 85, 86, 86, 88, 114, 118, 141, 153, 179, 195, 201, 203; woman's suffrage, 5, 9, 11–12, 51, 73, 83, 84, 142–43; prohibition, 68, 70
Revolution, The, 46, 47
Richmond, IN, 7, 23, 24, 29, 41, 125
Riesenberg, Henry C., 179
Riesenberg, Lucy, 114, 179
Riesenberg, Mrs. Henry C. *See* Riesenberg, Lucy
Rochester, NY, 58, 59
Roosevelt, Theodore, 110, 179
Rose, Ernestine, 26
Rosecrans William, 38
Ross, Hubert W., 127
Ross, Carrie Barnes, 1, 117–18, 127; (illus.), 103
Rule, Perry, 130
Rushville, IN: women meet in, 85–86

Sanitary Commission, 35, 36, 38–39, 48, 50
Sargent, A. A., 64
Saunders, Mollie, 184
Scott, Alexander, 149
Scott, Ida Gray, 124
Sebbelov, Gerda, 124; (illus.), 116
Seneca Falls, NY, 5, 18, 21, 22, 26, 90
Sewall, May Wright Thompson, 1, 10, 62, 63, 67, 70, 75, 76, 79, 80, 82, 83, 84, 85, 86, 87–88, 90–91, 92, 93, 95, 96, 97; (illus.), 89
Sewell, Theodore, 80
Shank, Samuel L., 112, 187
Shaw, Anna Howard, 138, 154, 169, 187, 188, 203
Shortridge, A. C., 48
Shortridge High School, 7
Shulz, Mrs. _____, 183
Sickler, Alma, 130, 142
Simmons, Abram, 160, 163
Simms, Mrs. Thomas, 187
Sixteenth Amendment, 9, 48, 50, 51, 64
slavery, 9, 15, 16, 19, 35
Smith, Louise, 98
Smith, Mrs. J. Cumming. *See* Smith, Louise, 98
Socialist Party, 110, 114
Sons of Temperance, 16
Spencer, W. W., 160
Stanbrough, Mrs. N. O., 115
Stanley, Elizabeth, 121
Stansbury, Ele, 160
Stanton, Elizabet Cady, 5, 21, 22, 35, 45, 46, 47, 55, 62, 79, 90, 197; (illus.), 17, 20, 26
Stanton, Harriot: (illus.), 20
State Federation of Colored Women's Clubs, 170, 184
Stephens, Anna D., 115
Stern, Mrs. Leon. *See* Stern, Sara Messing
Stern, Sara Messing, 1, 6, 117, 124, 127, 131, 172
Stilwell, Horace, 121
Stimson, Mrs. S. C. *See* Stimson Stella
Stimson, Stella, 103, 127, 130, 131–34, 135; (illus.), 149, 150
Stone, Lucy, 32, 45, 46, 47, 52, 55, 56, 62, 63, 71, 79
Stoops, Miss _____, 183
Stotenburg, Evan B., 118, 121
Stove Plate Molders' Union, 112

Stowe, Harriet Beecher, 28
Stuart, Allison, 155, 163
Stuart, Mrs. Weir, 187
Suffrage: divisions and disunity among organizations, 1, 2, 6, 10–11, 63–64, 79–80, 83, 86, 87–88, 96–98, 106, 118, 121, 122, 127–29, 134, 138–39, 140, 141–42, 143–45, 167, 168; opposition to, 1–2, 10–11, 12, 29, 54, 56, 58, 65–66, 67, 68, 104, 196; and prohibition laws, 2, 3, 10, 11, 82, 83, 86, 90, 130, 131–32, 135, 140, 151–52; marches and parades support, 2, 3, 11, 13, 122–23, 124–25,139–40, 142; and women's clubs, 3, 5, 11; and slavery, 9, 15, 19; temperance issues and, 9, 11, 15, 28, 55, 59–60, 65, 82, 88, 89, 90, 111; reasons to give women the vote, 35–39, 43, 44, 112, 192–93; and Fourteenth Amendment, 45–47, 51; and African American women, 52, 72; test votes by women in some states, 58, 59; women arrested for, 59, 164; white women support black suffrage groups, 61, 72, 75; political lobbying for, 64–65, 66, 82, 95, 98; women's organizations, 63, 64, 65, 70, 75, 76; interaction with political parties, 71, 73, 84–85, 87, 88, 97, 118, 120, 124, 138, 141, 142, 195, 198; organizations in Indiana need to reenergize, 79–99; some states grant to women, 79, 84, 88, 96; organizations merge, 85; brewers against, 87; women in Indiana attempt to vote, 88–90; movement reenergizes in Indiana, 101–34; organizations experience challenges, 102; and unions, 112; women form lobbying group for, 128–29; legal challenges to, 137, 155–56, 157, 159–61, 170, 189; federal amendment for, 138, 142–43, 155, 156, 159, 163, 164, 165; use of auto tours to promote, 139, 142, 143, 158–59, 168; groups attempt to merge, 140–41, 142, 152; some women oppose, 145–46, 147–48, 149, 162–63; and World War I work, 153, 154, 160, 162; women picket in DC, 153–54, 163–64; nativism, 179; court cases, 195, 196; publicity and public relations, 206;
Suffrage Amendment. *See* Nineteenth Amendment
Sunny Side (riverboat), 38–39
Susan B. Anthony Amendment. *See* Nineteenth Amendment
Swank, Emma, 1, 25, 29, 48, 51, 53, 56
Swift, Mary Ella Lyon, 145, 147
Swift, Mrs. Lucius B. *See* Swift, Mary Ella Lyon

Taft, William Howard, 110
Taggart, Thomas, 148
Tarkington, Mary. *See* Jameson, Mary Tarkington
Taylor, Nell M.: (illus.), 177
telephone: use of in suffrage message, 101, 130
temperance, 3, 10, 15, 16, 19, 28, 30–31, 41–42, 55, 59–60, 65, 67, 68, 70, 71, 73, 81–82, 108, 111, 135, 151, 201; and suffrage, 9, 11; and women's property rights, 16, 19
Tennessee, 201, 203
Terre Haute, IN, 11, 125, 127, 131, 147, 183; women meet in, 83, 86, 190–91; women on school board ballot, 102, 110
Terre Haute Brewery, 132
Terre Haute Saturday Evening Mail, 73
Thirteenth Amendment: woman support ratification of, 35–36
Thomas, Mary, 1, 7, 9, 10, 19, 20, 22, 25, 27, 28, 29, 30, 31–32, 33, 36, 38, 40–42, 48, 49, 50, 51, 52, 59, 63, 64, 65, 66, 67, 71, 75, 76–77, 80, 97, 111; (illus.), 30, 72
Thomas, Owen, 20, 31, 39
Thompson, Edwin, 80
Thompson, May. *See* Sewell, May Wright
Thompson, William H., 160
Thornton, William, 155–56, 157
Timmons, Mrs. John Wesley: (illus.), 133
Tipton, IN, 96, 98
Toph, Mrs. Ollah P., 124
Trainor, George, 46
Tresmire, Lizzie, 115
Turner, Margaret McClure, 205

U.S. Constitution: suffrage amendment to, 123, 124
U.S. Congress: women petition for suffrage, 98; and Nineteenth Amendment, 140, 159, 164, 165, 188, 192, 193
Uncle Tom's Cabin, 28
Underground Railroad, 16, 30
Underhill, Sarah, 27
United Mine Workers of America 112
Upton, Taylor, 102, 104

Vater, Thomas, 49
Vayhinger, Culla, 130, 150, (illus.), 150
Veatch, James C., 49
Vernon, Mabel, 164
Vicksburg, MS, 38, 39

Wabash Express, 83
Wade, Bertha, 98
Walker, C. J. (Madam), 117, 127
Wallace, David, 60
Wallace, DeWitt, 73, 74
Wallace, Zerelda, 1, 60, 62, 64, 65, 66, 70, 72, 75, 83, 85, 86, 197, 206; (illus.), 69
Warsaw, IN: women meet in, 75
Washington, DC, 153, 163; women picket, 192
Watson, James E., 201
Waugh, Alice, 98, 124
Way, Amanda, 1, 2, 9, 15,19, 20, 22, 27, 29, 30–31, 33, 38, 47, 48, 49, 50, 52, 56, 59, 64
Way, T. A., 15
Westfield, IN, 115
Whallon, Carrie, 142
Whitaker, Minnie, 184
White, Emma Eaton, 130, 139, 160, 167, 194, 197, 203
White, Mrs. E. T.: (illus.), 149
White, Mrs. Edward Franklin: (illus.), 150
Whittemore, Margaret, 163, 64
Wiley, Anna, 164
Wiley, Harvey, 164
Wilhite, Mary H., 48
Wilson, Woodrow, 13, 110, 118, 122, 140, 143, 154, 164, 167, 192, 193, 196, 203
Winchester, IN, 230
Winslow, W. W., 121
Winter, Mary, 115; (illus.), 110
Woman's Christian Temperance Association, 55, 59–60, 150
Woman's Christian Temperance Union (WCTU), 10, 79, 80, 83, 86–87, 88, 90, 95, 97, 101, 103, 108, 127, 128, 130, 131, 150
Woman's Club of Greencastle, 92–93
Woman's Committee of the Indiana State Council of Defense, 170, 175, 180, 184
Woman's Crusade, 59
Woman's Department Club, 128
Woman's Franchise League (WFL), 1, 3, 11, 13, 101, 102, 106, 108–9, 110, 111, 112, 114, 115, 117, 118, 119, 121, 122, 123–24, 125, 126, 127, 128, 134, 135, 137, 138, 139, 140, 141, 142, 143–44, 147, 148, 152, 153, 155, 157, 158, 159, 160, 161, 162, 163, 164, 167–68, 169, 170, 171, 175, 180, 183, 188, 189, 190, 191, 192, 194–95, 196, 197, 198, 200
Woman's Journal, 47, 49, 50, 53, 121
Woman's Legislative Council (WLC), 1, 128, 130, 131, 134, 135, 144, 151, 158, 159, 167, 194
Woman's Party, 138, 139, 153, 160, 162, 163–64, 171, 192
Woman's Press Club, 170
Woman's Suffrage Act of 1917, p. 151
"Woman's Temperance Army," 30
Women in Industry, 171
women: politics, 2, 3, 5–6, 13; and Civil War work, 9, 12, 35–39, 43, 44, 54, 56; conventions, 11–12, 14, 15, 18, 19, 20, 21, 22, 23, 24–25, 26, 27, 30, 32, 47–51, 55, 56, 59, 62, 63, 64, 70, 71–72, 75, 76, 83, 84, 85–86, 87, 90–91, 95, 96–98, 140–41, 148, 152, 163; work in World War I, 12, 154, 167–75, 180–89, 191, 195–96; property rights of, 15, 16, 18, 19, 28; reforms and reformers, 18–19, 28, 30, 41, 108, 109, 172–73; employment of, 24, 25, 30, 37, 41, 43, 48, 51, 84–85, 101, 104, 108, 111, 157, 171, 172, 173–75; wages of, 30; temperance, 30–31; support Thirteenth Amendment, 35–36; suffrage groups split, 46, 47, 48, 51; reasons not to have the vote, 49–50; reasons for suffrage, 53–54; test vote in some states, 58, 59; arrested for voting, 59; rights of, 60, 67; form clubs, 91, 92–96; petition and lobby for suffrage, 101–34, 189–92; relationships with the press, 101, 108; automobile tours and parades, 101, 114–16, 127; use telephone in spreading suffrage message, 101, 130; become active in local elections, 102, 103, 104, 110; work for partial-suffrage law, 104–6, 118–20, 130; use of public relations, 108–9, 110, 112, 114–17, 121–22, 124–25, 127; and political parties, 111, 118, 120, 140; register to vote in Indiana, 137, 154, 155–56, 157–58, 168, 170, 191; canvas for signatures, 191–95; vote in 1920 election, 204–5, 206; picket Washington, DC, 192; run for office, 205
Women's Committee of the Council of

National Defense, 188
Women's Council, 127
Women's Division of the National Council of Defense, 154
Women's Equality Day, 201–3
Women's Press Club, 128
Women's School Commission Organization, 103, 104
Women's School League, 104
Women's Section, 169
Woollen, Evans, 93, 94
World War I, 153, 154, 160, 162, 167–68, 169, 175, 179; women's work for, 12, 154, 167–75, 180–89, 191, 195–96; suffrage work continues during, 180; end of, 193–94
World's Congress for Women, 87, 88
World's Congress of Representative Women, 90
Wright, Georgia, 86
Wright, Henry C., 19
Wyoming: women vote in, 96

Yancey, Simon P., 65
Young Men's Christian Association, 127

Zionsville, IN, 115